THE POLITICAL ECONOMY
OF THE WORLD BANK

D1571519

MICHELE ALACEVICH

The Political Economy of the World Bank

The Early Years

A copublication of

Stanford Economics and Finance, an imprint of Stanford University Press,

and The World Bank

Stanford, California

The Political Economy of the World Bank: The Early Years was originally published in Italian in 2007 under the title *Le Origini della Banca Mondiale: Una Deriva Conservatrice.* © 2007, Paravia Bruno Mondadori Editori.

A copublication of Stanford Economics and Finance, an imprint of Stanford University Press, and the World Bank.

Stanford University Press   The World Bank
1450 Page Mill Road   1818 H Street NW
Palo Alto, CA 94304   Washington, DC 20433

This work is exclusively distributed and sold in the USA, its dependencies, and Canada by Stanford University Press. Throughout the rest of the world, the work is exclusively distributed by The World Bank.

Printed in the United States of America on acid-free, archival-quality paper

Library of Congress Cataloging-in-Publication Data

Alacevich, Michele.
  [Origini della Banca mondiale. English]
  The political economy of the World Bank : the early years / Michele Alacevich ; translation by the World Bank.
      p. cm.
  Translation of: Le origini della Banca mondiale, c2007.
Includes bibliographical references and index.
ISBN 978-0-8047-6065-2 (cloth)—ISBN 978-0-8047-6066-9 (paper)
  1. World Bank—History.   I. Title.
HG3881.5.W57A4213 2009
332.1'532—dc22   2008041300

Typeset by Westchester Book Group in 10/14 Janson

To my grandfather Ferruccio

Contents

Preface

This book is about the early years of the International Bank for Reconstruction and Development (IBRD), commonly known as the World Bank,[1] when it faced the issue of development for the first time, which is now central to its mission. The book concerns mainly the way in which the Bank interpreted its mission and, more specifically, with how its persona came into being: what events gave shape to it, what cultural and ideological baggage it carried, and in what historical context it took place.

Today, the World Bank takes an all-inclusive approach to development. It can be very instructive to study the antecedents of this approach during the years when it was still believed that economic growth is not only a necessary but also a sufficient condition for the development of a country. Doing so helps us understand why this concept of development did not succeed. Of course, as Paul Streeten rightly reminds us, even during the 1950s "sensible economists and planners were quite clear (in spite of what is now often said in a caricature of past thinking) that growth is not an end in itself, but a performance test of development" (Streeten et al. 1981, p. 9). However, in

---

[1] It is useful to clarify from the beginning the name of the institution. The expression "the World Bank" was created by the media soon after the institution was established. The actual name was the *International Bank for Reconstruction and Development* (IBRD). When the IBRD was joined by its first two affiliates, the *International Finance Corporation* (IFC), established in 1956, and the *International Development Association* (IDA), established in 1960, the expression "the World Bank" was used at an official level to indicate IBRD and IDA together (but not the IFC). Later, the entire group was called *the World Bank Group*: IBRD plus IDA, IFC, the *International Centre for the Settlement of Investment Disputes* (ICSID), established in 1966, and the *Multilateral Investment Guarantee Agency* (MIGA), established in 1988. In this book, I will primarily use "the International Bank" or simply "the Bank" because this was what the institution was called in the documents that I examined for the years being considered.

fact that awareness did not have any impact on development policy or bring about any expansion of the social and cultural change that is inherent to the process of development.

Thus, this book makes a contribution to the study of the "prehistory" of development understood both in its economic and social dimensions. In this regard, studying the early years of the World Bank provides an excellent context for observation for three reasons. First, during its history there was a clear delineation between the "growth" phase and the "social objectives" phase. Second, hints of opposing voices could already be heard during its first years of activity. Finally, there was a sudden change in the mandate of the institution: from supporting the reconstruction of postwar Europe to helping developing countries. The transition from one to the other was a formative moment and redefined the institution. It is thus a very fertile terrain for exploring the signs of conflict among various approaches to development.

My aim is to help understand how the Bank made its choices of economic policy for developing countries when the problem of development appeared for the first time on its agenda; and, by analyzing the debates raging within the institution, to understand better its work in the context of the newly emerging field of development economics.

Referring to sociology, Robert K. Merton made a comment that can apply to all types of knowledge:

One way of identifying the alternative orientations, commitments, and function ascribed to sociology is by examining, however briefly, the principal conflicts and polemics that have raged among sociologists. For these presumably exhibit the alternative paths that sociology might have taken in a particular society, but did not, as well as the paths it has taken. In reviewing some of these conflicts, I do not propose to consider the merits of one or another position [. . .]; I intend to consider them only as they exhibit alternative lines of development in sociology that are influenced by the larger social structure and by social processes internal to sociology itself. (Merton [1961] 1973b, p. 54)

The study of conflicts in development economics and at the World Bank allows us to identify the values and variables at stake, the available options in the field to stimulate development in poor countries most effectively, and ultimately how one direction prevailed over the others, leaving its imprint on the institution. This reflection is particularly interesting in the case of the International Bank because of the historical consequences of those distant events. That initial imprint hardened the Bank so that it had difficulty adapting to the new sensitivity to social issues, which emerged in development economics and at the United Nations during the 1960s. Studying the first years of the Bank helps us understand its evolution, at least until the end of the 1960s and the beginning of the 1970s. In those years, the need to free itself of its original imprint forced the Bank to undergo a radical transformation. In essence, it became more an *agency* for development than a *bank*.

This study is based on documents from the World Bank Group Archives and the Lauchlin B. Currie papers collection, held at Duke University. This rich archival material was made available for the first time to researchers. This is especially true for the documents held in the World Bank Group Archives, covering many aspects of the life of the Bank in the late 1940s and early 1950s. Roger Sandilands had already discussed the Currie papers in several articles and in *The Life and Political Economy of Lauchlin Currie* (Sandilands 1990, 2004; Sandilands and Laidler 2002; for a specific analysis of Sandilands's work on the Currie papers, see Sandilands 2009). However, I had the opportunity to explore the Currie papers more in-depth as regards the relation between Currie and the Bank.

A few words about the structure of this volume. The first chapter discusses the historiography that serves as the foundation for the book. It refers to a varied literature that uses periods of transition or crisis in the history of an institution to understand its dynamics and mechanisms. Several disciplines, including history, sociology, economics, and evolutionary biology, use a methodology that combines analytics and deep historical research to understand the mechanisms of change. This book favors this eclectic approach, which aims to break "the taboos against association with the *Polscis*, *Sociogs*, and other tribes" (Leijonhufvud [1973] 1981, p. 350).

The second chapter describes the period during which the Bank, having reduced its support of European reconstruction, turned to developing countries. The first instance of meaningful activities in a developing country was Colombia, where the Bank sent its first General Survey Mission in 1949. Colombia was a very important test case for the Bank; for this reason, it provides a privileged point of view for looking at the actions and pronouncements of the Bank on development policy. Moreover, the

Colombian mission was the first trial by fire for the Bank, a moment when the views that had matured within the institution confronted the outside world. The internal tensions that arose then and ended with the complete break between the Bank and the head of the mission (the economist Lauchlin Currie) are especially helpful in understanding better the evolving journey of the institution.

The third chapter explores the tensions between Currie and the Bank, and in particular, between Currie and the economist Albert Hirschman, who replaced him as the Bank's envoy to Colombia. It deals with the debates that raged within development economics at a time when the discipline was taking shape as an autonomous field. The chapter analyzes simultaneously the theoretical debates and the practice of the debaters themselves. Presenting these stories allows us to evaluate better their real scope, partly resizing them and partly revealing the real mechanisms of the conflict. Albert Hirschman, one of the founders of development economics, wrote *The Strategy of Economic Development* based on his Colombian experience. This story is revisited using archival documents that have never been used before and thus give us new insights into the history of the field of development economics.

The fourth and final chapter concentrates again on the International Bank and in particular on the lending instruments created by the Bank for developing countries. Once again, the Colombian experience provided the backdrop for weighty discussions within the Bank about what the institution should be financing and whether it was appropriate to use "impact loans" and "social loans" in certain situations. Ultimately, for reasons that are explained in this chapter, the Bank adopted a rigid and conservative behavior as a closed financial institution. It refused to adopt more articulated and inclusive policies at least until the second half of the 1960s. Then, faced with a growing disappointment within the development community, the Bank was forced to change.

Acknowledgments

This work was born as a doctoral dissertation at the University of Milano, Italy. My first and major debt of gratitude is to Paola Villa, my Ph.D. supervisor during the research. Her intellectual generosity and support have been very stimulating and encouraging. Earlene Craver, Axel Leijonhufvud, and Giorgio Fodor gave me fundamental advice during the outline phase of the research. Roger J. Sandilands shared with me opinions, literature, and advice on countless occasions, with openness and enthusiasm. I heartily thank him for his generosity and friendship.

Within the World Bank, François Bourguignon, former chief economist and senior vice president, Jean-Jacques Dethier, research manager, and Elisa Liberatori-Prati, chief archivist, supported my work, encouraged publication of this book in English and gave me valuable and inspiring comments. I also received useful comments and support from Biagio Bossone, Barbara Buckingham, Elizabeth Currie, Alan Gelb, Maria Lardner, Branko Milanovic, Trudy Huskamp Peterson, and Bertha Wilson. Valentina Kalk gave me invaluable and essential support in the revision of the translation from Italian.

I am also indebted to Jake Abbott, Lluis Argemi, Pier Francesco Asso, Kai Bird, Elisabetta Croci Angelini, Annalisa Angelini, Giovanna Devetag, Marino di Marzo with Fulvia and Marina, Sheila Dow and the participants to the Budapest 2005 Workshop "Research Bank on the World Bank," Stefano Fiori, Louis Goodman, Mattia Granata, Wendy Harcourt, Shanda King and Cooper Bethea, Ivo Maes, Perry Mehrling, Donatella Minuto, Andreas Ortmann, Daniela Parisi, Sandra Peart and David Levy and the participants at the 2008 Summer Institute for the Preservation of the History of Economic Thought, Claudio Picozza, Jacques Polak, Paolo Ramazzotti,

Mayya Revzina, Giulio Sapelli, Pasquale Lucio Scandizzo, Asuncion St. Clair, Paul Streeten, Claudia Sunna, Fernanda Tuozzo, Antje Vetterlein, Michael Ward, and Chris Wright. Four anonymous referees provided detailed and very helpful feedback.

While I was searching for source materials, I spent several months at the Rare Book, Manuscript, and Special Collections Library at Duke University, Durham, North Carolina, and at the World Bank Group Archives, Washington, D.C. The competence and professionalism of their staff are outstanding. I am especially grateful to Elizabeth Dunn, Laura Micham, Eleanor Mills, and Janie Morris of the Rare Book Library at Duke for their kindness and professionalism.

Finally, my deepest thanks go to Margo Beth Crouppen, acquisitions editor, Mariana Raykov, production editor, and Jessica Walsh, editorial assistant at Stanford University Press, and to Barbara Goodhouse, production editor at Westchester Book Group.

All the people I mentioned contributed to the outcome of my research, and to all of them I am indebted. Of course, the errors and deficiencies still present in the book are entirely mine.

THE POLITICAL ECONOMY
OF THE WORLD BANK

CHAPTER ONE

The World Bank and Development

It is the privilege of early youth to live in advance of its days in all the beautiful continuity of hope which knows no pauses and no introspection. One closes behind oneself the little gates of mere boyishness—and enters an enchanted garden. Its very shades glow with promise.

—JOSEPH CONRAD, *The Shadow Line*

Certain periods in the life of the International Bank for Reconstruction and Development (IBRD) can be particularly enlightening in understanding its history and development. Naturally, *what* to look for and *how* to look are closely connected issues in practice, although they may belong to different spheres in the researcher's experience, namely "passion" and "reason." *What* has already been briefly discussed in the Preface. *How* requires more space and structure and is the subject of this chapter, which discusses the approach that guided my analysis. I first investigate the historical context of the events that will be analyzed in subsequent chapters. Then, after examining the work of other scholars who (positively or negatively) informed my research, I discuss the methodology that I consider appropriate to study the history of a multilateral financial institution.

Historical Context

The IBRD is one of the two international institutions created by the Bretton Woods Conference in 1944. Its original mission was to help the postwar reconstruction of devastated European countries and the development of poorer member countries. In 1946, the year it became operational, the Bank soon postponed its second objective indefinitely. In 1947, the Bank granted loans for about a half billion U.S. dollars to subsidize the balance of payments of recipient countries for whom foreign currency (essentially dollars) to purchase raw materials and machinery necessary for reconstruction was vital. The Marshall Plan, announced in the same year and implemented in 1948, overlapped with the work of the Bank, although with two major differences: first, the intervention was bilateral and not multilateral, and, second, the financial commitment (approximately $4 billion per year) was substantially larger. The Bank was caught off guard and suddenly was faced with the fact that its usefulness in Europe had greatly diminished and that it would need to change its mission. The Bank found a new raison d'être in providing economic assistance to what were then called "backward" or "underdeveloped" countries.

Until that time, with a few notable exceptions, development as a topic had been all but ignored in academia, and there was little research on the economic condition of dependent territories (dominions and colonies), except in cases where it was useful or necessary for metropolitan territories (Meier and Seers 1984). The Cold War, President Truman's policy of containment, and local conflicts tightly bound the economic development of these territories (and the emancipation promised by both superpowers, the United States and Soviet Union) to the dynamics of the confrontation between the Soviet and Western blocs. As Gunnar Myrdal lucidly observed:

> The fate of the underdeveloped countries [has become] a matter of foreign policy concern in the developed countries. [. . .] It should be remembered that the economic and social conditions of the South Asian countries today are not very different from those existing before the disintegration of the colonial power system. [. . .] On the whole, the masses in South Asia in pre-war times were as poor and their lives as miserable as they are now. Their poverty and misery did not, however, induce economists to take any

great interest in their situation [. . .]. Practical intervention along such lines was then not within the realm of political feasibility. Still less was there a feeling of urgency about such action. (Myrdal 1968, pp. 8–9)

Walt W. Rostow, in his double role as economic historian and as director of the Policy Planning Staff of the U.S. State Department, declared, "We must demonstrate that the underdeveloped nations—now the main focus of Communist hopes—can move successfully through the preconditions into a well-established take-off within the orbit of the democratic world, resisting the blandishments and temptations of Communism. This is, I believe, the most important single item on the Western agenda" (Rostow [1960] 1990, p. 134).

The World Bank had to consider this new reality in order to prepare projects that were appropriate to the needs of its new clients. From mid-1947 until the end of 1948, the flow of loans disbursed by the Bank almost completely stopped, and the entire institution focused on research, collecting data, and preparing missions.

The Bank favored placing the management of daily operations in the hands of internal managers instead of the executive directors. The latter were representatives of the governments of member countries and could potentially interfere politically. This remained a controversial point because the political weight of some executive directors, primarily the United States, often played a fundamental role in determining the Bank's policies. As for financial soundness, the Bank presented itself to the capital markets as a trustworthy institution in managing investments. Lastly, the Bank structured its loans around individual and well-defined *projects*. These became its main vehicle, instead of the development *program*, which was more complex and seemed more difficult to monitor.

Methodological Framework

While transition dynamics and the role that transition periods have in the life and evolution of institutions have been the subject of very interesting analysis and reflections by some social scientists, the specific literature about the history of the Bank has rarely paid attention to the institution's transition periods and has often neglected a major aspect of all transitions, that is, uncertainty. In this chapter, I will briefly examine and discuss the literature useful to our inquiry. Borrowing from Francis Bacon's terminology, I will first put forth my criticism of the existing analyses of the Bank (*Pars Destruens*, that is, the destructive part of my argument); subsequently, I will present an approach which is, in my view, particularly fruitful in analyzing institutions' transitions (*Pars Construens*, that is, the constructive part of the argument).

PARS DESTRUENS

In part, the reasons for the policy choices of the Bank were linked to its early difficulties—for example, raising capital in a climate that was initially hostile toward international institutions.[1] From this point of view, these choices seem necessary and indisputable and often have been presented as such. Such an interpretation makes any analysis of how the institution made these choices seem redundant. Some historical narratives leap from the "reconstruction" phase to the "development" phase, overlooking the transition between the two periods.[2] Other narratives take into account this transition but describe it as a transformation in which, despite its difficulties, all actors involved agreed to the ultimate goal, which in turn would guarantee the success of the institution.[3] Because the World Bank has proven to be a successful model, at least by its own measures of productivity (loan volumes and yields), such historical accounts appear perfectly adequate. Undoubtedly, they answer many questions satisfactorily.

However, these are post-facto reconstructions that do not necessarily correspond to the actual events. This is the risk of those studies that use the success of an institution as the lens for interpreting its history; the history, in turn, is used to prove the rationality of the earlier choices made by managers.

An example of this approach can be found in the introduction to a collection of biographical essays about the past presidents of the Bank from the beginning until the 1990s. It is worth quoting at length:

The nature of the institution changed over the years. The report of Commission II, entrusted by the Bretton Woods conferees with working out the charter of the IBRD, concluded that "it was accidentally born with the name Bank [. . .] mainly because no satisfactory name could be found in the dictionary for this unprecedented institution." Nevertheless this designation seemed to define adequately the institution's behavior for the first fifteen years of its life. The Bank took pain to present itself as a sound financial undertaking and adopted standards common to commercial financial institutions. Economic backwardness was regarded as a problem that could be dealt with by relying on the normal process of financial intermediation, that is, by raising capital in the richer countries and transferring it to the needy ones. Once the depth and complexity of the problems faced by the developing countries were recognized [. . .] the concept of the Bank as a financial institution modelled on traditional investment banks gave way to a new vision of a development finance institution.

These changes in orientation were neither accidental nor automatic; they reflected decisions by the Bank's leaders. The Bank's presidents, each in his fashion, recognized the needs of the member countries and sought to satisfy those needs. They moved the institution to identify appropriate ways of intervening and to respond to the needs of its members. (Kraske et al. 1996, p. 4)

Looking at it this way, the Bank went from one phase of its existence to another following a process of progressive accumulation of information and skills and adapting to the reality faced by the institution in all its complexity. This is a mechanism found in many learning experiences in human societies. This analysis contains some undeniable truths: the presidents and the top management of the World Bank were principal agents of the changes in economic policy and decisions of the institution. However, as argued above, this approach is partially misleading.

What is missing is the accidental nature of the change. As a matter of fact, the presidents and top management were not the only ones in the institution to express a point of view about what to do and how to do it. Clearly, the presidents and top management were very influential actors and ultimately determined the direction of the institution; but they are not entirely representative of a large and complex organization such as the Bank. Of course, change is caused by the way the institution interacts with the world around it. However, this obvious consideration does not mean that change occurs through a sequence of external stimulations and internal responses led by top management, as if it were a gradual adjustment. The institution facing the world surrounding it is part of that world. It goes through changes (or resists change) in response to external and internal stimuli and in light of how it views itself, its mission, and its history.

Certainly, as the Bank went through different phases, it had to position itself vis-à-vis those changes, and its top management had a fundamental role in these positioning efforts. However, how this process developed, what criteria and conventions inspired it, and what effects it produced depend on many different variables. We are not questioning here the "centrality of management in strategic planning," which was one of the pillars in the analysis of Alfred Chandler and many others (including Louis Galambos, whose analysis of the World Bank is discussed below). Instead, we are questioning its comparison to what has been defined as "managerial reductionism" to explain this centrality—a reductionism that impoverishes and excessively simplifies the analysis (Sapelli 1990, p. 11).

Another example of the limits of the above-mentioned approach can be found in the first major account of the history of the International Bank, the volume published by Edward Mason and Robert Asher in 1973. My research exposes the debate about economic policy choices that the Bank faced in the 1940s and 1950s. As will be shown in the following chapters, this debate anticipated many themes that emerged again in the 1960s and 1970s. As my research shows, in exercising economic policy options at the beginning of the 1950s, Bank management deliberately excluded some forms of investment and acted in favor of others. Mason and Asher propose a diachronic sequence of different approaches to economic development. Such approaches, however, while indeed diachronic, were often proposed at the same time, generating a conflict for this very reason. Mason and Asher's reflections ignore the conflict and give the impression that the institution evolved naturally from a reductionist vision of development (development as mere economic growth) to a more complex and multidimensional vision, which includes economic and social aspects, in the way that an individual goes from childhood to adolescence to maturity. The two scholars conclude that

> there are recognized fields of development lending that the Bank has to date avoided. Housing, with some minor exceptions [. . .] may be the most conspicuous example [. . .]. Public works projects, intended primarily to

provide jobs for the unemployed and underemployed, are also examples [...]. We mention these, not because we want the Bank to finance every conceivable type of project, but because, from the point of view of development, some hitherto neglected fields may deserve a high enough priority to replace fields for which external finance has become less important [...]. As the Bank has amassed more information and more experience, and has become less of a bank and more of a development agency, its advice has become more relevant and more useful both to the borrowing government and to others interested in assisting that government.

The World Bank, in summary, appears to have earned its right to play not just *a*, but *the* leading role in nurturing and coordinating the international development effort during the 1970s. (Mason and Asher 1973, pp. 721–22)

This reflection—like Kraske's—is neither false nor wrong. The Bank did change policies between the 1960s and the 1970s. Moreover, it also changed its *nature*, as the two authors rightly point out (less *bank* and more *agency for development*). However, the Bank did not reach the 1970s through a linear path of cumulative learning but through the passionate confrontation of opposing views of development policy. Colombia was indeed a perfect case study of such confrontations, as will be shown below. Yet the many pages that Mason and Asher dedicate to Colombia (1973, pp. 649–57) rely solely on the conclusions of two of the Bank's reports published in 1970 and completely ignore the tensions that raged within the Bank.

Two articles about the World Bank published in 1995 by Louis Galambos and David Milobsky, in which they refer explicitly to Chandler, present a very interesting overview of the changes at the Bank through the decades (Galambos and Milobsky 1995a, 1995b). The authors describe the evolution of the internal structure of the Bank, and the two decisive reorganizations of 1952 and 1972, as a process similar to large modern corporations. In particular, the second reorganization of the Bank moved it "toward the structure of the most powerful and fastest growing organizations in the world economy during those years—that is, toward the model provided by the decentralized multinational corporation, the so-called M-form or multidivisional company" (1995a, p. 158). According to Galambos and Milobsky, the various groups of top managers that the Bank had over the years were responsible for these structural changes. Galambos and Milobsky present a clear analysis of the changes that took place in the institution and the strategies that shaped them. Of course, the space of two articles cannot render justice to the complexity of the mechanisms of strategic change or to the recurrences of certain strategic proposals (at times the expression of a minority, at times of a majority, of the participants in the internal debate).

PARS CONSTRUENS

The study of institutions is central to all social sciences, but there is a dichotomy between the deductive approach similar to that of marginalist economics and more historical and descriptive approaches.[4] A major feature of a historical approach is that it thoroughly examines elements of uncertainty and explains the alternatives that were in conflict at a given historic moment. The ways of historical change are complex and do not lend themselves to mechanistic interpretation; change does not follow a linear path.

In a conference held in Rome in 1980, Albert O. Hirschman warned against forgetting the "thick description" of Clifford Geertz and the much-maligned *histoire événementielle*—the history of events (as opposed to the history of the deeper structures of human societies). Hirschman used the example of the study of a revolution, but he was clearly discussing the method:

> Following in detail the process of a revolution gives us a strong feeling, as the structuralist approach does not, for the many might-have-beens of history [. . .]. As a result, the event-minded historian is less likely [. . .][5] to declare that, given such a structural condition, the outcome was preordained. [This] emphasis on the revolutionary process [. . .] in effect promises to restore a few degrees of freedom we were in danger of losing to the structuralists. (Hirschman [1980] 1986, pp. 171–72)[6]

Alfred D. Chandler had offered a similar contribution several years before: "[The historian] is more concerned, I believe, with the real alternatives facing men, and why men took the alternatives that they did" (Chandler 1970, p. 145).

In this view, the real options and the choices that derive from them become the focus of the research. According to Mark Granovetter (1990, p. 100), it is by studying the beginnings, the "formative" periods of an institution, that a researcher is in the best position to identify possible options for its evolution. Hirschman also favors the moments of transformation, transition, and change. The convergence is substantial: to understand the mechanisms of change of an institution, we need observation based on historical facts and sensitivity to the alternatives, what Hirschman refers to as "the many might-have-beens of history." This is what Bertolt Brecht, in 1938, resolved to do when he wrote *Julius Caesar*: "Not even for an instant should I allow myself to believe that things had to go *per force* the way that they went."[7]

Once this starting point and sensitivity have been established, it is possible to reconstruct the persistent and historic reasons of some shortcomings that institutions sometimes carry with them throughout their history. In other words, it becomes possible to identify the processes that contribute to institutional "path-dependence." The concept of "path-dependence" was applied at first to technological change. Paul David's article about the QWERTY keyboard is the most famous example. By examining the history of the clearly inefficient keyboard that was successful on the market, David showed the existence of self-reinforcing mechanisms that, thanks to the growing revenues as a result of the adoption and repeated application of the same technology with no regard to its relative efficiency, restrict ("lock-in") development to a determined path of growth, thereby preventing the pursuit of more efficient solutions.[8] However, the validity of the concept applies more broadly. As David put it: "It is sometimes not possible to uncover the logic (or illogic) of the world around us except by understanding how it got that way" (David 1985, p. 332). The "lock-in" concept is only implied here, and, when there is a process involving time, one can probably also recognize a path-dependence mechanism. However, it would be a misunderstanding to have an excessively structural and deterministic interpretation of the concept of path-dependence. In fact, "the dynamic process itself takes on an *essential historical* character" (David 1985, p. 332, emphasis in the original).

This research focuses neither on the first period (reconstruction) nor on the second period (development) in the history of the World Bank but on the more uncertain interim period, when convictions were questioned and the institution prepared itself for a new mission. Only in light of this can we offer an interpretation of the genesis of the policies that were to guide the Bank in subsequent years. This interpretation is not so much an *ex post* evaluation as a recognition of the intense debates that were taking place during that historic moment. I find support for this interpretation in the words of Leonard Rist, then head of the Economic Department of the Bank, to explain how the Bank made evaluations and operational decisions: "Policy was not 'formulated.' It was formed. It evolved. It resulted from events. And it changed with different loans [. . .] policy formulations have been extremely rare."[9]

The study of the internal debate and the attention given to specific events provides many otherwise unobtainable elements that can explain the journey later taken by the institution. To understand the history and the development of the Bank, the various options that were rejected and the reasons for rejecting them are just as revealing as the options that were accepted and later offered to explain the successes achieved.

I propose a reading that favors *ex ante* observation, because it reconstructs the uncertainty and fatigue of the journey and exposes the options opening up at a particular moment in time. Though we may know what we are looking for, though we may know what we are doing, walking without knowing the destination means gambling at every fork in the road and feeling like we are walking in a labyrinth. Reconstructing the history of an institution without taking all of this into account would mean following Ariadne's thread too fast back to the starting point of the institution. Such a hasty reconstruction of past events runs the serious risk of not recognizing those fundamental moments that were turning points and not reflecting on the debates that took place there.

For these reasons, the initial years of an institution, and more generally the moments of junction and transition, are especially well suited for this kind of historical reconstruction. In keeping with the metaphor of a journey, they are more like a clearing from which many paths depart than like a fork in the road.

CHAPTER TWO

The Currie Mission in Colombia, 1949–1953

In tracing the evolution of IBRD assistance to member countries in development programming, the historian quickly discovers that all roads lead not to Rome, but to Bogotá.

—EDWARD MASON AND ROBERT ASHER,
The World Bank Since Bretton Woods

Between 1949 and 1954, the years during which the International Bank transitioned from its mission of "reconstruction" to "development," the relationship between the Bank and Colombia was especially important for both entities. The Latin American country was an important counterpart for the Bank, because the Bank wanted to establish a long-lasting collaborative relationship and it emphasized this relationship by considering Colombia a kind of "laboratory" for the definition of more general policies for developing countries. For its part, Colombia wanted to establish a strong relationship with an institution that could attract funds and resources necessary for its development. For a historian, therefore, the relationship between the Bank and Colombia helps to highlight the more general dynamics of the institution during this period. It helps understand how the Bank concretely experienced its transition from reconstruction to development and how it forged its policies.

The first section of this chapter gives a broad context and defines the transition and the nature of the first contacts between the Bank and Colombia.

The second section describes the continuation of these contacts, especially when they intensified. It specifically covers the progress of the relationship between the Bank and Colombia and focuses on the "Currie Mission" of 1949 and its developments. The third section highlights the growing tensions between the institution and Lauchlin Currie, who only two years before had been hired by the Bank for a prestigious position of responsibility. In these tensions, one can detect traces of the dynamics that were central to the process of shaping the economic policies of the International Bank.

The Importance of the Colombia Mission for the Switch from Reconstruction to Development

With the advent of the Cold War and the resulting foreign policy of the United States, the changed international economic and political scenario forced the Bank to rethink its own activity suddenly and radically, only two years after its founding. In this quick and sudden change of scenario, the Bank found in Colombia an ideal partner to refocus its own strategy. This section will analyze the birth of this long-lasting relationship.

END OF THE RECONSTRUCTION PHASE

In 1948, the Marshall Plan was launched. It was a major and direct effort of the United States to sustain European postwar reconstruction. With a budget of approximately $4 billion per year, the Marshall Plan marginalized the role of the International Bank in Europe. The Bank, whose loans for reconstruction totaled $497 million by the end of 1948 (Kapur, Lewis, and Webb 1997, p. 71), had to come to terms with the new situation.

> So far as European reconstruction is concerned—in the words of the 1948 Bank's *Annual Report*—substantial loans by the Bank have been precluded primarily because of the uncertainties which have existed, first with respect to the shape and content of the European Recovery Program and later with respect to the manner in which loans by the Bank could best be brought into harmony with that program. (IBRD 1948, p. 5)

One year earlier, Bank president John McCloy had suggested at a meeting with the executive directors: "I think we are going to be driven into a very different field sooner than I thought, into the development field."[1] By now, this had become inevitable.

The uncertainty caused by U.S. bilateral activity in Europe led the Bank to pause its operations, except for two small loans: one to Chile ($16 million, in March 1948) and one to the Netherlands ($12 million, in July 1948). At this point, the institution needed to deepen its knowledge of the social, political, and economic conditions of developing countries—knowledge that was almost completely lacking.

The mission that the Bank sent to Colombia between July and November of 1949 was the most important episode during this phase.[2] The Bank had sent other missions to member countries before 1949, but those missions had the goal of implementing or evaluating specific projects that were or would be financed by loans from the Bank. The goal of the Colombian mission was broader and more ambitious. According to the preface of the final report of the mission, the goal was to formulate "a development program designed to raise the standard of living of the Colombian people" (IBRD 1950a, p. xv). For this reason, both the International Bank and the Colombian government, together with some national interest groups (e.g., manufacturers and professional engineers), were optimistic about the outcome of the mission. For its part, the Bank was particularly interested in the trailblazing role of the mission. Because this was the first mission to feature such a broad vision—"the most ambitious [mission] undertaken so far by the Bank," according to an internal document[3]—its success would establish a conceptual framework for future missions. That is, it would have a central role in drawing up instruments for analysis and action, which the Bank would need in its new role of assisting in development, even beyond the specific case of Colombia (IBRD 1949, p. 10; 1950c, p. 23). This was one of the main characteristics which Bank president McCloy always underscored when referring to the mission to Colombia. As he said in a telegram to a possible candidate to head the mission: "This is first comprehensive mission to be sent out by Bank and may form a pattern for what I believe will be one of most important aspects of Bank activity in development field."[4] From its point of view, Colombia had everything to gain from hosting a mission that would examine the general social and economic conditions of the country and that would shape the position of the Bank (albeit informally)[5] concerning the opportunity to help finance its development.

Colombia had already hosted two brief Bank missions, but they were operational missions. The first was organized to deepen the Bank's knowledge of the Colombian fiscal system; the second was sent to identify specific projects that the Bank could consider for loans (Mason and Asher 1973, p. 162). These two missions and the General Survey Mission of 1949 came from the same request for funding submitted by the Colombian government to the Bank in July 1948. However, the discussion about possible loans had been going on since 1947.

In addition to the reasons that were relevant to the individuals and institutions of those years, we should look at why a researcher would want to explore the events of this period. In part, the reasons coincide with those that had already been perceived at the time. It was a period of transition during which the International Bank was building the foundation for its new phase of activity. The Colombian mission was one of the most important events of this period. However, there are also the reasons of the historian who observes these events in perspective. Some of the individuals involved in the Colombian project and what came after were highly regarded economists who made important contributions to their field. One such scholar was Albert Hirschman, who was sent by the Bank as a consultant to Colombia in 1952, while Lauchlin Currie, who was the head of the General Survey Mission, is almost unknown today. However, we should remember that, at the time, the situation was reversed. Currie was better known; he was a former manager of the Federal Reserve Bank under Marriner Eccles and an economic advisor to the U.S. president, Franklin D. Roosevelt. Although Albert Hirschman had significant experience with the Marshall Plan and the Federal Reserve and had already published an important and well-received book entitled *National Power and the Structure on Foreign Trade*, he did not yet have the same prestige and authority as Currie. Earlier, Hirschman had published several articles about the Italian economy, which certainly constituted his first study of the problems of economic development.[6] However, it is the Colombian experience that would shape his most mature thinking, earning him a place among the "pioneers in development" (from the title of the book by Meier and Seers 1984). On the other hand, Lauchlin Currie, probably because of his decision to move to Colombia and to remain there for the rest of his life, maintained his reputation as a well-known economist only among those who for professional reasons shared his research interests (including monetary issues, political economy, development economics, and urban planning).[7] In other words, he was unknown outside some professional niches. Therefore, the Colombian experience was important personally and professionally for both men and one must study it to understand their intellectual journeys and their outcomes.

INITIAL CONTACTS BETWEEN THE COLOMBIAN
GOVERNMENT AND THE IBRD

Colombian president Mariano Ospina-Pérez initiated the first approach by the Colombian government to the Bank on April 28, 1947, just a few weeks after McCloy became head of the Bank. In the terse language of a telegram, Ospina-Pérez announced the arrival in Washington of the Colombian governor Emilio Toro, to ask for a loan "for indispensable urgent reconstruction Colombian economy."[8] The Bank immediately collected information on the Colombian economy.[9] Three months later, the Latin American Division identified the main issues to examine: the critical state of the budget and fiscal policy of the country, as well as the serious conditions of the domestic transportation infrastructure, a prerequisite for assessing the potential for national economic development. As for production, the Bank highlighted the balance of trade deficits both for the agricultural sector and for consumer and capital goods. The main recommendation was to undertake a "field investigation" as soon as Colombia formally applied for a loan.[10]

The documents do not mention the visit of Toro. However, they do bear witness to a second overture several months later by the Colombian ambassador to Washington. Through him, President Ospina-Pérez invited McCloy to take part in the Ninth International Conference of American States, which would be inaugurated in Bogotá on March 30, 1948.[11] On that occasion, William Iliff, who had just been appointed loan director of the Bank,[12] aired the idea, for the first time, that McCloy propose to the Colombian president a mission that would address the general conditions of the country rather than individual projects: "My Latin American people think that Colombia is a country of some potentialities and may be of some interest to us. We should be glad of the opportunity to send a mission there to make a general study of conditions. [. . .] When you are in Bogotá you might mention, quite informally, (say to the President) the possibility of our sending such a mission."[13] The Colombian trip proved to be dramatic: on April 9, the leader of the Liberal Party in Colombia, Jorge Eliécer Gaitán, was assassinated by a certain Juan Roa Sierra during the conference.[14]

Gaitán was a very popular and charismatic figure. As a young intellectual who grew up in Italy under the extremist unionist Enrico Ferri, in the 1930s he took part in the founding of the most important group of the radical left in Colombia, the Unión Nacional Izquierdista Revolucionaria (UNIR). In 1935, he joined the Liberal Party. During these years, he became very well known as a radical leader despite the important responsibility he had as mayor of Bogotá during the first government led by Alfonso López Pumarejo (1934–38), as minister of education under Eduardo Santos Montejo (1938–42), and as minister of labor during López Pumarejo's second administration (1942–44). After the moderate conservative Ospina-Pérez won the presidential elections of 1946, groups from the extreme right initiated a series of intimidating acts and aggressions against liberals, party offices, and any form of protests against this violent campaign. The following year, after a landslide victory by the liberals in the parliamentary elections, Gaitán took over as head of the Liberal Party and withdrew the liberal ministers from the government. At the same time, he supported the general strike of the Confederación de Trabajadores de Colombia (CTC), which denounced the oligarchy in power that was largely conservative but with many representatives from the Liberal Party. His next step was to organize a massive popular protest in Bogotá at the same time as the founding conference of the Organization of American States (OAS), to protest the continuous violence suffered by leftists, often tolerated or even supported by the government (Casetta 1991). It was in this awkward situation that Gaitán, who seemed poised to win the presidential elections of 1950, was assassinated. A popular reaction immediately exploded into a violent revolt in the capital, the *Bogotazo*, which spread to other cities and then to the countryside.[15]

In addition to the dramatic turn of the events in the capital and through-out the country, the dialogue between the Bank and the Latin American states also became difficult because of these governments' positions on some topics that were delicate in U.S. foreign policy. Several days after the *Bogotazo* explosion, an internal Bank report stated:

> It should be borne in mind that prior to the events of April 9, the conference was not going very well in any case, the main stumbling blocks being: a) the reluctance of some countries to commit themselves to joint action against foreign-inspired subversive (i.e. Communist) activities [. . .]; b) the issue of the European colonies in the Western Hemisphere, which was bound to cause much embarrassment to the United States; and c) the question of long-term financial aid, which a number of Latin American countries are unwilling to accept if the United States makes it a previous condition that facilities for foreign private capital investment should be liberalised. [. . .] Latin American countries consider anti-communist action, intergovernmental financing (through the IBRD, the Eximbank or a possible Inter-American bank) and treatment of foreign capital as independent things which stand on their own merits and not as conditional upon each other.[16]

In the postwar years, the United States was particularly sensitive to the anticommunist struggle and the liberalization of overseas investments, and the International Bank seemed stuck on the same positions. This mix of commercial openness and anticommunist political struggle was typical of the time, and the Bank acted accordingly. It is important to remember that the Soviet bloc refused to participate in the Bretton Woods institutions and denounced them as instruments of capitalistic imperialism. As a result, only U.S. capital was available for transnational investments. In these early years, Bank management was walking a fine line between the Bank as a multilateral organization and as a resource for "intergovernmental financing," which also meant treating it as a bilateral institution. The multilateral character of the institution was intertwined with the difficulty of differentiating it from the policies of its primary "shareholders," mainly the United States. Throughout its history, this relationship between the institution and its primary donors developed dynamically, passing through some phases in which the Bank could be independent and others in which it had to adapt to the positions of its primary member countries.

In spite of the political crisis, the Colombian government was able to continue its relationship with the Bank. During McCloy's visit to the country, a development program was presented, based on some large projects: an iron and steel plant, a soda plant, a program to build roads and railroads, and a plan for irrigation and agricultural development. The management of the Bank did not see a valid reason to delay preparing a loan strategy for the country. On the contrary, "the situation is no more unstable in Colombia in the long run than it is in France and Italy."[17] If anything, the political crisis provided a more pressing reason to intervene. The primary goal of the Colombian mission about to arrive in Washington was to "obtain financial assistance urgently needed by Colombia as a result of the economic losses suffered by that country from the disturbances that had occurred last April."[18] A Bank mission to Colombia remained the object of preparations.

The semiofficial request on June 1, 1948, by the Colombian ambassador Restrepo Jaramillo for a Bank loan of $60 million, changed to $87 million on June 20, created the occasion for the mission.[19] A series of meetings between Bank staff and Colombian representatives helped define the terms of reference. The mission, made up of just a few people, arrived in Colombia on July 22, 1948, and stayed briefly only to examine the projects that seemed best launched, that is, railroads, roads, rivers and ports, and agricultural equipment.[20] In the meantime, the Bank turned to New York to contact several U.S. companies and institutions that could provide firsthand information on the economic conditions in Colombia or that were interested in investing in the country.[21] The Colombian industrialists, organized into the Asociación Nacional de Industriales (ANDI), were mobilizing to obtain government guaranteed loans from the Bank that would directly support their activities.[22]

The documents that could be examined in the archives of the International Bank do not cover the period of the mission, but the conclusions reappear in other documents that were written in the following weeks. The members of the mission had found themselves in a situation rather different from what they had imagined before they left. Among the identified projects, in fact, only the one about purchasing agricultural equipment continued to be discussed. It was not possible to evaluate the transportation infrastructure (rivers, ports, railroads, and roads), its condition, or the action needed. Beyond this, however, there was a more fundamental issue: the broader condition of the national economy. The country was experiencing serious inflation primarily caused by the government using central bank loans to finance the budget deficit. The exchange rate was considered unrealistic, and the currency should have been devalued.[23] Finally, the trade balance had had a deficit for two years in a row.[24] The mission of the Colombian government to Washington, which had originally made the request for the loans, had the mandate to discuss these problems with the Bank and primarily with the International Monetary Fund, which had also sent a mission to the country.[25]

A general lack of data about the economic conditions of the country exacerbated the difficulties of the Bank mission to Colombia. The summary of the answers by the government to a questionnaire from the International Bank about some national economic data is very telling: most responses were "no data available" or "sketchy data."[26] There was no information about land use or capital investment in sectors such as mineral extraction, manufacturing, electric energy production, or transportation. Major time series, including series on manufactured products, number of production plants, number of employees, and investments, when available, did not go back farther than three years. The data were very approximate, even for the primary national product, coffee, and for basic macroeconomic indicators, such as gross national product and the rate of savings and investment. A document produced several months later testifies to the serious difficulty of finding information. Several fundamental questions remained unanswered, such as the average salary of industrial workers, the principal areas of artisanal manufacturing and even an exhaustive list with the name and location of the major manufacturing plants in the country.[27]

Given this situation, the Bank opted for a two-pronged strategy. The short-term strategy focused on some specific projects that should help stimulate internal production and alleviate the pressure on the trade balance, albeit indirectly. A plan to purchase agricultural equipment was approved as well as a new soda production plant and three small electrical plants: Planta de la Ínsula, Central Hidroeléctrica del Río Anchicayá, and Hidro-Río Lebrija.[28]

The long-term strategy would go into effect only with the decrease of inflationary pressures and after additional studies had collected new information for a more broadly based program.[29] However, some long-term objectives were already clear: reorganizing the credit system to allow easier and larger flows of domestic investment to private sector activities; legislation to establish explicitly a role for the Colombian Banco de la República as the guarantor of IBRD loans to private businesses in the country;[30] and, finally, a fair and transparent policy toward foreign investments in the country (that is, explicit assurance that there would be no expropriations).[31]

In sum, the end of 1948 was a crucial moment: a clear and workable strategy was defined through the Bank's analysis of a country that had primarily been unknown to the institution and its staff, although it was considered one of the most advanced among developing countries. On November 24, 1948, the need for a General Survey Mission was recognized by the most important body of the Bank that oversaw the loans, the Staff Loan Committee.[32] The mission was formally approved at a political level a week later in a letter from the Bank vice president, Robert L. Garner, to Emilio Toro, who had become executive director of the International Bank:

> The Bank will be prepared to consider financing the foreign exchange costs of these projects [the purchasing of agricultural equipment and the three electrical plants, while the plant for soda production had to wait for additional evaluation] subject to the Bank being satisfied, as a result of its examination, that they are technically feasible and economically sound. Such consideration, however, is dependent upon the adoption by the Colombian Government of a vigorous financial policy which is designed to remedy certain elements in the Colombian financial situation which are hampering the economic development of the country.
>
> Also [. . .] it will be necessary for Colombia to pass legislation permitting the Colombian Government to guarantee the repayment of principal and the payment of interest and other charges on any loans made to Colombia by the IBRD.
>
> The IBRD's consideration of the above projects constitutes part of the short-range program whereby the Bank hopes to assist Colombia in its economic development [. . .]. To this end, the Bank considers that an integrated overall development program would be most helpful [. . .]. The Bank would be willing to form an economic mission which would be prepared to make an overall economic study.[33]

Figure 1   Port of New York, agricultural equipment for Colombia.
SOURCE: Co Ln 18, 18 CO 9, World Bank Group Archives.

Another brief mission of technical experts left soon after to focus on three projects that were under way.[34] Several days later, Toro forwarded the enthusiastic response of Colombian President Ospina-Pérez to Garner.[35]

In early 1949, further and deeper thought was given to the short-term plan of action, and the plan was consequently limited. After an additional brief technical mission, the projects on which the Bank decided to intervene were reduced to two: a loan to the Caja de Credito Agrario to purchase agricultural material and an electric power station (La Ínsula Hydro Project). The Bank postponed the two other electrical plants and the soda plant. The official reason was the lack of a detailed implementation plan, but what was most pressing to the Bank's staff was to avoid excessive financial exposure for Colombia before the General Survey Mission. The additional exposure would have limited the country's ability to absorb new loans when the mission took place several months later. Colombia was

Figure 2   Port of New York, agricultural equipment for Colombia.
SOURCE: Co Ln 18, 18 CO 8, World Bank Group Archives.

expectedly disappointed: it claimed that larger investments would produce greater yields, to be used for new, larger investments downstream. Despite this, the first of two loans, used for agricultural material,[36] was granted in August 1949 (see Figures 1, 2, 3, and 4). By then, the General Survey Mission had already begun.

The Collaboration Between Lauchlin Currie and the IBRD

THE MISSION COLLECTS INFORMATION

When the mission to Colombia was approved at the end of 1948, the Loan Department and primarily the Economic Department started a preliminary survey to systematically collect information about the country. The collector and organizer of this preliminary effort was Paul Rosenstein-Rodan, who had worked in the Economic Department since August 1947.[37]

In part, these data could be gathered from other institutions that were operating or preparing to operate in Colombia at the time. The U.S. De-

Figure 3   Caterpillar tractor imported with the 1949 agricultural loan, Valle del Cauca, Colombia.
SOURCE: Co Ln 18, 18 CO 4, World Bank Group Archives.

partment of Agriculture was one of the most active institutions, having already sent a mission to Colombia to study its agricultural conditions. The Export-Import Bank had given credit several times to the Colombian Central Bank and the Caja de Crédito Agrario, Industrial y Minero, and was working with the Food and Agricultural Organization of the United Nations (FAO) on three possible irrigation projects. Finally, the Institute of Inter-American Affairs was active in the field of public health. It was possible for the Bank to find enough material on the agricultural sector because of the prior involvement of other institutions. Other sectors were less

Figure 4 Tractor imported with the 1949 agricultural loan, Valle del Cauca, Colombia.
SOURCE: Co Ln 18, 18 CO 6, World Bank Group Archives.

well covered. However, even the material on agriculture provided little more than general information.[38]

The Colombian territory is dominated by the Andes. The mountains, following the meridian lines, impeded communications between the regions of the country: the tropical coastal areas; the valleys with a temperate climate; and the eastern territories, which are also tropical and further divided into two zones, the *llanos* in the north and the *selva*, or rain forest, in the south.

Population was growing significantly. In 1900, it totaled 3,880,000. The 1938 census registered a population of 8,700,000 (IBRD 1950a, p. 5), but there were estimated to be more than 9.5 million people in 1942 (Casetta 1991) and 11 million in 1950 (IBRD 1950a, p. 5). More than 70 percent of the population lived in rural areas, primarily the high plains of the Andean slopes, and the same percentage of the labor force was employed in agriculture. Only four cities had populations greater than 100,000: Bogotá, Medellín, Barranquilla, and Cali.[39] The vast majority of the population lived in extreme poverty. A 1948 memorandum from the U.S. State Department recorded that "80 percent of the people can't be taxed because of underconsumption [. . .]. Last year more than a million children could not go to school in Colombia because there was no money for teachers or buildings [. . .]. 90 percent of the people of Colombia have never worn shoes."[40]

Marketing of coffee, the most important production item in the country (this includes both agricultural and nonagricultural products) was monopolized by a national federation of producers who purchased the entire production from individual growers. Globally, Colombian coffee production was second only to Brazil. A monopoly had also been imposed on the cultivation and commercialization of bananas by the United Fruit Company through its subsidiary, Magdalena Fruit Company,[41] and on the distribution of sugar and cotton by two other cartels. Coffee and bananas were the two major items exported by the country (see Figure 5).

Beyond these two products, almost all remaining agricultural production supplied the domestic market. The commercialization of products for domestic consumption was not at all organized. The backwardness of the agricultural sector persisted mainly because of strong tariff protectionism. A system of multiple tariffs could selectively impede the import of goods from abroad at competitive prices.

Other important exports included products from the extractive industry: oil, gold, and platinum. Colombia was the largest producer of gold on the Latin American continent, but the three most important mines (responsible for 40 percent of national production) were owned respectively by a U.S., British, and Canadian company. However, petroleum was the most important extractive product. Its extraction began in 1921 with the awarding of a thirty-year license to the Tropical Oil Company, a subsidiary of Standard Oil of New Jersey. In 1951, the approaching expiration of the license and uncertainty about the Colombian government renewing it had discouraged Tropical Oil Company from making new investments. As a consequence, the Colombian share of world production had been declining for some time (less than 1 percent by the end of 1948).[42]

Figure 5 A banana cargo ship in the Colombian port of Santa Marta.
SOURCE: Photo by Hamilton Wright, 1956, Co Ln 68, 68 CO 25, World Bank Group
Archives.

The labor force of the country, which was primarily employed in subsistence agriculture or on large plantations, did not have any specialized
skills. From the beginning, it was clear that an unskilled workforce was
a major obstacle to the modernization of the country. The Bank and
others looked to the Tennessee Valley Authority programs as examples
for spreading advanced agricultural techniques to the rural population.[43]
As for the financial condition of the country, the government was trying to
meet the requirements of the Bank for stability. The Colombians assured
the Bank that the 1949 budget had been prepared according to sound criteria, that foreign debt had been renegotiated with the creditors, and that the
monetary policy had been set up in agreement with the International Monetary Fund, with the principal goal of reducing inflation.[44] Surprisingly,

the same document attributed the net improvement in domestic political stability to the positive consequences of the *Bogotazo* incidents:

> Until the eventful April 9th, the political struggle between the historical parties, Conservative and Liberal, had such characteristics of violent aggression and lack of understanding that a normal development of the administration work seemed a hopeless task [. . .]. The April riots [. . .] created a different and milder climate in the political field which made possible a good understanding between the parties, and their cooperation in search of the permanent well-being of the Republic.[45]

Naturally, this was straining the point, because the Colombian government wanted to reassure the Bank. Actually, several months later, the head of the Colombian mission commented about the political situation of the country:

> The political situation is very tense. The two parties are getting themselves in a position where it is difficult to see a peaceful and orderly way out. [. . .] If the report of the Canadian Electoral Mission is made public, it will leave the situation even worse than before as the Mission, in private conversation with me, more or less threw up its hands at the possibility of instituting an honest system before the coming elections.[46]

As for the fragile industrial sector of the country, at the time, information was almost nonexistent. Therefore, in order to provide here a more thorough picture of conditions in Colombia, it is necessary to refer to the data that the mission collected subsequently during its time in the country and to supplement them with another publication that appeared a few years later (Hirschman and Kalmanoff, 1955).

The industrial sector in Colombia was born only during World War I, when the scarcity of supplies hit global markets. As a consequence, a new generation of diversified businesses emerged and joined the few existing companies, which were mainly specialized in food and beer production. However, the most significant growth was in the 1930s, in response to the reduction in international trade. One can see the importance of these years for the Colombian industry in the increased production in some key sectors between 1934 and 1938: the production of cement grew by 400 percent;[47] sugar production by 200 percent; the production of electricity by 400 percent. Although industrial production diversified, it was still concentrated in the four largest cities: Bogotá, Medellín, Cali, and Barranquilla, where 70 percent of industrial production and 80 percent of investments were concentrated. On the eve of World War II, an oil refinery, plants for the manufacturing of iron products, as well as plants for the production of bottles, textiles, shoes, and building material were added to the food industry. A few years later, new tire production plants were also created. The few national industries were mainly labor intensive. The largest amount of value added in the manufacturing sector came from industries with low capital investment and low productivity: textiles alone made up 18.6 percent, followed by food (18.1 percent), and beer and nonalcoholic drinks (15.8 percent) (Hirschman and Kalmanoff 1955, Table 5, p. 16). Moreover, the country imported almost all rolling stock and wheeled vehicles, industrial and agricultural machinery, machinery for road construction, chemical and pharmaceutical products, paper and paper products, iron and steel (IBRD 1950a, pp. 87–89).

PUTTING THE TEAM TOGETHER

Together with the problem of collecting information, the mission also had to be organized logistically. Considering the novelty and breadth of the objective, it needed more specialists than the two or three that were normally sent on technical missions. In addition, a search was in progress for a high-profile, competent head of the mission. A Bank document of January 10, 1949, seems to mention the first choice of Bank management, John Williams of the Federal Reserve Bank of New York.[48] The choice was important. Williams had been a protagonist in the debate in the early 1940s about how to organize the new international monetary order after the war.[49] Williams, however, did not accept, and his name disappears from the documents.

The position was then offered to Douglas H. Allen, former president of the Rubber Development Corporation (a U.S. governmental agency created in 1942 to guarantee the supply of rubber to the United States), and to Earl B. Schwulst, vice president of the Bowery Savings Bank of New York. Both declined the offer.[50] Although there is virtually no information about these two individuals, it is clear that the senior management of the Bank was conducting the search in familiar grounds, the U.S. financial and entrepreneurial circles. This attention given to Wall Street was not exclusive; the next choice was Lionel Robbins, the famous economist from the London School of Economics, who was probably nominated because of his role as representative of the United Kingdom during the negotiations with the United States during the war, which led to the Bretton Woods Conference. Robbins also found it impossible to accept the invitation.[51] Lauchlin Currie, who finally did lead the mission, was contacted soon after and, by mid-April, the agreement was reached.[52]

Born in 1902 in Nova Scotia, Canada, Lauchlin Currie graduated from the London School of Economics in 1925 and continued his studies in the United States. He earned his Ph.D. from Harvard University and afterward taught there as an economics instructor (Sweezy 1972, p. 117). During those years, Harvard's Economics Department was building itself up after a period of crisis, undergone during the years of World War I (Mason 1982, p. 410). From the second half of the 1920s, intellectuals of the caliber of Joseph Schumpeter, Wassily Leontief, Gottfried Haberler, Sumner Slichter, and, from 1937, Alvin Hansen, the most important representative of American Keynesianism, joined the department. Harvard also served as a laboratory for the younger generation, including Alan Sweezy and his younger brother Paul, John Kenneth Galbraith, Paul Samuelson, Lauchlin Currie, and Harry Dexter White, the future architect of the Bretton Woods Conference. Even before Harvard became "the principal avenue by which Keynes's ideas passed to the United States" (Galbraith 1971, p. 40), several members of the faculty, especially the younger ones, were independently reaching conclusions about fiscal policy that were similar to those that John Maynard Keynes would propose later. As David Laidler and Roger Sandilands have commented (2002a), the scholars who were most alert to contemporary economic reality during those years were open to the most diverse ideas, as shown in a memorandum on economic policy measures to stop the recession that was written in January 1932 by three young scholars from Harvard, Currie, Ellsworth, and White. In this memorandum, they proposed a quantitative monetary theory that appears to be much more typical of the Chicago School than influenced by Keynesian thought (Laidler and Sandilands 2002b). However, these same authors also proposed expansive fiscal policies, which were heterodox at the time. In particular, Currie studied in depth the role of money supply in the collapse of the U.S. economy (Currie 1934).[53]

During the 1930s, this group of young scholars migrated to Washington, D.C., where, as recalled by Galbraith, "there was a strong feeling [. . .] that key economic posts should be held by people who understood the Keynesian system and who would work to establish it. Currie at the White House ran an informal casting office in this regard" (Galbraith 1971, p. 45).[54] Before moving to Washington, Currie had garnered the support of a small group of colleagues for his open letter to the U.S. president. Taking issue with the general orientation of the Economics Department at Harvard, which was rather critical of the Roosevelt Administration, he applauded the government's economic policy as being courageous at last and for having the right outlook for a vast project of reforms (Sweezy 1972, p. 117). While the document was well received in Washington, it irritated the Harvard establishment (Barber 1996, p. 87). They were happy to let Currie go when Jacob Viner called him to Washington in 1934. Viner also called Currie's good friend Harry D. White, who had moved to Lawrence College in Wisconsin. The two men were to form the "Freshmen Brain Trust" to help Roosevelt develop the policies of the New Deal (Laidler and Sandilands 2002a). Their first assignment was at the Treasury Department. From there, Currie followed Marriner Eccles to the Federal Reserve Bank, where he worked to create conditions that permitted a more active fiscal policy (Barber 1996, p. 88).[55]

In 1939, Currie was appointed as President Roosevelt's personal economic advisor. In this position, he was able to insist even more effectively on the need for the expansive policies and public spending that he had supported with Eccles at the Federal Reserve Bank. Currie aimed to create the conditions for a "high-consumption and low-saving economy."[56] This aim could be achieved by combining a highly progressive taxation system with a redistributive policy, mainly in the sectors of health, education, and welfare. As such, "the humanitarian and social aims of the New Deal" could be perfectly reconciled with "sound economics."[57] These policy options were later called "Curried Keynesianism" (Barber 1996, p. 126). In 1942, the war strengthened the policy of massive state investments, which, in the plans of the Keynesian economists in the government, should have continued after the war, as "a comprehensive social welfare program as well as [. . .] air and water pollution abatement, a national grid pattern for electric systems, public transportation for cities, and so on." This would be an integrated program, which was supposed to create sixty million jobs, as Roosevelt said in his 1945 State of the Union address.[58] In reality, military spending, a "Keynesian" instrument during the war, remained a priority after the war, when the conflict turned "cold." Such spending became a decisive obstacle for "liberal Keynesian hopes for abundance, security and progress" (Jones 1972, pp. 130–32).

After Roosevelt's death, Currie left the White House to join the Board of the Council for Italian American Affairs, an organization created to support the Italian government in postwar economic and political reconstruction as well as its confrontation with the Communists.[59]

In 1948, the U.S. citizen Elizabeth Bentley admitted that she had conducted espionage for the Soviets during the war. In her confession, Bentley declared that for many years until 1945 the economist Nathan G. Silvermaster, who had worked at the Treasury and Agriculture Departments and at the Committee for War Economics, had organized a group of spies in Washington. Bentley cited several people whom she thought had contacts with Silvermaster. Among the most important were Lauchlin Currie and Harry D. White, the former right-hand man of the treasury secretary, Henry J. Morgenthau, Jr., and the principal architect of the Bretton Woods Conference. At that time, White was also the U.S. executive director of the International Monetary Fund. White and Currie had only indirect ties to Silvermaster and the proof against them was almost nonexistent, but they were still victims of Joseph McCarthy's hallucination. They asked to appear before the House Committee on Un-American Activities to defend themselves against the accusations, and they both testified on August 13, 1948. Badgered hotly by a young Richard Nixon, White gave particularly dramatic and passionate testimony. As he was returning to his house that evening, he felt ill and died three days later of a heart attack (Sandilands 2000; Boughton 2001). Lauchlin Currie was able to defend himself and return to his job. A few months later, the vice president of the Bank, Robert Garner, asked him to lead the Colombian mission.

As with other people whom the Bank had approached earlier, it is not clear how Currie was selected. As we have seen, he had been a point man for the New Deal and a personal economic advisor to Roosevelt. Robert Garner, on the other hand, although he saw himself as a "Mississippi Democrat" (Garner 1972, p. 163), considered Roosevelt and the New Deal a national calamity:

> [Roosevelt] wanted a balanced budget and many other good things. I voted for him. I think that was reasonable, though I'll never forgive myself for it. He had been in office only a few months when he began to repudiate everything he had declared in his campaign. He instituted the New Deal. He took us off the gold standard. He began to run terrific deficits [. . .] his vicious attacks on bankers and businessmen assured the long continuation of depression.
>
> Roosevelt was a man completely without principle, had a shallow mind and, I think, did more harm to this country than anyone else in history. (Garner 1972, pp. 163–64)

The New Deal provided Robert Garner with the opportunity to become active in politics in order to curb Roosevelt's initiatives.[60] Despite these precedents, it is certain that Garner contacted Currie, and, after being persuaded that Currie was not a Socialist and was not especially partial to the public sector at the expense of private entrepreneurship, he appointed Currie as head of the mission (Currie 1981, p. 54; Garner 1972, p. 289).

The mission was made up of fourteen members. It is interesting to observe its composition in detail (IBRD 1950a, pp. xiii–xiv). In addition to Currie, who was recruited externally,[61] three members came from the Bank: Gordon Grayson, Currie's deputy; David Gordon, who was responsible for services and community facilities; and Jacques Torfs, economist. The chief economist of the mission was Richard Musgrave, from the University of Michigan, who had been strongly recommended by Alvin H. Hansen.[62] Four other members were consultants from the following fields: highways and waterways; industry, fuel, and power (Carl Flesher, from the Kellex Corporation, New York); general transportation; and railroads. Two additional consultants were assigned to agriculture, and two others to health and welfare (see Figure 6).

Upon Rosenstein-Rodan's suggestion, a staff member from the International Monetary Fund participated in the mission to take care of issues

Figure 6   The Currie Mission members. Front, left to right: Raymond C. Smith, Juan de Dios Ceballos (Institute for Industrial Development, Colombia), Lauchlin B. Currie, Jaime F. Cordoba (Banco de la República, Colombia), Haywood R. Faison. Rear, left to right: Frederick C. Gill, Roger Anderson, Richard A. Musgrave, Jacques Torfs, Joseph White, Gordon Grayson, Juan Antonio Montoya, Carl W. Flesher, Wilford E. Johns. Two members of the mission do not appear in the picture: David L. Gordon and Joseph W. Mountin.
SOURCE: Colombia Mission 1949, World Bank Group Archives.

related to the balance of payments.[63] This experiment would fail because of the lack of understanding between the Bank and the Fund, who were both eager to have jurisdiction over issues related to foreign currency exchange. The Fund in particular resented the fact that the Bank discussed this topic in its reports (Sandilands 1990, p. 161). When the final report of the Currie mission was officially presented to the directors of the Fund, "they objected strongly to the Bank's dealing with problems which lie within the Fund's jurisdiction."[64] Cooperation between the Fund and the Bank on monetary policy remained a prickly subject for a long time. Leonard Rist, the director of the Economic Department of the Bank, remembers:

> Our friends in the Fund, the research department of the Fund, were somewhat miffed when they found out that we investigated balance of payment, monetary policies, central bank policy and matters like that [. . .]. At the beginning I tried to resolve it through periodic luncheons with my colleague at the Fund. They always ended up with my having told him what I was doing and he having not had time to tell me what he was doing. At one time he even went so far as to tell me that he didn't think the word "balance of payment" should be used in the Bank. So that was the end of our luncheons.[65]

It is because of this bumpy start that the Fund would reluctantly assign staff to subsequent Bank missions. The Fund would be available only on a case-by-case basis, "so as to avoid the possibility that on some future occasion a Bank mission might cover some important monetary or exchange problem in its report without this report having been reviewed by the Fund Board" (Horsefield 1969, p. 342).[66]

A team of fourteen Colombian consultants supported the mission as its technical-political liaison. This group consisted of high-level representatives of five ministries (Hygiene, Commerce and Industry, Public Works, Agriculture, and Education), the Banco de la República, and three government agencies (Railroads, the Institute of Nutrition, and the National Steel Corporation of Paz de Río).

The various competences of the different members of the mission were supposed to provide a better understanding of the economic, financial, industrial, and agricultural conditions of the country, as well as its communication and transportation infrastructure, public health, hygienic conditions, and public services. According to a telegram that McCloy sent to Robbins, the goal was "to make recommendations as to desirable rate of investment, appropriate fields for development, priority to be assigned various undertakings, projects suitable for International Bank financing, measures to promote local investment and attract foreign private capital, economic stabilization and reform measures, etc."[67]

Figure 7   The first members of the mission just landed in Bogotá, July 11, 1949.
Left to right: Gordon Grayson, Lauchlin Currie, and Robert Garner, greeted by
the head of the Colombian National Bank, Martín del Corral.
SOURCE: Sandilands 1990, p. 160.

On July 10, accompanied by vice president Robert Garner, the first
members of the mission left Washington. The next day they landed in Bogotá (see Figure 7).

THE FIRST IBRD GENERAL SURVEY MISSION,

COLOMBIA 1949

The mission was supposed to last slightly more than two months, but it
went on for almost four, from July 10, 1949, to November 5, 1949. The
various members operated with significant autonomy. They traveled widely
across the country, trying to collect as much information as possible. They
dedicated the final weeks to writing a first draft of their sector evaluations,
which would make up the final report presented by the Bank to the Colombian government.

Lauchlin Currie coordinated the project. He worked closely with the
other members and intervened when he thought that his presence would be

useful in the relationships with the officials of the outlying local governments, who were supposed to supply information. Of course, he maintained
direct contact with the Colombian government and with the International
Bank.

The documents covering the period of the mission are restricted to the
letters between Currie and Robert Garner. Because it was a frenzied period, the narration had the style of a chronicle, but Currie's writing is very
effective in describing the difficulty of coordinating the work of many
people in different locations, the challenges of communication, personal
initiatives, the enthusiasm and harmony, transportation on unpaved roads,
the relations with local officials, in sum, the adventure of the mission. The
following text from Currie speaks for itself.[68]

> When I returned to Bogotá on Friday afternoon, I found things a little
> disorganized. Faison and White, for example, had taken off the previous
> Tuesday for a 20 day trip without having consulted me on their itinerary,
> and I would have made certain changes if I had been consulted. For
> instance, they spent nearly a week getting down the Magdalena [valley]
> and budgeted another week for Cartagena, Barranquilla and Santa Marta,
> which I think is rather extravagant time, so I have written them suggest-
> ing that they cut shorter and spend more time on the roads of Medellin
> and Cali.
>
>   Then there was another little tempest in the teapot, when Caballos,
> whom you will remember, asked Torfs whether the Mission would be
> prepared to study immediately problems of a related exchange. Then they
> proposed to introduce a law into Congress giving the Banco de la Repub-
> lica power to change it. That is the law which you will recall that you and
> I heard mentioned several times. Torfs had not heard of it previously and
> got a little excited, told Anderson [the International Monetary Fund
> representative in the mission], and also made an attempt to see the general
> manager of the Bank to see whether or not the rate was going to be
> changed immediately. Arango didn't see him but sent word to him to keep
> his shirt on. In the meantime, Anderson spent all day last Wednesday
> drafting a cable to the Fund, apprising them of this possibility of a change
> in law and what not, but the whole thing has subsided now. I had a little
> conference with Caballos when I got back and I think he understands now
> that he shouldn't take those matters up with individual members of the
> Mission.

Also, I found that Torfs and Musgrave had gone off to see the Minister of Finance and interviewed him at some length, and had been quoted in the papers subsequently, or rather remarks were attributed to them, saying that Colombia needs a sound budget. But on the whole, I don't think any damage has been done and a lot of good work has been accomplished while we were away.

Smith goes to the Cauca Valley this week and Flesher leaves early in the week for Medellin. Flesher is spending this weekend out at the proposed steel plant.[69]

Among other things, the problem of news leaks was not limited to the possible contacts of individual members of the mission with the press:

We found that despite instructions to the contrary, any dictation given the girls [i.e., the typists] is passed back to the Bank [the Colombian central bank, which housed the offices of the mission], so we are using our machine more. Flesher had a half-completed record stolen the other day when he went out to lunch. I am trying to tighten up on security precautions but don't be too surprised if some newspaper has a scoop purporting to give our views on something or other.[70]

One month into the mission, Currie wrote:

Everything continues to run smoothly here and everybody keeps well. I flew over to Medellin on Saturday to check up on the transport people and what they were doing. The trip was very worthwhile as I found that they had embarked on a rather arduous and painstaking detailed survey of the transportation facilities of Colombia. I convinced them that what was needed was a more selective approach, and we picked out what seemed to be the five or six more pressing problems and devoted the bulk of our attention to that.

Our friend, Gonzalo Majia, got Mr. Faisan to drive down by car on the road to the sea. They had a pretty hectic day, leaving at five in the morning, and I met them when they got back at six in the evening. Majia looked like something the cat brought in. He apparently lost his nerve in the first car and got out and followed in the pick-up car and followed all the dust. Even that didn't quite satisfy him so he took the wheel and nearly had a bad accident. Subsequently, he played us a rather dirty trick in return for the interest we have shown in his own project, by inspiring a long story in *El Tiempo* today to the effect that the Mission was recommending the paving of a road from Bogota right through Medellin to Turbo. I meditated issuing a denial or correction, but then I decided that we might as well get hardened to this sort of thing and just grin and bear it [. . .] I gave permission to Torfs today to bring his wife down for the remainder of our stay here.[71]

Unfortunately, the political situation worsened significantly during the fall. Currie again commented:

We have had the shooting incident in the Chamber. The next day was very tense, but passed off without incident. I think the affair rather shocked and sobered the country. The sale of liquor was prohibited for three days and the Army was very much in evidence, but there were no particular disturbances and liquor is again flowing freely. The Banco [the Central Bank of the country, which hosted the offices of the International Bank's Mission] laid in considerable quantities of rice, potatoes and canned goods and beds, evidently being prepared for a siege, and there was a considerable run on grocery stores in general.[72]

Despite the explosive political situation, the mission concluded its work without major incidents. On October 28, 1949, in a farewell ceremony organized by the Colombian Central Bank for the return of the mission to Washington, Currie proudly described the accomplishment:

Our terms of reference were very broad. They were to diagnose the current situation in Colombia and to suggest a sound plan of development to the end of raising the standard of living of all Colombians within a period of five to ten years [. . .]. Since our basic aim is to raise the standard of living we have had perforce to cover a very broad field. We will have recommendations, as quantitative and specific as possible, in the fields of agriculture, industry and fuels, all forms of transportation, housing, the provision of municipal services, such as power, water, et cetera, health and sanitation, education and in the broad field of fiscal matters, money, banking and exchange [. . .]. I may remark in passing that a study of Colombia, while fascinating to an economist, constitutes an extraordinarily difficult assignment. While the country is much smaller geographically, and in population and wealth as say the United States, its study is a much more difficult task than would be the study of the United States by a group of foreign experts. In the first place, some of the basic data are not available in a form suitable for the type of planning we envisage. A considerable part of the time of the Mission has been spent in compiling and arranging such data. We have, for example, constructed for the first time series of national income and of capital formation [. . .]. We have constructed a balance of international payments for Colombia. We have constructed a money series which enable us to determine exactly the source and causes of changes in the money supply. We have developed basic data on housing, health and sanitation, and on the adequacy of existing municipal services and the requirements for the future. We have assembled basic statistical material in the fields of highway and air transport not hitherto available and have made estimates of traffic flows on the highways [. . .]. We have done considerable work in assembling material on the standard of living of different classes in different areas. We have rearranged and reclassified data in the fiscal field.[73]

The results of a mission with such a large breadth of topics made many institutions curious, including international organizations, U.S. governmental agencies, and private businesses. After the return of the mission and even during the writing of the final report, they asked for access to the information (and were also asked to send comments).[74]

THE CURRIE MISSION REPORT

From early November 1949 until the summer of 1950 when the report was published, Currie was busy with its preparation. The report was to be presented to the Colombian government and the public between July and August 1950. This was the conclusion of the first phase of the new course that the Bank had taken toward member countries who wanted to establish an ongoing collaboration with the institution (see Figure 8).

The report of the Colombian mission and its presentation to the Colombian government and to the public, represented "a *first* in the history of the Bank."[75] The primary focus of the report was "on the task of raising the standard of living of a whole people in a relatively short time" (IBRD

Figure 8   On August 13, 1950, the president of the World Bank, Eugene R. Black (left), presents the summary of the Currie Mission report to the Colombian Ambassador in Washington, D.C., Eduardo Zuleta-Angel.
SOURCE: Colombia Mission 1949, World Bank Group Archives.

1950a, p. 355). The report stated, "In Colombia, the standard of living of the majority of the people is so low that there can be little controversy as to what things are most urgently needed" (IBRD 1950a, p. 353). In general, during the first half of the twentieth century, one could see visible improvements in industrial production, foreign trade, the development of a banking system, and infrastructure, which provided a positive picture of the efforts to modernize the country. However, these improvements developed from such a low basis that they remained far from achieving significant results. The report added, "The great majority are inadequately fed, clothed, and housed. Their health is poor and life expectancy short. A large proportion is illiterate" (IBRD 1950b, p. 2). Raising the standard of living of the Colombian people implied the creation of conditions for better health, an adequate and balanced diet, some education, vocational training, higher productivity at work, and in general the development of intellectual capabilities of individuals, clothing and shelter, and opportunity for leisure activities (IBRD 1950b, p. 3).

One of the main obstacles to this program was not so much an unequal distribution of income as the very low salaries. In a passage of the report, Currie clearly stated what path was to be taken:

> The possibility of making the basic elements of a satisfactory living standard generally available depend upon (1) the size of the national product in relation to population, (2) the distribution of income among the population, and (3) the division of the national product between consumers' goods that can be enjoyed now and capital goods that will increase production in the future. *Of these, the most important is clearly the first.* (IBRD 1950b, p. 3; author's emphasis)

Thus, first of all the goal was to raise productivity faster than the population, whose growth rate was very high.[76]

The adopted approach was to address these problems within a larger and multifaceted framework: "only by a generalized attack throughout the whole economy on education, health, housing, food and productivity can the vicious circle of poverty, ignorance, ill health and low productivity be decisively broken" (IBRD 1950a, p. 356). *The Basis of a Development Program for Colombia*, therefore, covered all the themes and sectors that together were supposed to provide a description of the economic and social conditions whose improvement was essential for the development of the country. On one hand, the actions that the mission considered fundamental dealt directly with both production (agricultural, industrial, and energy) and infrastructure (transportation). On the other hand, they dealt with the standard of living of the population (health and housing). Because of the importance of the agricultural sector within the country's economy, success in raising the standard of living depended primarily on increasing the productivity in this sector.

The mission was disappointed by the use of the land in the various regions: the most fertile soil in the most heavily populated areas was used almost exclusively for raising cattle, while food crops were small and often cultivated on poor land in steep zones where it was impossible to mechanize (IBRD 1950a, pp. 61–74). The mission proposed measures to penalize the underutilization of land in order to push farmers toward higher-yield methods of cultivation, that is, greater productivity. The proposed instrument was a regressive tax on the land when productivity fell below the normal level of production for that particular land. An institute created for this purpose would have prepared a map of the average productivity of the different regions of the country and the lands that went below the identified levels would have been taxed more (IBRD 1950a, pp. 384–86).

In the area of industrial production, the mission focused considerable attention on heavy industry, primarily on the advisability of opening an integrated steel plant in Paz de Río–Belencito (IBRD 1950a, pp. 417–26). This particular focus on a single plant was due to the great enthusiasm of the Colombian government (with obvious patriotic-nationalistic nuances) for a plant that would give the country independence from foreign imports of a strategic good such as steel. In the next chapter, I will discuss the details of this project when I explore the economic policy options during those years. Regarding the conclusions of the mission report, suffice to say that they were strongly against the plant, because it was considered oversized and inefficient. The alternative proposal was to open a much smaller plant on the Caribbean coast to melt down imported scrap (IBRD 1950a, pp. 426–28).

The transportation system, the third topic presented in the report, was still so fragmented that there was no direct connection between the capital, Bogotá, and the northern coast until the end of the 1950s (Abel and Palacios 1991, p. 587). The Colombian transportation infrastructure was so inadequate that the mission recommended only a few concentrated investments, first of which was a railroad along the Río Magdalena (IBRD 1950a, pp. 448–53). Although responding to the countless needs of the various local communities, many small investments would not have made a sufficient impact on the national economy nor would they have solved the main problem, which was to create a new network of interregional connections.

Another serious gap in the infrastructure was the production of electricity, which the government had already started to address. The mission estimated that the total power produced by Colombia's power stations should be almost doubled in a few years (IBRD 1950a, pp. 208–9 and 514–34).

The central sections of the report discussed actions that would have a direct impact on the living conditions of individuals. Public health was a priority issue for the mission, and Currie had already highlighted its crucial importance before the mission began. One of his first notes reported a conversation he had had with a U.S. businessman who was knowledgeable about the Colombian society. The two agreed that "one of the most urgent needs of the country [is] improved health [. . .]. The health of the people is bad."[77] It was necessary to increase access to potable water and to storm drain and sewer systems. It was important to promote public health awareness by training the information providers, such as doctors, nurses, and teachers (IBRD 1950a, pp. 492–98, 503–12, and 543–48).

Another sector that would directly influence the standard of living of a large portion of the population was construction. In this field, the mission suggested active government intervention by creating an agency charged with developing plans to finance and build housing for the masses that were swelling the cities. However, they hoped that soon the governmental agency could devote itself to incentive and oversight, leaving the financing and construction of housing to businesses and private cooperatives (IBRD 1950a, pp. 535–39).

Various sections of the report dealt with fiscal and monetary issues and the balance of payments. With respect to these issues, there was a lot to be done. First, it was necessary to reorganize the national accounting system to make it more accurate and precise. Second, the fiscal system needed to be simplified and made more efficient. Indeed, tax evasion was too high. Third, the Central Bank needed to be empowered to exercise effective control over the reserves of commercial banks. Finally, commercial tariffs needed to be simplified (IBRD 1950a, pp. 551–80). However, on this point the report recommended a closer analysis by the International Monetary Fund. This appears as a recognition on the part of the Bank of the role and competences of the Fund, which had expressed disappointment at the mission when it took positions on international trade issues that the Fund considered within its exclusive jurisdiction.

The total amount projected for all the interventions was approximately 5 billion pesos, of which one billion was for imported goods (IBRD 1950a, p. 593).[78]

The publication of the report on August 14, 1950, triggered many reactions and criticism from various parts. In Colombia, emotions ran high regarding the suggestions for agricultural reform. The Association of the Colombian Farmers counterproposed with several ideas that found support even inside the International Bank. In an article published on January 2, 1951, in *El Siglo*, one of the leading Colombian newspapers, the president of the Colombian farmers, Carlos Echeverri Cortés, denounced Currie's proposals as being unrealistic and punitive. On one hand, the limited and vague knowledge of the lands of the country, together with the great variability in the weather, did not allow an equitable definition of the threshold of minimum productivity under which the regressive tax would apply. On the other hand, Cortés maintained that it was "casi criminal" (almost criminal) to criticize a productive class to which the banks would not issue credit and which could not market its products because of a poor transportation system:

> We should not reach the absurdity of taxing land that cannot be cultivated without offering its owners the credit necessary to achieve the proposed goal in advance. How can you cultivate the land with short term loans of 60, 90 or 120 days? How can you ask farmers to build dams, irrigation, and develop necessary but costly infrastructure, without having the necessary capital, without the adequate credit and effective support from the banks? To dream does not take much, and it takes even less to propose policy about national issues without comprehending the Colombian reality. (Echeverri Cortés 1951, p. 1)

Similar criticism came from the FAO, which had carefully studied the Currie report. These criticisms, however, were based on a preliminary analysis that was quite different from the one offered by the president of the Association of the Colombian Farmers. Herbert Broadley, the director general of the FAO, complained about the fact that "the report does not go into the social and political factors which lie behind the monopolization of the best land by a relatively small class of wealthier people," a class that was probably well represented by the farmer's association.[79] The World Health Organization (WHO), on the contrary, had an "excellent impression" about the analysis and recommendations in the report.[80]

I have already mentioned the criticism by the Fund. I should add that, in addition to questioning the competence of the Bank on fiscal and monetary policies, the Fund questioned matters of substance. Jacques J. Polak, then a young economist at the Fund, complained to his friend Paul

Rosenstein-Rodan about the inadequacy of the foreign capital forecasts that were needed to implement the development program proposed by the report: "One would naturally expect a comprehensive study like that of the Curry [*sic*] Mission Report on a Development Program for Colombia to contain some estimate as to the amount of foreign capital that would be required in the execution of such a program. It is most surprising, therefore, to find that in this report no real allowance is made for foreign capital."[81]

It is useless to analyze this past diatribe further, especially because too many elements are missing to draw acceptable conclusions.[82] However, it is interesting to note that this criticism conveys well the common wisdom of the time that the development of a country primarily depended on the rate of investment, which in turn depended on domestic savings and/or on foreign capital. Moreover, a generally shared opinion assumed that there was a direct and fairly straightforward correlation between these elements, thus it was possible to predict the growth rate of the national economy given certain rates of investment. Even though Currie had declared that he was attempting to illustrate "the dynamics of economic development through an analysis [. . .] of the processes which determine the volume of capital formation" (IBRD 1950b, p. x), the Fund maintained that the Bank was not the right place to conduct this type of analysis.[83]

In academic circles there were opposing views, of which good examples are Frederick T. Moore (1960) and Joseph J. Spengler (1954). They both conducted overall analyses of the results achieved by the first general survey missions of the Bank to developing countries.

Spengler was positive in his evaluation of these results, although he noted several aspects that could have been more deeply explored. For example, he highlighted favorably the great attention that all missions devoted to institutional, political, and extra-economic factors. Frederick Moore's opinion was decidedly more negative: "If the mission reports of the International Bank for Reconstruction and Development are meant to be documents on which development programs and decisions can be based, then they appear to have failed to achieve that objective, except in the most broad and general terms" (Moore 1960, p. 93). According to Moore, the historical-economic analysis and the statistical apparatus were without doubt useful, but what was missing was the formulation of a consequent economic policy, what he called *"political arithmetic* on the program and the alternatives" (1960, p. 90). Although Moore was probably too severe in his overall criticism, this point was apropos. In Colombia, two agencies were eventually established in order to extrapolate a concrete program of development from the report.

THE COMITÉ DE DESARROLLO ECONÓMICO (1950–1951)
AND THE CONSEJO NACIONAL
DE PLANIFICACIÓN (1952–1954)

During the months that the General Survey Mission spent in Colombia, the International Bank completed evaluating the projects that the two technical missions had considered within the framework of the short-term plan of action. As a result, in August 1949, a loan of $5 million was granted to the Colombian government through the Caja de Crédito Agrario to purchase agricultural machinery.

The growing political tensions during the last months of 1949 impeded the closing of the loan for the electric power station at La Ínsula. Although the high price of coffee kept the trade balance positive for the time being and provided a precarious stability to the country, the political situation was becoming worrisome. Colombia was in a state of emergency, and civil and political liberties were severely limited. In addition, many representatives of the Bank expressed fear that "the granting of a loan might be construed as an endorsement of the Colombian regime; it seems certain that the Government would try to make it appear so."[84] The loan for La Ínsula ($2.6 million) would not have been granted until the end of the following year, on December 28, 1950.[85]

Aside from these two specific outcomes, the Bank decided not to initiate any new loans to Colombia before the Colombian government endorsed the Currie report.[86] The Export-Import Bank, a U.S. government bilateral credit agency, followed suit, and, after having granted a $10 million loan on August 12, 1948, blocked additional disbursements to the country.[87]

Currie himself convinced the Colombian president Ospina-Pérez to appoint an independent committee to study the report of the 1949 mission and draw up some action plans and investment priorities. This committee was named Comité de Desarrollo Económico and was established on September 28, 1950. Modeled on the British Royal Commission, it was made up of six eminent individuals representing the two major political parties of the country, conservative and liberal.[88] Currie, whose appointment with the International Bank had come to an end, was hired as a consultant to the Comité to assist the members in the analysis of the report. Jacques Torfs, Carl Flesher, and Frederick Gill, who participated in the General Survey Mission, also took turns consulting on specific issues (Sandilands 1990, p. 168).

Obviously, the Bank followed this step with great interest but decided to refrain from taking a direct role and to wait to open a dialogue with the Colombian government only after all the recommendations of the Comité were made public.[89] Currie's personal involvement with the Co-mité led to some confusion among the press and the public concerning direct involvement of the Bank. This caused the Bank to emphasize that, although interested in the outcomes of the Comité, it would not take a direct role for the time being.[90] This step back by the Bank allows us to move faster through this phase with the help of Sandilands's synthesis (1990, pp. 169–74).

The Comité welcomed most of the recommendations in the final report. An initial success was achieved when inflation was controlled, which until then had been about 30 percent per year. The Central Bank strengthened its power over means of payment, thus ushering in a rather long period of stable prices.

The suggestions regarding development policy for the transport sector were also accepted. Many local building sites, which absorbed significant financial resources, were closed to redirect efforts in the building of major arteries that would eventually link the various regions of the country. These major works included the railroad that ran along the Río Magdalena, a canal between the town of Cartagena and the northern railroad termi-nus, and the upgrade of the most important highways.[91] The airlines were liberalized despite the strenuous, yet predictable, opposition of the airline Avianca, which had a monopoly in this sector. An independent authority for civil air transportation was established, and the monopoly of Avianca ended.

For these infrastructure works, the Comité obtained a $16.5 million loan from the International Bank during the first months of 1951 thanks to the initiative of the secretary of public works, Jorge Leyva. Although this initiative greatly increased the prestige of the Comité within the country in the short term, it may have weakened it in the long term, because it showed that final conclusions from the Comité were not indispensable for the Bank to grant loans to the country. In addition, by breaking up the loans for individual projects, the Bank and the Comité would have lost the ability to link the flow of funds to the Colombian government's acceptance of a comprehensive and integrated investment program, thus giving up much leverage (Currie 1981, p. 63).

The Comité was unable to oppose the political pressure to create an integrated steel mill in Paz de Río in the poor and distant region of Boyacá. It was obviously impossible for such a large plant to break even economically. The domestic market was too small to absorb the potential production of such a plant, and exports would have been insignificant because the local minerals were not of high quality and transportation was expensive. Nevertheless, the Paz de Río steel company was able to move forward with its project. The initial budget of approximately $40 million quickly increased to $160 million in 1955 and $200 million in 1959, "a sum that almost equaled the net amount borrowed for all purposes in the 1950s by Colombia from public agencies abroad" (Sandilands 1990, p. 171).[92]

The Comité did not agree with Currie on the proposal of a regressive tax on underutilized land. As we have seen, this proposal caused a chorus of protests and arguments that found support even within the Bank. There was no doubt that implementing this proposal would require a staggering effort to update the real estate registers. Some asked how well the mission's agricultural recommendations had been thought out.[93] The issue was dropped. The Comité did embrace the proposals from Richard Musgrave for issues related to fiscal policy. Some of them were eventually implemented.

In addition to consulting to the Comité, during those months Currie agreed to lead a new mission sponsored by the Colombian government on reforming public administration. This mission produced a report that was to be studied by a committee to extract a series of reforms. The lack of interest for this mission on the part of the Bank and the weakness of the committee set up to study the report (three people, with no support staff) quickly led to the termination of the implementation phase with nothing concrete coming from it. The only novelty in public administration came from the Comité de Desarrollo Económico, which, with Currie's input, reorganized the Ministry of Agriculture.

The Comité also established a new council for national planning, the Consejo Nacional de Planificación. The Consejo was to report directly to the president of the Republic and would prepare a broad platform for economic and social development for the country, mediate between different positions in civil society, and filter requests presented to the president. Preparing more detailed programs would be left to the different ministries under the general coordination of the Consejo, since it was primarily "an advisory not an executive body" (Sandilands 1990, p. 174).

The new body consisted of three people: Emilio Toro as president, and Jesús María Marulanda and Rafael Delgado Barreneche as advisors. All three were well-known figures and were particularly respected by the vice president of the Republic, Roberto Urdaneta Arbeláez.[94] Other consultants from the United Nations and the International Bank were to support the three members of the Consejo. However, of the seven experts requested by Toro, only two economists appointed by the International Bank joined the Consejo: Albert Hirschman and Jacques Torfs, then one of the major experts in Colombian matters.

At the beginning, the Consejo primarily looked at monetary policy, thus filling an institutional void that the Colombian Central Bank had been unable to cover. The Banco de la República was the only authority in the country in charge of managing monetary issues, but, because many of its directors were also private bankers and thus clients of the Banco themselves, the policies of the central institution had suffered from this obvious conflict of interest. The most serious problem caused by this situation for the institution was its inability to decide the discount rate in a completely autonomous manner (Sandilands 1990, p. 175).

In addition to monetary issues, the Consejo studied many individual projects for the industrial development of the country. Proposed mainly by Hirschman and Torfs, this approach conflicted with the more articulated and organic vision of a general program proposed by Currie. At the time of the establishment of the Consejo, Currie was conducting economic and administrative research for the Department of Caldas (Currie 1979). Currie joined Toro's Consejo only in August 1952. Together with Enrique

Peñalosa, a Colombian colleague in the Consejo, Currie helped develop monetary policies and reproposed the reform of the national public administration, which was again unsuccessful (Sandilands 1990, p. 175). With Peñalosa, Currie also prepared two urban development plans for the cities of Barranquilla and Bogotá, which will be further discussed in Chapter 4. For now, suffice to say that these plans aimed at facilitating economic growth and improving the standard of living of the population.

The Evolution of the Relationship Between Currie and the World Bank

TENSIONS WITHIN THE COMITÉ DE DESARROLLO ECONÓMICO

Relations between Currie and the International Bank had already been complicated since the time of the Comité. The first indication of tension can be found in early 1951 in a letter from Torfs to Rist, then head of the Economic Department of the Bank: "I forgot to add that Dr. Currie's contract expires on February 20. This may account for certain tensions here which, added to the altitude, do not make work in Bogotá particularly pleasant."[95]

The contrast between the two economists in the Comité was catalyzed by the agenda that the committee should have followed. "In Dr. Currie's opinion," Torfs wrote to Rist, "the Committee should discuss and pass on all specific programs (Air, Water, Rail, Transport, Education, Health, Public Utilities, Agriculture, Housing) before being presented a general investment program [. . .]. I do not agree with this view [. . .]. The Committee can no more afford to lose time or prestige."[96] This last reference was to the fight that the Comité had just lost on the issue of Paz de Río. However, Torf's disappointment referred more broadly to Currie, who was inclined to present a comprehensive program, thus delaying the phase of implementation. As we have already seen, Currie's approach was challenged in practice by the loan that the Bank granted to the minister of public works in early 1951 to improve the national transportation infrastructure, even though the Bank considered it "very important that an over-all plan of development be pursued as a result of the extensive studies of the Currie Mission and the Committee."[97]

Torfs did not share Currie's emphasis on issues related to public administration. In this case also, Bank management abstained from supporting Currie's position. One of the very few available minutes of a Staff Loan Committee meeting records Garner's reflection on the issue raised by Torfs during a brief visit to the offices in Washington: "On Public Administration matters you can give them only your personal opinion since the Bank has not had a chance to formulate their views. You can say that the Bank thinks the economic recommendations should be completed first before Public Administration matters are taken up."[98]

In sum, the management of the Bank distanced itself from Currie in early 1951 at a critical time for the Comité. The fight with Empresa Siderúrgica Paz de Río about the advisability of an integrated steel plant had just been lost. The agenda of the Comité had to be defined, while Torfs was challenging Currie's strategy on the overall program and the focus on public administration.

The expiration of Currie's contract as chief advisor of the Comité has been mentioned above. Elmer (Tommy) Burland, a new Bank consultant who had just arrived in Colombia, considered it obvious that Currie would be reconfirmed, and thus he informed the offices in Washington.[99] Garner responded to Burland's letter:

> Dear Tommy, I think it would perhaps be helpful if I explained to you our position on one or two matters.
>   In your letter No. 8, you touched on the expiration of Currie's contract with the Colombian Government. Currie himself also mentioned this subject in a letter to me on February 15, and suggested that I might express to the Colombians my hope that his contract would be extended. On the whole, I would prefer not to do that.[100]

In part, the context taking shape from these documents is confusing: after reading Garner (and learning from him and from Torfs that Currie seemed concerned about not having his contract renewed by the Colombian government) it seems that it was actually the Colombian government that wanted to unload Currie. However, on the same day that Garner wrote to

Burland, the latter received strong assurances from Toro that the Colombian minister of finance intended to keep Currie as chief advisor of the Comité.[101] Rather, it was Martín del Corral (an important figure of the Colombian financial oligarchy, member of the Comité, and future president of the Consejo Nacional de Planificación) who eventually revealed the hostility from Washington against Currie:

> There is a feeling in some quarters of the International Bank that Dr. Currie may have exhausted his usefulness in Colombia [. . .]. If there exists any such feeling, I should like to correct it [. . .]. A major share of the credit for [the Committee's] accomplishment to date is due to Dr. Currie. Although handicapped throughout by totally inadequate staff, and engaged at the same time in directing a Public Administration Mission, he never missed a session and always had material ready for the consideration of the Committee [. . .]. I personally take considerable pride in the objectivity and technical competence of our reports, and this again is due in large part to Dr. Currie. Although anyone who proposes reforms is certain to be criticized, the Colombian people know that he is working for the good of the country. Even the opposition press has recently favorably spoken of his work [. . .]. I think, therefore, that so far from his usefulness has exhausted [*sic*], he has never been in a more strategic position to insure the success of the Plan.[102]

The basis of these feelings and rumors is unclear. What is clear is the final position of the individuals and institutions involved. The Bank did not want Currie to be reconfirmed as a consultant to the Colombian agency that would maintain relations with the Bank. On the other hand, the Colombian government considered Currie's contribution precious and did not intend to give it up.[103]

This became extremely clear when the Consejo Nacional de Planificación took the place of the Comité as the governmental agency for the national economic development. Documents about the Consejo reveal persistent difficulty in implementing its program smoothly and a general dissatisfaction and frustration of almost everyone involved.

THE DIFFICULT BEGINNING OF THE CONSEJO NACIONAL DE PLANIFICACIÓN (1952–1953)

The Consejo Nacional de Planificación was established on April 25, 1952. There was some hesitation regarding its function and its goals from the beginning. First, there was a problem of internal political equilibrium. The Consejo consisted of three people, of which one was liberal (Toro) and two were conservative (Delgado-Barreneche and Marulanda). In the Colombian political scene, which was very tense and constantly on the verge of authoritarianism, this was a serious problem. Although the government considered introducing a fourth member with a liberal orientation, this was not pursued. This imbalance caused the Consejo to lose the aura of independence that had belonged to the Comité. Second, the part-time availability of the members of the Consejo and the very limited dimensions of the financial and economic consulting office raised doubts about the ability of the group to achieve any concrete results. To overcome this problem, identified by the members of the Consejo even before it was officially established, the Bank sought and obtained, in the name of the Colombian government, the collaboration of Albert Hirschman, "an economist of outstanding ability and integrity."[104] After noting that the Consejo was understaffed, Hirschman listed the tasks that he expected to face: "public finance, monetary and credit policy, national accounting, investments in industry and agriculture, foreign trade and payments, social security, education, health, etc."[105] Despite the large quantity of work that awaited him, both Hirschman and the Bank maintained that the Consejo should not request the assistance of other experts. As Garner wrote to Toro two weeks after the establishment of the Consejo, "We feel strongly that there should be only one 'Economic Advisor' to the board."[106] Other foreign experts would have to recognize Hirschman as the "final authority" in formulating recommendations to the Consejo.[107] Meanwhile, on March 15, 1952, Hirschman landed in Bogotá.[108]

The Bank's position was repudiated by the facts. Toro's response to Garner allows us to understand the complications that developed soon after:

> We are in perfect accord with your views as to having one top economic consultant at the head of all the foreign and national experts and are

satisfied that Mr. Hirschman be that man now. Our first idea—that of having several experts in their own field and all more or less with the same standing—sprung from the belief that it would make it difficult to obtain the services of first class men if they were aware that they would come under another expert. You know that—in general—these technicians are quite susceptible. But if that is not the case, it is a much more practical and lasting arrangement to have a director, a "boss," if the expression is allowed [. . .]. As you well remember a Public Administration Mission made a very thorough study of our Governmental organization and presented an excellent study and recommendations for very urgent and important reforms in that field. Very little has been done on that and the Planning Board is going to push that ahead forcefully.

No amount of planning will be effective if there is not the appropriate administrative machinery to carry it on; that is a truism.

The Board has asked me to obtain your confidential opinion upon the following point: As Doctor Currie is very well acquainted with that matter, and very enthusiastic about that work, would there be any inconvenience if we engaged his services—restricted to that field alone—as consultant in it? Doctor Currie has peremptorily been advised by me that Mr. Hirschman will be the top economist and that everything would have to be cleared with him and that he would be the "boss" in the office in charge of the experts. He accepts that.

Currie has also been warned by me as to what his attitude should be with [regard to] his fellow workers and the complaints that they have had in the past about his ungenerous and aborvent [*sic*, perhaps abhorrent] dealings with them. On the other hands the hard times he has gone through of lately have moderated his egoism and ambition to overshadow his co-workers—at least for the time being. We think he could be very useful in the said restricted field.[109]

Evidently, the diverse opinions that emerged during the times of the Co-mité exploded as personal conflicts, and relationships deteriorated. Garner's response was extremely cautious:

So far as concerns the Currie matter, this raises questions of obvious delicacy. You know the various considerations involved as well as I do and the decision is necessarily one which you will have to make. Since you have asked my personal views, however, I feel impelled to state that, were I in your position, I would not engage Dr. Currie for the proposed assignment. My main reason would be that, despite his broad experience and obvious intellectual qualities, Dr. Currie is not, in my opinion, a leading expert in the field of public administration. [. . .] In addition, I believe that employment of Currie on the staff of the Planning Board might, despite the best of intentions on every side, embarrass Hirschman. At the present time, Currie knows a great deal more about conditions in Colombia and the economic problems of the country than does Hirschman. If he should become a leading adviser to the Board, even if only in the public administration field, I believe it would be only natural for him to be looked to for economic advice because of his past experience and activity and because of Hirschman's as yet relative unfamiliarity with Colombian circumstances.[110]

Garner's concern was justified. Since the Bank and the Consejo had entrusted Hirschman, a man with Currie's experience would have overshadowed him and weakened his role as chief economist of the Consejo. Evidently, however, Garner's concern was not enough, and Currie, who had completed the Colombian government mission to Caldas, was recruited by the Consejo,[111] much to the disappointment of Hirschman:

Dear Dick:
    [. . .] things here move not only slowly, but on occasion also erratically.
    What has happened is that the Council has been asked by the President to lend its help in a number of administrative reform problems and that the Council decided to hire Currie, who has just completed a survey of the Caldas province, as a consultant on these matters [. . .]. The situation in the Council continues somewhat confused, not only because of the absence of a secretary-general, but also because of the rather vague nature of Currie's new assignment. I was told that he was to be strictly a temporary consultant on administrative problems; in practice, however, it was probably inevitable that he should have become an economic adviser as well. Since we are not always in agreement, we have already had several open discussions between ourselves during Council meetings on such matters as fiscal and monetary policy. I need hardly say that this is not only unpleasant (Currie's operating methods do not help matters), but also serves to confuse the Council members. In fact, we are getting exactly into

the situation of "confusion and conflict" against which Mr. Garner warned Dr. Toro in his letter of May 13.[112]

Three weeks later, another staff member of the International Bank who was visiting Colombia confirmed Hirschman's discomfort.[113] However, almost simultaneously the situation seemed to change significantly. Based on Hirschman's account, it seemed that Currie had stepped aside:

Dear Burke:

[. . .]. This is the second letter I am writing you in three days. I am very happy not to have to send you the first one which dealt in some detail with the unpleasantness which had arisen here in connection with Currie's participation in the work of the Planning Council. At the end of that letter, I told you that I was still confident that I could handle the situation myself, but added that I would not mind a little help from the Bank. As events turned out, Currie took it upon himself to resolve everything by committing one of those blunders which are not forgiven here. You will no doubt be given all the details by Koster and his companions. Looking back on it now, the whole episode reminds one of Napoleon's Hundred Days, with the fortunate difference that Currie's comeback lasted only about half as long![114]

This was certainly good news for Hirschman. His conflict with Currie could finally be shelved, but not all problems were resolved. First of all, Hirschman's position within the Consejo was not satisfactory. According to a draft memorandum about restructuring the internal staff, Hirschman should have continued being the economic consultant on monetary and financial issues, alongside another economist of the same stature for investment plans and programs. Hirschman criticized this setup for two reasons, one objective and one subjective. On one hand, the proposed reorganization of the duties of the economic consultants would have led to additional internal conflicts; on the other hand, it would have excluded Hirschman from a field in which he had developed a great interest.

It was fairly clear that the set-up contained many opportunities for conflict, especially considering that the Board of the Consejo was already divided politically. Disagreements between economic consultants would have been amplified and not mediated by the Board. In addition, the division of responsibilities would not have been as straightforward as it appeared in theory. The activities of the two consultants would have been inherently contradictory: the financial affairs consultant would be affected by "deflationary bias" and the programming consultant by "inflationary bias." "Moreover," Hirschman concluded, "I am convinced that our Colombian friends do not mind very much if the possibility of conflict is built into the staff organization of the Council. They just love to play one foreign expert out against the other: [. . .] it permits them to make their bow to foreign expert opinion and at the same time provides them with an alibi for doing exactly what they want."[115]

The second and more subjective reason for Hirschman to object to the setup is made explicit here: "I did not give up my Federal Reserve position to advise on the raising or lowering of reserve requirements in Colombia."[116] Hirschman had made himself available for a long period of time to consult in a new and stimulating field, the economic development of a country. Consequently, he was understandably unwilling to manage only the monetary side of the task. He predicted—and threatened—that his frustration would undermine the operational capabilities of the Consejo: "Since I have no intention to set myself up here as a purely monetary expert and to examine projects only from the point of view of their compatibility with monetary stability, the proposed staffing pattern has even less chance to result in good working relations than might otherwise be the case."[117]

Because the Consejo intended to continue with the staff reorganization and had asked the International Bank to collaborate, the head of operations for the Western Hemisphere, Burke Knapp, suggested sending Torfs to Colombia as "planning adviser pro tem."[118] Torfs would have been responsible for developing an "overall plan" and implementing the individual projects in it. Together with Hirschman, with whom he was on good terms, he could also assess whether the roles of "financial" and "program" advisor could exist on the same level, as the troika of the Consejo originally thought, or if one role should be subordinate to the other, as Hirschman maintained. The Bank was aware that this did not address the problems posed by Hirschman, but it could not go too far in opposing the Consejo's guidelines. The Bank hoped that Hirschman and Torfs could work together well.[119] Torfs landed in Bogotá on October 21, 1952.[120]

Hirschman was probably disappointed by this solution and by the fact that he had to continue dealing professionally with Lauchlin Currie. The "50 days" of Currie were not really 50 days. We do not know what "blunder" he committed, because the Bank's management did not leave any written record. What is certain is that, even though the error was serious, he was still forgiven. The president of the Colombian Republic asked the Consejo to study the reform of the national public administration. Lauchlin Currie, who was getting ready to start a mission to evaluate possible projects in the northern city of Barranquilla, would have managed the extension of this research to other administrative departments of the country, as he had done for the Department of Caldas.[121]

In the opinion of Bank management, however, this was too much. The letters and reports from late 1952 and early 1953 testify to the level of frustration and bitterness regarding the "Currie issue" and the persistent inefficiency of the Consejo. Knapp, ultimately responsible for Colombia, was furious. In a letter to Torfs, he wrote: "Dr. Currie's continued intervention in the affairs of the Planning Office is intolerable [. . .]. We should tell the Colombians very frankly that we cannot continue to lend our support to this activity unless Dr. Currie is *completely* removed from the scene," or, in the version to Hirschman, "unless [Currie] is completely eliminated from the picture."[122]

Knapp thought seriously about withdrawing Hirschman from the mission, although "Albert's retirement would mean serious interruption to the continuity of the program in Colombia."[123] Knapp would have been happy to have Hirschman in his department at the Bank,[124] and pulling everyone out might have made it possible to appoint one consultant to cover the two roles of "financial and monetary advisor" and "planning advisor," as originally envisaged. During those days, Knapp contacted economist Bruno Foa in New York. "Naturally," Knapp reasoned, "a prerequisite in getting Foa interested would be to assure him that Dr. Currie was eliminated."[125] Between November and December, both Garner and Knapp expressed this conviction to Toro.[126]

In situations of head-on conflict like this, without contemporaneous documents to reconstruct the facts, it is difficult or impossible to understand who is right and who is wrong; it is also useless. First of all, the correspondence reveals a basic inability to communicate, certainly fed by the difficulties encountered in trying to expedite the work of the Consejo. A report from Torfs to Knapp is the best example of the personal frustration and the confusion surrounding the organizational difficulties of the Consejo. It is worth quoting at length:

> The question of the management of the Office was brought to a head by the draft of a letter to Mr. Garner, in which Dr. Toro said, in substance, that he was going to run the Office for the next four months. The Secretary-General told me privately that this was not acceptable to him, because the management of the office was his responsibility [. . .]. Anarchy reigned as a result. [. . .] Dr. Delgado Barreneche said he did *not* agree that Dr. Toro or any member of the Council should manage the Office. The members of the Council were appointed to pass on recommendations already produced by the Office. Therefore, somebody, whether the Secretary-General or one of the advisers, was to run the show. The present Secretary-General was not able to do it[,] neither was the past one, and it seemed impossible to get a Colombian to fill the job. Therefore, the Planning Adviser was to be the manager of the Office [. . .]. I concluded that the matter required further exploration, and provoked a meeting between Dr. Toro, Hirschman, Arango and I. What came out of this meeting is that in Dr. Toro's view we were all co-equal, but that I was more co-equal than Hirschman and Arango, and also that the Planning Adviser was expected to be responsible for operations over which he had no authority [. . .]. We had—for the moment and probably for a long time—to abandon any hope of "selling" a rational organization of the Council. [. . .] There are already two "co-equal" foreign advisers. Even if one of the two would bow out, the remaining adviser would be confronted with the fact that he is "co-equal" with the Secretary-General [. . .]. I think that the only way out, the only way to obtain some type of leadership is to work it out through mutual consent of the "co-equals."[127]

These difficulties poisoned relationships and made communications and the exchange of opinions ever more complicated. Torfs wrote about Currie in a confidential report to the International Bank: "The fact is that he is still there, and still intervenes in discussions on monetary and fiscal issues, and deliberately sabotages the work of Hirschman."[128] Torfs also had personal difficulties:

I would like to present some very personal views: I have had in the past, and still have a difficult mission in Colombia. Not only I had to formulate—and to some extent invent—the "overall approach" as it applies to Colombia, but I have been involved, through no fault of my own, in very painful operations and exposed myself to violent personal attacks in order to defend the interests of the Bank.

Also, my Colombian assignments have been extremely frustrating in nature. I have already started several times, and am now in the process of starting once again projects I will have to abandon when half way, or a third of the way through. If well handled by my successors, I shall receive very little credit for them. If badly managed by them, I shall share the responsibility.

Finally, the fact that I gave much of my time in recent years to the study of Colombian problems unavoidably resulted in my being assigned more Colombian problems [. . .]. I simply feel that I have been given ample opportunity to experience the less attractive aspects of a work I like, and little possibility of enjoying its more favorable aspects.

The possible appointment of Foa as "planning advisor," therefore, did not seem to Torfs a fair solution: "I would appreciate it very much if the Bank could consider my candidacy for the job of permanent planning adviser here."[129]

The situation had reached a point of impasse. Currie's position was personally defended by the president of Colombia, making it impossible to break his contract.[130] Moreover, Emilio Toro had a very different opinion from the Bank management about the contribution of the consultants to the Consejo. He would not easily give up working with Currie:

Dear Bob:

[. . .]. It is quite evident that Dr. Currie has come to be a phantasmago-ric obsession for some of these technicians.

But in consideration of the fact that Dr. Currie is doing work which, as I say, was ordered by the President and that under these circumstances you find it difficult for the IBR [sic] to induce a proper candidate to assume the post of Economic Advisor, the only alternative that remains is to prescind of looking for one, for the time being [. . .]. Wholly in the spirit of frank cooperation, allow me to advance some short observations about this so important matter of technical personnel: Hirschman is a good man in his restricted field of monetary matters, but as Director of Programs, to plan the development of a country in all its aspects, he falls short and very short.

He lacks broadness of concept, leadership, initiative, personality and has difficulties in expressing and getting consideration for his ideas.

When I compare the work done by the IBR Economic Mission to Colombia in four months; the task accomplished by the Administrative Mission in five months and the service rendered by the Committee of Economic Development in nine months, all under the direction of Currie, with the work that the planning office has accomplished in seven months, under Hirschman, I feel appalled [. . .]. Coming back to "the Currie obsession" let me express the following: some of the Colombian bureaucrats and quite a few foreign experts resent him. This is just natural: one cannot reform without hurting some one, nor direct and correct the work of "experts" and hold their gratitude.

But little if any of Currie's work and recommendations have been found erroneous or unfounded and after discussion and resistance they finally received general approval. The respect for him grows every day in the country.

Believe me yours sincerely,
Emilio Toro

P.S. My good friend and companion in the Council, Doctor Marulanda, who happens to be at my office at this moment, has read this correspondence and he agrees with me fully.[131]

Currie continued his study on the departmental administrations and in particular on urban development program for the cities of Barranquilla and Bogotá. Knapp and Garner decided to stop fighting over the issue of the head of the internal staff of the Consejo. Instead, they resumed collaboration with the Consejo to recruit other consultants for more limited issues.[132] This decision left Torfs and Hirschman "rather surprised."[133] They continued to work together on the overall program and on specific studies about electric power production, trends in exports, and the reform of national financial institutions.[134]

THE END OF THE AFFAIR

On June 13, 1953, General Rojas Pinilla overthrew the government of Urdaneta Arbeláez in a coup d'état. Emilio Toro quit the next day as a sign of protest, but the tensions that had developed in recent months within the Consejo and the bitterness about seeing Lauchlin Currie continuously marginalized were also factors in his decision. The following is a letter handwritten by Toro to Currie and sent from the Chatham Bars Inn in Cape Cod on July 28, 1953:

> Dear Dr. Currie,
>
> I have been hiding from my friends to make possible the "complete relaxation" that my [. . .] doctor also considered indispensable for my health.
>
> I don't know how Dr. Zuleta discovered me here and called me today on the phone. Amongst other things he informed me that Mr. Garner is going tomorrow to Bogotá.
>
> I availed myself of the opportunity and told Zuleta that I authorized him to inform Garner directly (they are going to meet today) that my resignation from the Council was due—amongst other motives—to the fact that I was little satisfied with the way the work of that Board was being accomplished and that I considered changes had to be made in personnel.
>
> That Torfs was mediocre—quite mediocre—as Director of Programs.
>
> That you should be appointed for that all important post.
>
> That the real important task accomplished by the Consejo had been done by you in the regional planning or inspired by you.
>
> That misappreciations, intrigues and jealousies had *reduced* you to a secondary position in the Council and that that situation should be remedied.
>
> That was exactly what I told him—somewhat more in detail. He was in accord and was going to say so to Bob.
>
> Although I will not return to the Consejo I will always do whatever might be in my power to see it functioning well.
>
> I cherish the hope that the Director of Programs be a strong enough character to lead the Counsellors firmly.
>
> This place is a most luxurious hotel. The weather is perfect and the spot is beautiful. It has a private beach and golf course at 50 steps from my apartment. Wish you were here.
>
> Cordially,
> Emilio Toro[135]

Lauchlin Currie, frustrated by the internal tensions and the difficulties that his plan for Bogotá was facing, and worried and in disagreement with the most recent political events, completed his mandate as consultant for the Consejo in February 1954. He retired to a farm near the city of Albán, approximately fifty kilometers from Bogotá (Sandilands 1990, p. 176). The International Bank, on the other hand, considered the political change in Colombia as having a minor impact on the relationship it had with the country and continued its collaboration essentially unaltered.

CHAPTER THREE

Economic Development in Theory and Practice

We are forced to think that humanity can only proceed through polemics, and that changing proportions and measures is necessary for humans that fight for affirming their ideals.

— FEDERICO CHABOD, *Storia dell'idea d'Europa*

The second chapter discussed the relationship between the International Bank and Colombia during the years in which the Bank was reorienting its work from the reconstruction of Europe to the development of its poorest members. The Colombian case was an important test for the institution and its new mission of development.

In this story, Lauchlin Currie and Albert Hirschman were key figures, both when collaboration was at its best among the various actors (the Colombian government, the International Bank, various Colombian government agencies, the Currie Mission, single members that made up the mission, and the public employees from Colombia) and during the periods of crisis and conflict. In some important episodes, Currie appeared to be the cause of conflict. The events of the Comité and then the Consejo are vivid testimony: on one hand, the International Bank was determined to distance him from all activities or institutions in which it was involved, and, on the other hand, the representatives of the Colombian government defended him and his decisions on different occasions.

The documents about this situation mention some disagreement about how the work should be organized and about the most efficient solutions for certain problems, but they also—and primarily—record a strong personal incompatibility among individuals. Personal and temperamental tensions helped worsen relations between Currie and the Bank. It is true that Currie had a harsh and thorny personality. This was confirmed even by people who sincerely admired his professional and personal skills. For example, Richard Musgrave, chief economist of the Colombian mission of 1949, congratulated Currie for the great success of the mission, which was due in his view to "[Currie's] proper combination of long-run patience with short-run impatience."[1] Robert Garner, notifying Emilio Toro that the Bank was determined to ask for the removal of Currie from the Consejo, justified this stance mainly because of Currie's "tendencies to antagonise many people and to create troubles."[2]

However, it is important to reiterate that, although external to the institution, Lauchlin Currie was a very important figure in the new direction taken by the Bank toward developing countries after the disengagement from European reconstruction. In particular, the Colombian mission should have served as a paradigm for future missions of the Bank, and its report was used for many years as a model for studying the general economic and social conditions of a country. In the specific case of Colombia, Currie *was* the Bank, to the point that the newspapers of Bogotá used to describe him erroneously as one of its top managers. *El Tiempo* defined him as "ex-vice presidente del Banco Internacional de Recostrucción y Fomento,"[3] probably to the displeasure of the officials in Washington.

Marginalizing one of the institution's most visible men because of mere personal disagreements seems excessive. Above all, this did not justify compromising the Bank's relations with the Colombian government (recall that Knapp had considered withdrawing Hirschman from the collaboration with the Consejo). To understand why the Bank wanted to get rid of Currie, the specific activities of Currie and Hirschman in Colombia should be seen through the lens of the broader scientific debate about economic development during the 1950s.[4]

The first three sections of this chapter summarize the main opposing positions within this debate and how they influenced or informed work at the Bank. In picking up the different lines of thought as they appeared in opposition to each other, as the specialized journals presented them at the time, and as they are often still presented even today,[5] I will lay the ground-work to demonstrate that the focus on conflict has been excessive and made at the expense of the many points of agreement that can be found within the diverse positions of the debaters. I agree with those who maintain that the debates within development economics were an essential element for the growth of the discipline. The goal of these reflections is not to demon-strate the uselessness of those distant debates but rather to show the points of contact that usually pass unnoticed.

The fourth and fifth sections of this chapter offer a deeper perspective of the conflict between Lauchlin Currie and Albert Hirschman. Chapter 2 chronicled the strife between Currie and the Bank and between Currie and Hirschman. The reasons offered so far for the disagreement between the two economists do not fully explain the irredeemable break between Lauchlin Currie and the International Bank. In this chapter I will explore two specific cases and determine whether they can help us understand this break. Currie and Hirschman were both linked to the International Bank in different ways and were considered representatives of two different approaches to the issues of economic development. Their disagreements about theory when they were both in Colombia can provide additional reasons for the break between Currie and the Bank. Consequently, these disagreements can shed light on the way the institution was taking shape as it considered different options for intervention in developing coun-tries. It will emerge that there was a difference between the debate as it appeared in *journals* and its origin *in the field*. The positions in the field were much closer to each other than the scientific debate led one to be-lieve. The final section reassesses the different positions from a sociolog-ical perspective.

Development Approaches: Balanced Versus Unbalanced Growth

As Pranab Bardhan noted, the study of economic development followed a path from the center to the periphery in economics. This marginalization was partially masked, however, by the fact that at the same time, develop-ment economics was becoming recognized as a specific discipline. In other words, it was gradually institutionalized but, at the same time, marginalized. "The classical economists of the 17th, 18th and early 19th century were, of course, all development economists" (Bardhan 1993, p. 130), but only after 1940 did *development economics* acquire a well-defined connotation as a discipline dedicated to the study of the causes of and solutions for economic backwardness. As we have already noted, one of the causes of this disciplinary institutionalization was the Cold War, which gave strategic relevance to some areas of the world that had been essentially ignored or had remained under the control of their respective colonial powers (Myrdal 1968; Rostow [1960] 1990). Perhaps even more important, it was only after World War II that many poor countries became autonomous states. Moreover, these countries saw the rise of intellectual elites who had studied in metropolitan countries and had come in contact with the ideals of modernization and industrialization typical of developed countries. It was in the name of these ideals that these modernizing elites often became champions of independence movements (Myrdal 1968).[6] From the very moment when its relevance was being institutionalized, development economics moved to the edges of the so-called mainstream.

BALANCED GROWTH

The first rising season of this discipline produced a considerable body of serious thought (Hirschman 1981a). The seminal article by Paul Rosenstein-Rodan (1943) on the problems of industrial development in eastern and southeastern Europe set the terms for the discussion that would develop over the coming years.

Rosenstein-Rodan recognized an "agrarian excess population," that is, a condition of "disguised unemployment" in the agrarian sector that made the productivity of the excess population equal—or close to—zero. The solution proposed by the author was to transfer excess population to a newly established industrial sector. This sector, he added, should be treated "like one huge firm or trust" (Rosenstein-Rodan 1943, pp. 202 and 204).

Although Rosenstein-Rodan did not explicitly mention "balanced growth," this was what he was proposing when describing the industrial sector as an indivisible and unified enterprise. The assumption was that only by developing many businesses like departments of an enterprise, each equally essential to its operation, would it be possible to create external economies that would have made the industrial sector profitable and economically sustainable. First, the many new businesses appearing on the market would have taken the initiative to train the workers in the new specializations. Second, the individual businesses would stimulate mutual demand through their needs for intermediate goods or through the demand for consumption goods by their workers. Rosenstein-Rodan's example was a shoe factory: if taken alone, it would die from an insufficient demand, because agricultural workers could not afford shoes and because there was not enough demand from its own workers, the only ones with enough money to buy shoes:

> If, instead, one million unemployed workers were taken from the land and put, not into one industry, but into a whole series of industries which produce the bulk of the goods on which the workers would spend their wages, what was not true in the case of one shoe factory would become true in the case of a whole system of industries: it would create its own additional market [. . .]. The industries producing the bulk of the wage goods can therefore be said to be complementary (Rosenstein-Rodan 1943, p. 206).

This example is useful to summarize Rosenstein-Rodan's ideas on economic growth. First, a large-scale plan was needed to avoid the bottlenecks of the private sector. Second, the industrialization program was not supposed to focus only on the "basic industries," like transportation, iron and steel, heavy machinery, and power generation: "The quality of 'basic' industries is not confined [. . .] to some public utilities. We have seen how complementarity makes to some extent all industries 'basic'" (Rosenstein-Rodan 1943, p. 208).[7]

Third, we should note the virtual absence of international trade in Rosenstein-Rodan's proposal. Some sections draw attention to the need for some exports in order to have a stable balance of payments. In general, however, foreign trade was marginal and not considered part of the complementarities needed for industrialization.

Finally, the article set the groundwork for subsequent work covering the need for an initial phase of decisive and concentrated development, in order to achieve the minimum scale and scope for the newly created industrial sector to sustain itself. This was the concept of the "big push." Rosenstein-Rodan described this process in a later article:

> "There is a minimum level of resources that must be devoted to [. . .] a development program if it is to have any chance of success. Launching a country into self-sustaining growth is a little like getting an airplane off the ground. There is a critical ground speed which must be passed before the craft can become airborne."[8] [. . .] Briefly, this is the task of the big push theory. (Rosenstein-Rodan 1961, p. 57)

Ragnar Nurkse took up many of these ideas in a rich and original essay, *Problems of Capital Formation in Underdeveloped Countries*. The issue was to find a way to break the "vicious circle of poverty" that rigidly bound together the incentives to invest, the share of the national income devoted to savings, private consumption, and the size of the market and that held them in equilibrium at a low level. In the following two quotations, one can notice parallels with Rosenstein-Rodan's themes of complementarity and the need for an intense and concentrated effort:

> The difficulty caused by the small size of the market relates to individual investment incentives in any single line of production taken by itself. At least in principle, the difficulty vanishes in the case of a more or less synchronized application of capital to a wide range of different industries. Here is an escape of the deadlock; here the result is an over-all enlargement of the market. People working with more and better tools in a number of complementary projects become each others' customer. Most industries catering for mass consumption are complementary in the sense that they provide a market for, and thus support, each other. (Nurkse [1953] 1962, p. 11)

In Nurkse's vision, the leading role should have been played by the Schumpeterian innovative entrepreneur. As Nurkse put it:

> In our present context it seems to me that the main point is to recognize how a frontal attack of this sort—a wave of capital investments in a number

of different industries—can economically succeed while any substantial application of capital by an individual entrepreneur in any particular industry may be blocked or discouraged by the limitations of the pre-existing market. (Nurkse [1953] 1962, p. 13)

The fact that the role of Joseph Schumpeter's entrepreneur was played by private entrepreneurs instead of bureaucrats in some nationally planned economy (as Rosenstein-Rodan meant, although he opposed the Soviet model) is a minor issue. The main point was to intervene on different fronts concurrently and with a speed that would create enough lift so that the entire economic system could take off.

However, Nurkse was more skeptical than Rosenstein-Rodan regarding the capacity of poor countries to accumulate the capital needed to succeed at industrialization. Inspired by James Duesenberry's writings on the "demonstration effect" (1949), Nurkse maintained that the marginal propensity to save in these countries would have proven to be decidedly lower than in industrialized countries when the latter went through their first phase of industrialization. Having little faith in shortcuts that relied mainly on income transfers from developed countries, Nurkse believed in the necessity for developing countries to establish more stringent financial policies that would enable a more efficient collection and use of internal resources (Nurkse 1952).[9]

UNBALANCED GROWTH

The analyses underlying the balanced growth approach were welcomed by the majority of scholars who were beginning to take an interest in development economics. These reflections "while being themselves novel and heterodox, were rapidly shaping up in the 1950s as a new orthodoxy on the problems of development" (Hirschman 1984, p. 87). In an explicit reaction, however, some researchers advocated considering the process of economic development as essentially *un*-balanced.

There were two main supporters of this second approach: Albert O. Hirschman and Paul P. Streeten. As Hirschman underscores (1984, p. 87n1), both independently published their works in support of a path of unbalanced growth between 1958 and 1959.[10] Of the two, Hirschman's work was known best for its radical criticism, for he questioned the ultimate meaning and the overall usefulness of the theory of balanced growth.

> My principal point is that the theory fails as a theory of *development*. Development presumably means the process of *change* of one type of economy *into* some other more advanced type. But such a process is given up as hopeless by the balanced growth theory which finds it difficult to visualize how the "underdevelopment equilibrium" can be broken into at any point. [. . .] The balanced growth theory reaches the conclusion that an entirely new, self-contained modern industrial economy must be superimposed on the stagnant and equally self-contained traditional sector. (Hirschman [1958] 1963, pp. 51–52; emphasis in the original)

Thus, for Hirschman, the theory of balanced growth came down to a static comparison between two hypothetical images. It was like considering two states of equilibrium: an equilibrium of "underdevelopment" and an equilibrium of "development," without facing the process of transformation from one condition to the other. Hirschman was therefore particularly vehement in his opposition to the dominant point of view:

> How many a Western traveler to an underdeveloped country has been bewildered and dismayed by the ubiquitous poverty and inefficiency, by the immensity of the task, and by the interlocking vicious circles! The temptation is strong then to leave all this backwardness alone and to dream of an entirely new type of economy where, in the words of the poet, *"tout est ordre et beauté!"* (Hirschman [1958] 1963, p. 52)

At the base of Hirschman's criticism was the deep-seated conviction that posing the problem in terms of a missing element (primarily, capital) was fundamentally misleading. This presupposition indeed led to thinking that it was sufficient to import or, in some way, acquire the missing ingredient in order to foster development.

This common conviction was strengthened by the generalized application of the models produced by Roy Harrod in 1939 and Evsey Domar in 1946 to analyze problems of growth in *developing* countries. However, these models had been originally designed to study short-term financial cycles in *developed* countries. Therefore, it was very inappropriate to try to derive instruments from them that could be empirically applied to stimulate growth in poor countries. As William Easterly summarized, "Domar's model was not intended as a growth model, made no sense as a growth model, and was repudiated as a growth model over forty years ago by its creator." Nonetheless, he added, "Domar's growth model became, and continues to be today, the most widely applied growth model in economic history" (Easterly 2002, p. 28). According to the summary of this apocryphal tradition—the so-called Harrod-Domar model—a country's growth rate is directly proportional and strictly correlated to the investment rate, which depends in turn on the savings rate of that country. An easy equation calculates the amount of capital needed to obtain the desired rate of growth. The difference between this amount and the capital effectively saved in a country defines the financial gap that must be overcome in order to obtain the target rate of growth. Aid from international institutions, therefore, was part of this general mechanism for transferring funds (Easterly 2002, p. 29; Hirschman [1977] 1981b).

On the contrary, Hirschman considered the resources and the elements necessary for development as latent, hidden, perhaps unavailable but nonetheless existent. In an oft-cited passage, he stated: "Development depends not so much on finding optimal combinations for given resources and factors of production as on calling forth and listing for development purposes resources and abilities that are hidden, scattered, or badly utilized" (Hirschman [1958] 1963, p. 5).

On closer examination, this concept was not completely new. It is worth noting that it also appeared in the writings of the scholars whom Hirschman criticized. For example, Rosenstein-Rodan and Nurkse had spoken of "disguised unemployment" in agriculture in an attempt to appreciate and expose hidden or badly utilized resources. The difference was in the breadth and variety that Hirschman considered typical of these "latent resources" (Hirschman [1958] 1963, p. 6). The issue was thus not only to create capital by productively employing an underutilized work force in a society that did not know anything about saving. Rather, it was necessary to bring to light existing but unused capital, a "latent or misdirected entrepreneurship, [. . .] a wide variety of usable skills," and then "*combine* all these ingredients" (Hirschman [1958] 1963, p. 6, emphasis in the original). Hirschman's interest was in the dynamic aspects of development, that is, on the *process* of development.[11] He stated: "Our approach leads us to look for 'pressures' and 'inducements mechanisms' that will elicit and mobilize the largest possible amounts of these resources" (Hirschman [1958] 1963, p. 6).

A first direct consequence of this approach was the at least partial use-lessness of the efforts devoted to identifying and removing alleged "obsta-cles to development" (for example, extended families, the lack of organized work habits, the lack of raw materials or capital, the lack of an entrepre-neurial mentality, the inefficiency of the public administration), the elimi-nation of which would enable development. Hirschman gave them much less importance. Their removal could at some times be postponed, at other times would be useless, and at still other times the obstacle could be trans-formed into an advantage (Hirschman [1965] 1971c).

The supporters of unbalanced growth did not focus their analysis on the lack of this or that productive factor, which, when mixed with others, would have led to a process of economic growth. Instead, they focused on a form of weakness in the very process of the mixing. The apparent scarcity of specific factors or "prerequisites" became a symptom of insufficient ca-pacity to assemble and sustain these very factors in the development pro-cess. In sum, they brought to light another scarcity, which was different in quality and importance. Streeten underscores: "One aspect of the case for unbalance is that it highlights the spots where action is needed most ur-gently, and thus economizes in a resource often in short supply, viz. the power to take decisions" (Streeten 1959, pp. 182–83).

Second, but just as important, these scholars thought that it was no lon-ger necessary to concentrate the effort needed to industrialize a country in a short period of time. The "take-off" metaphor crashed. As Hirschman wrote to André Gunder Frank in 1959:

> If one wants to move [straight] from one equilibrium position to the next, then, because of the discontinuities and invisibilities *that I take for granted*, the "big push" or "minimum critical effort" is indispensable. But if we assume that intermediate positions of development-stimulating disequilib-rium are sustainable at least for limited time periods, then we can manage to break down the big push into a series of smaller steps.[12]

This change in perspective was significant. The focus was exclusively on the *process*. This perspective fostered the research into all those mechanisms, sequences, and instruments that served to stimulate investments or had a contagious effect. As Hirschman stated, "Development theory and policy therefore face the task of examining under what conditions development decisions can be called forth in spite of these imperfections [in the process of the formation of decisions], through pacing devices or inducement mechanisms" (Hirschman [1958] 1963, p. 26).

It was therefore a search for "hidden rationalities" (Hirschman 1984, p. 91) that, through apparently perverse or defective processes, could stimulate effective sequences of investment. By showing the way, forcing certain future decisions, and inducing the increase of the demand of a product through growing availability of another (the "induced needs"), a single investment was able to generate entire sequences of new investments. It could motivate new, previously frustrated potential investors and supplement scarce decision-making capacity. Hirschman defined this as "complementarity" of investments, a concept that was fully explored through the idea of "backward" and "forward linkages" in *The Strategy of Economic Development*.

The "linkages" led to the dismissal of synchronic solutions to the problem of industrialization (for example, the "big push," "critical minimum effort," "take-off") and replaced them with sequential solutions that were more appropriate to developing countries. In the 1950s, Alexander Gerschenkron was known for his studies about the processes of European industrialization. He refuted the concept of a one-size-fits-all model that could be applied to countries that were industrialized first (the "first-comers") and to those that followed later (the "late-comers"), and he developed the concept of "substitute factors" (Gerschenkron 1962; but the most important essays are from 1952 and 1957). Hirschman took inspiration from Gerschenkron's approach in his analysis of developing countries, and he underscored "sequences [. . .] that seemed questionable or *al revés* (the wrong way around) from the commonsense point of view" (Hirschman 1984, p. 94).

For example, in his discussion on the relationship between foreign trade and economic growth, Hirschman sustained (contrary to the prevalent opinion) that "countries tend to develop a comparative advantage in the articles they *import*" (Hirschman [1958] 1963, p. 122; emphasis in the original). Imports mark a path, provide proof that an internal market exists, and very probably, once they pass a certain threshold, will be substituted by national production: "Imports thus reconnoitre and map out the country's demand; they remove uncertainty and reduce selling costs at the same time, thereby bringing perceptibly closer the point at which domestic production can economically be started" (Hirschman [1958] 1963, p. 121). Among other things, this implied a different attitude toward trade policies: "Infant industry protection should not be given *before* the industry has been established but should become available, if at all, only once this event has taken place" (Hirschman [1958] 1963, p. 124; emphasis in the original).

More generally, the concept of "linkages" aimed at defining all the processes and sequences that proved effective in promoting additional investment in sectors or interconnected productions. This would lead to investment decisions that would have been more difficult, had they not been made in a sequential process (that still remained spontaneous).[13]

Reflecting on the most appropriate technologies for developing countries, Hirschman observed that economic processes that could tolerate a lower margin of poor performance were particularly useful to developing countries lacking industrial traditions, to the extent that these processes could exert pressure toward more efficient and higher-level performance. Thus, they could force these countries to move toward a standard of productive efficiency comparable to developed countries. Hirschman gave the example of air versus road transportation. A less industrialized country would need to provide its air transportation service with a high standard of maintenance, because poor performance would lead to intolerable levels of risk. On the contrary, the country could tolerate poorly maintained roads because this implied a lower level of risk.

By generalizing, Hirschman highlighted production activities in which the *process* was central rather than the *product* (Hirschman [1958] 1963, p. 147). An example of a process-centered industry is iron and steel production, where the machinery dictates the pace and the performance of the worker. On the contrary—for example, in woodworking and housing—workers can follow their own pace and habits in creating the product. These reflections revealed a "hidden rationality" in the priority given by some developing countries to capital-intensive (centered on the process) production rather than labor-intensive (centered on the product) (Hirschman [1958] 1963, chapter 8).

Thus, these hidden rationalities functioned as "substitute factors," to use Gerschenkron's words, for some of the cultural prerequisites of industrialization (specific ethics or motivations for success). They also undid the usual recipe that advised developing countries to economize their scarce resources (capital) instead of the abundant one (labor). Hirschman favored a dynamic vision that focused on creating mechanisms to stimulate processes of growth. These mechanisms would be functionally equivalent to the ability to make decisions (also a scarce resource in Hirschman's and Streeten's views).

In addition, Streeten observed that the process of unbalanced growth would allow more efficient use of resources in the long run. On the contrary, balanced growth, if at all possible, would inevitably lead to untimely or inefficient investments, because it requires a condition of equilibrium throughout the development process. Therefore, Streeten also insisted on the "process" as the fundamental factor. It is somewhat paradoxical that Streeten based his own position on the work of Schumpeter, who was also hailed by the supporters of balanced growth.

> Schumpeter considered this kind of investment [characterized by "complementarities"] as the key to the understanding of economic growth. Progress depends upon the adaptation of passive sectors to the active sector in which innovations originate. [. . .] "We must recognize that evolution is lopsided, discontinuous, disharmonious by nature. [. . .] The history of capitalism is studded with violent bursts and catastrophes. [. . .] Evolution is [. . .] more like a series of explosions than a gentle, though incessant, transformation."[14] (Streeten 1959, p. 181)

Development Approaches: Program Loans Versus Project Loans

While discussions about theories of balanced and unbalanced growth were *en vogue*, another dichotomy ignited debate among development economists: the appropriateness of loans linked to broad development programs versus loans for individual projects.

PROGRAM LOANS

As one might expect, balanced growth was conceived and promoted through planning policies, that is, through investments aimed at *programs*. We have seen that Rosenstein-Rodan recommended considering the entire industrial sector "like one huge firm or trust." Only an investment effort big enough to involve an entire manufacturing sector could jump-start the development process; individual projects would not reach critical mass. In addition, taking into account the *composition* of the investment programs was considered fundamental, as was a reflection on the effects that fiscal and monetary policies could have had on initiatives in the industrial sector.

It was crucial to reach an investment level that would maintain not only high employment rates but also sustained growth in labor productivity (Dasgupta 1965, p. 54). A growth in consumption to the detriment of investments was considered a danger to avoid carefully. Addressing the possibility of growing salaries and inflationary pressures, the Indian economist A. K. Dasgupta proposed "a system of controls very much on the lines of war-time controls" (1949, reprinted in Dasgupta 1965, p. 37). This radical position, which was still influenced by a postwar climate, can be better understood in light of John K. Galbraith's analysis several years later.[15]

> For India and the Indian Government, economic development is a political imperative. Perhaps—just perhaps—if development were left to market incentives, it would proceed as rapidly as under public auspices, or more rapidly. But suppose it did not. Suppose the private vision and entrepreneurship were lacking. Or the capital. Who can be sure? [. . .] Then to count on free enterprise now would be a dreadful risk. (Galbraith 1958, p. 591)

During those years, India was committed to carrying forward its second five-year plan, centered on the development of heavy industry, which the Nehru government considered a priority for the economic development of the country. At that time, this plan was praised or criticized as an autochthonous version of a socialist economy. In reality, the Keynesian Nehru[16] and the Keynesian Galbraith (who became an economic advisor to the Indian government after his diplomatic tour of duty), considered it the only realistic path toward economic development.

PROJECT LOANS

Both the program approach and the theories of balanced growth were subject to severe criticism. In an article written at the end of the 1960s, Albert Hirschman summarized the numerous criticisms directed against the program approach during the years (Hirschman [1968] 1971b).

First, an aid program linked to a complex program of economic intervention rather than an individual project would probably touch macroeconomic issues, such as the relationship between investment and consumption, the relative sizes of the public and private sectors, or exchange rates and the system of prices. By changing these variables, it is certain that some groups within a receiving country would positively benefit from the reforms, while other groups, at least in the short term, may be harmed. Therefore, according to Hirschman, a first and general consequence of a program approach would be to stimulate internal opposition that a single project, however important, could not do.

Second, an aid program risks becoming useless or redundant. A government receiving an aid package to pursue some macroeconomic targets needs to be already committed to those targets, regardless of the aid received. Thus, the aid is useful only to "remunerate the virtue [. . .] where the virtue spontaneously appears" (Hirschman [1968] 1971b, p. 277). On the other hand, if one believes that aid could push a government to pursue policies that it would otherwise not have considered, then the task becomes much more difficult, that of "introducing virtue into the world" ([1968] 1971b, p. 278), and it would be doomed to failure because governments are most often reluctant to having their hand forced. Along this line of thought, multilateral lending institutions have historically concentrated on fiscal and monetary indicators, which, unlike the real applicability of program loans, are easy to monitor. As a consequence, these institutions have paid ever less attention to economic growth or social justice, the assumed main goals of the aid.

Therefore, according to Hirschman, an aid policy centered on individual projects, albeit less ambitious, would be more realistic and ultimately more efficient.

The Debate on Development Reverberates Inside the IBRD

Within the Bank, the debate between different approaches to stimulate development of poor countries took the specific form of a discussion between those who supported program loans and those who supported loans for individual projects.

CONFLICTING APPROACHES: PROGRAM VERSUS PROJECT

The report of the Currie mission clearly took the side of those who favored a program approach, and Lauchlin Currie often underscored the need to prepare an integrated development plan. In August 1950, in a speech to the American Academy of Political and Social Sciences, he declared:

> It appears essential that the attack on the problem be incorporated in a comprehensive, overall program that provides for simultaneous action on many fronts. Economic, political and social phenomena are so inter-related and interwoven that it is difficult to effect any significant and lasting improvement in one sector of the economy while leaving the other sector unaffected [. . .]. Poverty, ill health, ignorance, lack of ambition, low productivity are not only concomitants—they actually reinforce and perpetuate one another. (Currie 1950, p. 5)

Supporters of project loans, instead, insisted that, according to the Bank's *Articles of Agreement*, "Loans made or guaranteed by the Bank shall, except in special circumstances, be for the purpose of specific projects of reconstruction or development."[17] Accordingly, the Bank could only gain the stable confidence of U.S. investors (the principal, and indeed practically the only, source of money that could be spent on international markets immediately following World War II) if it adhered strictly to this practice. Only individual and well-monitored projects would guarantee U.S. financial markets that the loans were administered according to sound criteria of responsible economic management (this topic will be resumed in Chapter 4).

Lauchlin Currie was not alone in promoting broad and multifaceted programs of development. Between 1947 and 1952 Paul Rosenstein-Rodan, then the most important economic theoretician at the Bank, opposed the institution's increasing propensity toward financing individual projects.[18] Specifically, Rosenstein-Rodan maintained that linking a loan to a single, well-defined project was illusory. He claimed that single-project loans would end up financing the marginal project that the beneficiary country would have abandoned had it not obtained a line of credit from the Bank. In other words, these funds would finance a project that a country would have probably accomplished anyway. It was a problem of "fungibility" of funds—their at least partial transferability from one destination to another that caused, in the words of Rosenstein-Rodan, the "psychoanalytical problem why a bunch of intelligent people committed what to an economist (not only to an economist, to any logical thinking people) must be rather an extraordinary shift in perspective in the wrong direction of giving so much emphasis to projects [. . .]. The bank thought it financed an electric power station, but in fact financed a brothel."[19]

To better understand the implications of the discussion, it is interesting to note how, as a reaction to the restrictions by the Bank on the use of the borrowed funds, the Colombian government deliberately used the legerdemain of "fungibility" during negotiations for a loan to increase supply of potable water in the city of Bogotá, which suffered from constant water shortages.[20] Since the Colombian officials knew it would be easier to receive funds for electricity than for potable water (which was mainly for private use), a preliminary report prepared by the office in charge of contacts with the Bank suggested applying only for a loan for the electricity project.[21] The total requested, however, would actually cover the funds needed for both the electricity project and the potable water one.

PROGRAM VERSUS PROJECT: THE BANK'S
CHANGING ATTITUDE

Even though the propensity of the Bank to disburse loans to individual projects was expressed in its *Articles of Agreement*, during the years of transition from European reconstruction to third world development there was a significant internal debate on the scope and extent of this mandate: more precisely, about the "special circumstances" defined by the *Articles* that would allow the institution to make exceptions. While this debate characterized the transition period, its substantive questions came earlier—

namely, does it make sense to make loans for individual projects? Is it realistic to propose integrated investment plans? It is worth noting that the conflict between the different options appeared only when the Bank started dealing with poor countries.

All the authors who wrote about the beginnings of the Bank agree that the first loans from the Bank financed large programs of reconstruction. The first and largest loan ever disbursed by the Bank, $250 million, was given to France in 1947.[22] Other loans to European countries all went toward "governments' reconstruction programs" and "deviated from what was expected to be the standard pattern for loans" (Kraske et al. 1996, p. 55). In the opinion of the Bank's vice president, Robert Garner, however, the loans for European reconstruction were supposed to be an exception: "The feeling at the time was that [they were] not to form a precedent for the normal operations."[23]

In other words, the Bank's top management did not think that it was part of the Bank's role to provide overall program loans to developing countries. Exceptions in favor of program loans had been made reluctantly, as in the case of the reconstruction of postwar Europe.

The Bank's documents, however, did not completely abandon the rhetoric of "planning" and "programs." During those years, programs of development that would frame the effort of modernization of a country were not at all uncommon, and many missions and institutions produced programs of this kind. As we have seen, the Currie mission received a broad mandate, and it produced an objective and complete survey of the economic and social conditions of Colombia. The Bank's publications remarked that "the Bank would prefer to [. . .] base its financing on a national development program, provided that it is properly worked out in terms of the projects by which the objectives of the program are to be attained" (IBRD 1950c, p. 8).

This notwithstanding, the Bank's operations increasingly financed individual projects—a propensity that would continue for many years. A publication about the goals and strategies of the Bank, prepared by its staff, summarized the issue:

> The Bank seeks in the case of each borrowing country to determine what are the appropriate investment priorities and then to adapt its program of financial assistance to meet the priority needs. Consistently with this approach the Bank has encouraged its members to formulate long-term

development programs. [. . .] The existence of such a program, particularly in countries whose investment requirements are large in relation to their available financial resources, greatly facilitates the task of determining which projects are of the highest priority in the light of their prospective contribution to the program as a whole. [. . .] If the Bank were to make loans for unspecified purposes or for vague development programs which have not been worked out in terms of the specific projects by which the objectives of the program are to be achieved, there would be danger that the Bank's resources would be used either for projects which are economically or technically unsound or are of a low priority nature, or for economically unjustified consumer goods imports. (IBRD 1954, pp. 44–45)

AUTOBIOGRAPHICAL NOTES

To take the next step in our discussion, it is important to consider Albert Hirschman's reflections on the circumstances that generated his theories. In the preface to his *Strategy of Economic Development*, published in 1958, Hirschman declared that his main purpose in writing the book was "to elucidate my own immediate experience in one of the so-called underdeveloped countries," that is "to reflect on my Colombian experience" (Hirschman [1958] 1963, pp. v–vi). His observations during his stay in Colombia—as he again explained in an article written in the 1980s— "remained key elements of the conceptual structure that I erected three years or so later in *Strategy*" (Hirschman 1984, p. 94).

Importantly—and this will be introduced in the following section—this conceptual structure was constructed in direct opposition to Lauchlin Currie. When Hirschman arrived in Colombia as a World Bank economic advisor, Currie had already been there for three years: initially as the head of the World Bank mission, then as economic advisor to the Colombian government. It was not long before the two economists reached the point of mutual intolerance. In a 1994 interview, Hirschman remembered this situation: "I felt a bit frustrated. In addition, we had conflicts with other American consultants [. . .] especially with one, Lauchlin Currie, a Canadian who had been part of Roosevelt's 'brain trust' and was a man of considerable intelligence" (Hirschman [1994] 1998, p. 81). It is thus worth deepening the theoretical nature of the conflicts between the two economists.

Currie Versus Hirschman: Monetary and Fiscal Policy

Disagreements between Lauchlin Currie and Albert Hirschman within the Colombian Consejo ignited when they worked together to address the monetary situation and budget planning of the country. In some respects, their opinions were truly different. However, on other issues, some of them important, their positions shared many points.

ANALYZING THE SITUATION

Currie and Hirschman shared similar assumptions on the monetary conditions of the country. The first available document on this issue is a memorandum prepared by Currie at the end of May 1952.

According to Currie, although there was no inflation, the rapid growth of government deposits posed an inflationary risk. Had the government spent these funds equally rapidly, this would have caused an increase in private deposits and a corresponding increase in reserves of commercial banks, thus causing the risk of a secondary expansion of credit and deposits. A suddenly increased availability of money in the hands of the public would have certainly caused a rise in inflation.[24] The Colombian government should have focused on controlling the debt of commercial banks with the Central Bank. By controlling the debt, the government could control the reserves of commercial banks and private deposits.[25]

One month later, Hirschman put forward a similar analysis, reporting an "inflationary trend." He continued: "The number of public works that are or about to be carried out [. . .] will turn themselves into a new source of means of payment in the public's hands and thus operate as persistent inflation factors."[26] Expanding on Currie's analysis, Hirschman pointed to a short-term, cyclical factor: the financing of the agricultural season while waiting for the produce to be sold, thus allowing the farmers to pay back loans taken out during the first half of the year. In spite of the seasonal character of this factor, in recent years the income had never been sufficient to cover all the loans.[27] Like Currie, Hirschman thought it premature to cool down this possible inflationary tendency, but he suggested monitoring the situation constantly and avoiding excessive levels of public spending.

The analysis of public accounts also confirmed the presence of inflationary stress. This was another point shared by the two economists. Hirschman noted that, even with a slight surplus in current accounts during the first six months of the 1952 budget, the amortization of public debt would have encumbered the entire surplus accumulated with the particularly well-managed budget of 1951. The resulting expansionary monetary policy would add to other spending already planned for the second half of the year for the National Police and the Ministry of War. As Hirschman put it, "It must be clearly understood that the release of this surplus means, from an economic point of view, the creation of new money."[28] Consequently, there would be a deficit and therefore "a decrease in the Government deposits in the Banco de la República."[29]

Unless the government could keep the spending of the various ministries under strict control, the problem would reappear even more severely the following year. Indeed, data available at the end of August 1952 showed that projections for all ministries exceeded the budget set by the government.

> The total expenditures according to the budgetary appropriations defined by the President were 614.9 million pesos. Nonetheless, the Ministers in their 1953 draft projects have not been able to keep within the limits set by the President. Up until now the total expenditures have been 718.8 million of pesos. This figure will continue to rise when the remaining Ministries (Foreign Affairs, Justice, Sanitation, Public Works) send their draft projects.[30]

Even without including the spending projections of the Ministry of Public Works, a spending ministry par excellence, the scenario for 1953 appeared very problematic, especially if one considers the cyclical expansion of money in the first half of every year as a result of loans to farmers.[31] Both Hirschman and Currie concluded that an inflationary movement that threatened the economic development and the social stability of the country was very likely.

HYPOTHESES

A first way of dealing, at least in part, with the emerging inflationary problem was to refinance the debt of the Ministry of Finance. This debt constituted about half of the predicted deficit; refinancing it had the purpose to defer the problem.[32]

The other half of the deficit posed more difficult problems. In their first estimates, both Currie and Hirschman considered it necessary to assess the spending items of the various ministries and to redistribute spending authority among them; by doing this the two advisors were attempting to reduce the enormous share allocated to the "public order" ministries—War, Police, and Justice—whose expenditures grew enormously after the events of April 1948 (the assassination of Gaitán and the *Bogotazo*).[33] These three ministries alone spent more than the ministries of Labor, Welfare, Public Services, Agriculture, Education, Hygiene, Trade and Oil, Communications and Telephones, and National Buildings, and the government contributions to the Agrarian Credit Fund, combined. On the other hand, the ministries of Agriculture, Hygiene, and Education accounted for only 14 percent of total spending;[34] a very small amount, considering the importance of their tasks. Currie and Enrique Peñalosa declared that "the objective must be to gradually modify the expenditures distribution in order to achieve a better impact on the wellbeing of the people."[35]

THE CLASH

The economic advisors of the Consejo were in complete disagreement on the revenue estimate for the following year. Currie and Peñalosa were rather optimistic: "In a country in a full development process like Colombia, income and taxable property grow every year."[36] Their estimate of the cash deficit was therefore quite small, equal to approximately 7 million pesos. They believed that, with a particularly favorable tax revenue, there would be a slight surplus.[37]

Hirschman reacted vehemently to Currie and Peñalosa's memorandum. First, he complained that the memorandum overlapped with a memorandum on the same subject, which the minister of finance was presenting to the president of the Republic at that time. Hirschman maintained that this struck a blow to the reputation of the Consejo, seemingly unable to coordinate with other institutions. It also jeopardized cooperation and trust with the ministries, which were fundamental for the Consejo to influence their spending policies effectively.[38]

Second, Hirschman thought that the exceedingly optimistic estimate of future tax revenues would have a decidedly damaging effect on the preparation of the coming year's budget:

> You have to be naive not to know that the preliminary calculations of the Budget Directorate were intentionally somewhat low. The Minister of Finance and the Budget Director have to wage a fight with the "overspending" Ministers in the first phase of the budget preparation and thus a conservative estimation of the Government income is a very important tactic in the difficult defense of a balanced budget. With the preparation and dissemination of a high and exaggerated estimation of the income the Council has gravely damaged the Minister of Hacienda and the Budget Director in this defense.[39]

Hirschman maintained that, ideally, Colombia should not only have a balanced budget but also a surplus. For this reason, revenues should be estimated at prudently low levels.[40]

As seen in Chapter 2, Hirschman referred to Currie's "blunder" in a letter to Burke Knapp. It is possible that this blunder (which Hirschman thought would eliminate his adversary) was precisely the publication of the memorandum written by Currie and Peñalosa. The dates of the memorandum and Hirschman's letter to Knapp are consistent with this hypothesis. Perhaps Hirschman believed that the disappointment of the minister of finance at Currie and Peñalosa's memorandum, which disempowered the minister in his fight against the spendthrift ministries, would have been enough to ask for Currie's immediate dismissal. However, this did not happen, and it is unclear whether the Currie-Peñalosa memorandum really bothered the minister of finance.

The main conclusion that can be drawn from this episode is that the differences between Currie and Hirschman were primarily tactical. As we have seen, they had agreed on the original analysis of the fiscal and monetary situation and on the solutions. The clash occurred on the opportunity to disclose the estimates of revenues for the following year and to what extent to disclose them.

This clash happened exactly in the period of high stress documented in Chapter 2. As an additional proof of the rock-bottom level of Currie and

Hirschman's tolerance for each other, it is worth noting that Hirschman also challenged the "unscientific" basis of the data presented by Currie and Peñalosa, and the discussion deteriorated into the nitty-gritty of the nature and the meaning of the numbers.[41]

Currie Versus Hirschman: Iron and Steel Production

The positions of Hirschman and Currie also differed over the advisability of establishing the Paz de Río integrated steel plant. To fully understand the impact of the dispute, it is worth reconstructing in detail the different positions. We will begin with Currie and the 1949 mission.

ANALYSIS OF THE CURRIE MISSION

At the end of World War II, steel production in Colombia was almost non-existent. In 1947, domestic production was only 7 percent of domestic consumption, thanks only to the recent installation of two steel plants with electric furnaces in Medellín and Pacho; the former to produce reinforcing rods and steel bars, the latter to make pig iron (IBRD 1950a, p. 90, table 20, and pp. 96 and 417).[42]

Because of the significant strategic national interest in steel production and the large scale of the proposed investments, which would have affected the entire strategy of industrialization of the country, the Currie mission gave special attention to this issue. The section of the report covering this topic was largely based on the work of Carl Flesher, the mission's expert on industry, fuels, and power. As was typical at the time, especially when dealing with developing countries, the report focused on the domestic market. There was little expectation that a local nascent industry could export its products, because of prices and/or quality (Krugman 1993). The mission estimated that in 1955 the internal market would be able to absorb about 150,000 tons of steel. However, about 44,000 tons would have been made up of large pipes, extruded sections, and steel for buildings that did not justify the high investments needed to establish a domestic production line. Thus, the remaining potential demand for future national production would have been about 100,000 tons per year (IBRD 1950a, p. 418). The government now actively pursued large-scale national steel production after a time when the country did not even reach 10,000 tons per year. The Currie mission endorsed these aspirations and evaluated options to best serve the goal.

When the mission arrived in Colombia, two options were already being considered. The first, backed by the government, involved building an integrated plant that took advantage of the domestic supply of iron and coal. The second had been proposed by some private groups and was more modest in nature. It envisaged the processing of scrap metal rather than an integrated plant.

The possibility of an integrated steel plant in Colombia had been studied for years. In 1944, the U.S.-based Rolling Mill Company, who had been asked to prepare a study, advised against it. The Koppers Company of the United States had different views, and in January 1949 proposed establishing a plant in the small town of Belencito, in the administrative region of Boyacá—a few miles from Paz de Río, where deposits of coal, iron, and calcium had been found. Koppers suggested a plant that could produce 200,000 tons a year and would cost almost $95 million. In October of the same year, Koppers's proposal was scaled down to about 100,000 tons a year that would cost a not insignificant $40 million (IBRD 1950a, pp. 419–20). It is very likely that Koppers's new proposal was made as an attempt to avoid criticism from the Currie mission, which had doubts on the profitability of a large integrated plant.

The government put constant pressure on the mission to accept the Paz de Río project, but Flesher and Currie thought otherwise.[43] The mission's final report criticized both proposals from Koppers. First, the mission maintained that the final cost would probably substantially exceed the estimates. Similar projects in Chile and Brazil just a few years earlier had their original estimates triple in size.[44] Specifically, the mission highlighted the fact that some essential costs had not been considered, such as "housing and community facilities; the establishment of central warehousing and branch warehouses for the efficient distribution of the final product; starting-up materials; personnel training and miscellaneous smaller items" (IBRD 1950a, p. 421).

Second, the methods of financing and incentives were not convincing. To implement the project, a government-owned firm, the Empresa Siderúrgica Nacional de Paz de Río, had been established in 1947. In an attempt to turn the Empresa into a public company, a decree (No. 4051, December 20, 1949) gave taxpayers the option of diverting 2.5 percent of their regular taxes to purchase its shares. However, although this might be an effective way to collect cash, it would not have an impact on the management of the plant: given the strategic importance of steel, the virtual impossibility of bankruptcy because of government's support, and the fact that all the necessary loans would be guaranteed by the government, it was easy to expect that the government would never give up tight control of the plant. The mission was concerned that management would be preoccupied with politics rather than economic and productive efficiency (IBRD 1950a, p. 422).

Third, a number of technical and geographical considerations advised against the implementation of the project: the low quality of the mineral at Paz de Río, the limited amount and the depth of the coal deposits, the lack of sufficient running water for the cooling system, and the high altitude, which would complicate the combustion process. Above all, the geographical location was highly unfavorable. A steel plant in Belencito would be isolated from the major transportation routes of the country. The product would have to travel to Bogotá by train, and from Bogotá it would have to be sent to final destinations by a second railroad with a different gauge. The isolation would have made Belencito unattractive for establishing other machinery plants, thus inhibiting the creation of a "growth pole." This, in turn, would have made it impossible to exploit the secondary products of the plant (for example, surplus gas beyond the need of the steel plant).

According to the evaluation of the mission, all these impediments would have significantly increased the price of the product compared to international market prices. Even the first, larger proposal of about 200,000 tons did not make a difference, as it would not generate economies of scale that would have made the project viable. The report concluded that "it seems apparent that the location of the proposed plant, on the one hand, and the smallness of the market, on the other, make it premature and inadvisable at this time to consider the erection of either the larger or the smaller integrated steel projects at Belencito" (IBRD 1950a, p. 425). Not even the expected development of a very depressed area such as the regions of Boyacá and Santander was a good enough reason to justify the project. Other, less costly and more profitable endeavors could be pursued, provided the steel plant at Belencito would not unbearably encumber the whole economy (IBRD 1950a, pp. 423–25).

The report proposed a different solution: to establish a smaller steel plant in Barranquilla, on the northern coast of the country, to transform imported scrap metal. The plant would consist of an electric furnace for scrap metal or for pig iron ingots, a rolling mill, a bar mill, and drawing mill. Unlike in Paz de Río, an additional power plant was unnecessary, as the existing one could support the energy demand of the new plant. Similarly, because Barranquilla was already well developed, it did not need an additional residential area. Most important, being entirely devoted to the transformation of scrap metal, this plant did not require a coke oven or a blast furnace. Its realization therefore seemed easier than the project in Paz de Río and also cheaper: less than $10 million, of which only half would be spent in imported products.[45] In conclusion, the International Bank would have only financed $5 million. Located at the terminus of one of the few internal waterways to the sea, this plant could supply the internal market of the country as well as other Caribbean markets (IBRD 1950a, pp. 426–27).

In addition to the establishment of a steel plant in Barranquilla, the report recommended expanding the metalworking plant in Medellín, which could take advantage of an abundance of electric power and could more than double the production of rolled sections and ingots with an investment of $500,000 (IBRD 1950a, p. 427). Obviously, the report from the Currie mission provoked bad feelings within the Empresa Nacional de Paz de Río.

INTERESTS AT ODDS

Soon after the report was published, headlines in the local newspapers reported the vehement arguments that immediately followed: "The Junta of Paz de Río Rectifies Currie's Judgment," "Boyacá Does Not Accept Currie's Judgment," "Currie's Plan Is Impracticable," "Mr. Currie's Report Is a Ghastly Analysis of Colombia."[46] Because the orientation of the commission had been clear even before the publication of the report, during the fall of 1949 and the first half of 1950 the Colombian government had been under constant pressure to keep the mission from vetoing the establishment of the steel plant at Paz de Río.

Regarding this issue, some documents of the International Bank from July 1950 reveal that the Colombian government had asked the Bank of France for a loan of $25 million to purchase some equipment needed for the steel plant, without mentioning it to the International Bank.[47] The Currie mission report had yet to be published (it would be made public on August 14, 1950), but an agreement existed between the International Bank and the Colombian government that provided for the latter to inform the Bank about any contacts with third parties for the purpose of obtaining additional loans. The reason for this agreement was to allow the Bank to have a clear vision of the financial conditions of the country and to discuss strategies *before* the government undertook additional debt.[48] Taking loans from other institutions would hamper the ability to honor the debts to the Bank or to pursue a development program that might have implied opening further lines of credit with the Bank. This initiative by the Colombian government appeared to question the usefulness of a General Survey Mission and its report.

While the report of the Currie mission was being published, the relationship between the Bank and the Colombian government dropped to its lowest point. The Bank considered Colombia "in default,"[49] and on August 22, 1950, a week after the publication of the Currie report, Robert Garner harshly protested to the Colombian minister of finance:

> It has been the Bank's understanding that it was the genuine desire of the Colombian Government to base its development plans and program on the results of the survey of the Colombian economy carried out by the Currie Mission and that was your Government's intention to have regard to the conclusions and recommendations of the Mission in channelling such resources (both domestic and foreign) as were available to Colombia for investment in economic development. It is therefore a matter of great disappointment to the Bank that on the eve of the publication of the Currie report, your Government, without any prior consultation with or notification to the Bank, should have so far committed itself to proceed with one single project which, if it is to be proceeded with in its present form, will absorb a substantial proportion of Colombia's investment resources.[50]

In particular, after recalling each of the terms of the agreement signed by the Bank and the Colombian government—"the guarantor will notify the Bank promptly of the particular proposal [to incur, assume, or guarantee any external debit] and prior to the time of taking the proposed action, shall afford to the Bank all the opportunity [. . .] to exchange views with the guarantor with regard to such proposal"[51]—Garner threatened to freeze the loans that were due:

> The full recognition and acceptance of these provisions is regarded by the Bank of the highest importance [. . .]. The Bank should have this confirmation before the President of the Bank could feel justified in recommending to the Board of Executive Directors the conclusion of the proposed loan to the Central Hidroelectrica del Río Anchicaya Ltda.[52]

It seems that the threat was effective: the loan for the power plant at Anchicayá was granted two and one-half months later, on November 2, 1950.[53]

As we saw in Chapter 2, the Colombian government established a committee to study the Currie report, the Comité de Desarollo Economico, which took office on September 28, 1950. The first topic in the agenda of the president of the Comité Martín del Corral was, expectedly, the Paz de Río plant.[54]

Within a month from its establishment, relations between the Comité and the Junta Directiva of Paz de Río seriously deteriorated. The consulting firm hired by the Junta, the U.S.-based Arthur G. McKee Company, sent its vice president, Mr. William A. Haven, to Colombia. Haven tried to undermine the authority of the Comité and its positive orientation toward the conclusions of the Currie report by arguing that no representative of the Comité had the competence needed to discuss the suitability and specifications of an iron and steel plant. At the same time, the Junta had purchased some advertising space in newspapers to denounce publicly the obstructionism of which it felt to be a victim. In addition to its own reasons, the Junta argued that the country needed to guarantee its independence from foreigners in the strategic sector of steel production, at a time of soft demand in the scrap metal market.[55] Evidently, the Junta was alarmed,[56] and the situation was tense: "There is little doubt"—wrote Jacques Torfs to his supervisor, Leonard Rist—"that the Cabinet is under terrific pressure to give up the stringent measures taken in accord with the over-all program [. . .]. Both conservative and liberal groups are attacking the Government for holding up Paz de Río."[57] Nonetheless, Currie wrote to the vice president of the IBRD, Robert Garner, that "the Committee is pretty solidly on our side."[58]

The new president of the Comité, Rafael Obregón, had written a note that partially seemed to confirm Currie's impression. The place for the new plant was Paz de Río, different from the location proposed by the Currie mission. This itself was a notable concession to the Junta, considering how the Currie mission had seriously criticized the undesirable location of the plant. However, Obregón was indeed solidly on the side of the Currie mission on virtually everything else. Recognizing the high cost of the plant proposed by the Junta, Obregón recommended that the committee study carefully the project proposed by the Currie mission, which was less costly and, most important, supported by the IBRD.[59] A large steel plant would be at the expense of other public works that were also considered necessary for the development of the country, and it would absorb an excessive amount of resources. Obregón affirmed: "We are all worried that its cost could affect other priority public works, such as roads, oil pipelines, agriculture, education, public health, etc. The funding available, both from national savings and international credit, is limited, and investment in one initiative takes away from others."[60] Two weeks later, a new document was ready, of which Currie had assiduously been preparing several drafts. This document recommended a compromise.

THE "INFORME DE LA MISIÓN PARA EL COMITÉ"
AND THE FLESHER SOLUTION

There was a general agreement that the new plant's output should be competitive with foreign imports, which until then had almost completely met the domestic demand for steel. This would ease the balance of payments. To this purpose, it was first necessary to assess the size of the domestic market. The "Informe" (report) used the estimates prepared by the Currie mission, about 100,000 tons per year.[61]

Also based on the Currie mission analysis, the Koppers Company's figure of $40 million was considered an underestimate. In the opinion of the

Comité, the total cost of the plant at Belencito–Paz de Río would have probably increased to $100 million. According to the evaluation of the "Informe," this number would have absorbed two-thirds of the capital available for the industrial sector of the entire country for one year.[62]

Finally, the financing resources did not seem adequate for the considerable size of the project. The Empresa de Paz de Río, which was determined to build an integrated plant, had managed to obtain a loan of $37 million (one-third German and two-thirds French), which was however frozen for the time being because of the Bank's complaint.[63] Additional spending, inevitable and probably larger, would be financed by the issuing of government bonds by the Banco de la República. The risk was, however, that the Banco itself would eventually have to purchase a large part of them, thus jeopardizing the anti-inflationary policies that the monetary authorities had been pursuing with great difficulty until then.[64]

The Empresa's forecast to produce at $20.76 per ton (one-third of the $61.71 per ton, estimated by the Currie mission, of the scrap metal plant at Barranquilla) was therefore considered clearly wrong; the production cost at Belencito would have probably been slightly higher than at Barranquilla. The "Informe" maintained that "all efforts geared towards low-cost steel production would be in serious jeopardy."[65]

The Comité harbored serious doubt: "We have to ask ourselves to what extent can a modern country make an important sector of its economy, such as the steel industry, independent from imports."[66] Both solutions—Belencito–Paz de Río and Barranquilla—were subject to criticism. On one hand, the Comité did not want to underestimate the strategic value that the government and the most influential opinion makers placed on independence from foreign markets in steel production. On the other hand, it recognized that the smaller plant in Barranquilla better met the economic reality of the country:

> It is true, though, that the national production of pig iron would eliminate the most serious raw material problem [. . .] and that an integrated plant would allow a much greater degree of independence. The cost of this independence is a greater capital investment. The type of plant needed for scrap transformation seems to be less expensive in the current stage of Colombia's industrial development than an integrated steel plant.[67]

The general inclination was toward the integrated plant. Such a plant was an explicit desideratum, for which it was necessary to find a positive response.[68]

Given the impasse of the discussion, the IBRD had once more sent Carl Flesher, the main author of the first proposal advanced by the Currie report, to Colombia with the task of recommending a new compromise, which the Comité eventually accepted. Flesher did not insist on the plant in Barranquilla and endorsed the case for expanding production at Medellín and Pacho. Part of his recommendations was the integrated plant at Paz de Río with its nearby deposits. This plant, however, would be much smaller than the one estimated by Koppers: from 122,000 tons of annual production envisaged by the original Koppers proposal to 60,000 tons per year; furthermore, the design of its coking plant, blast furnaces, and rolling mills would have to be greatly simplified in order to build them in Colombia.[69]

This proposal truly seemed to square the circle: On one hand, the national necessity to produce a strategic good (steel) without depending on the international scrap metal market was confirmed. One the other hand, it avoided a gigantic investment, which would have absorbed too many resources from other sectors that were just as important for the development of the country. Domestic manufacture of most of the equipment would also reduce spending in foreign currency (estimated at around $15 million). Finally, a smaller plant would allow management and local workers to gain experience without risking serious errors. The report concluded that "this type of plant could be built much faster and its development would be in tandem with the growth of the internal market. [This] plant will solve the dilemma created by previous projects."[70]

The Flesher proposal was officially adopted by a Comité document, the "Informe preliminar sobre el establecimiento de una planta siderurgica" (Preliminary report on the establishment of a steel mill). This second proposal drafted by Flesher achieved the outcome of "aligning the development of Paz del Rio with the Currie Plan with the favorable perspectives of a better financing scheme than the current one."[71] While drafting the "Informe preliminar," on the advice of the IBRD and in agreement with Currie, the Comité contacted several businesses to verify the feasibility of its proposal.[72] Among these, the Comité selected the American Salem Engineering

Company of Salem, Ohio, whose enthusiastic and confident president-owner Samuel Keener—"quite a high pressure salesman" according to Currie's judgment—arrived in Bogotá on December 9, 1950, to make initial contact and to present a draft proposal.[73]

Established during the Depression in 1934, Salem consulted on the construction of the widest variety of different plants, "from concrete to fruit processing plants, from steel mills to frozen food installations."[74] It was regarded as one of the most important steel mill construction firms in the world. It had offices in England and Canada and partnerships with companies in France and in Germany. Moreover, before the war it had owned about 90 percent of Friederich Siemens of Berlin, which manufactured and licensed open-hearth furnaces (also known as "Martin-Siemens furnaces").[75] During the war, it had collaborated with the Manhattan Project to build the atom bomb.[76] It had plants throughout North America and worldwide, except for Australia.

Salem's proposal met the priorities specified by the Comité to have an integrated steel mill that was independent from imported raw materials and not too costly. It was also important to save foreign currency and work with technologies that were as labor intensive as possible (this aspect related to the need for capital saving). Production would include ingots and rods, rolled sections, structural steel, and steel cable. A simple plant would also reduce dependence on foreign spare parts and technicians from abroad. The total cost would not have exceeded $20 million (including materials to launch production and employee room and board, which were not included in Koppers's estimates, according to the Currie report).

Salem proposed an incremental strategy, from relatively easy technology to cutting edge. It was important to follow a path by "starting at the beginning."[77] This incremental policy was corroborated by historical evidence, and it was advanced as the most appropriate policy to make the business grow consistently with its own experience, according to the method of learning by doing:

> Generally, it has been through the small plant approach that the steel industry has been developed through the world. Fully integrated plants came into existence through the orderly, profit-financed growth of small

companies [. . .]. As the simplified steel plant makes profits and operators become more skilled in the use of complicated equipment, orderly growth can be planned, thus eliminating many of the operational headaches and equipment choice mistakes which occasionally arise in fully integrated units [. . .]. The plant will be so designed that the addition of relatively inexpensive machinery would [. . .] increas[e] the number of products which could be made from the plant's steel production.[78]

This concept had been taken up and adapted to Colombia by the "Informe preliminar" of the Comité: "All current important industries in the country started on a modest scale and with relatively simple equipment that was later upgraded while the work force was trained, the markets expanded, and more capital became available."[79]

As of December 15, Currie seemed confident about the positive outcome of the new compromise: "Things are done cheaply and si[m]ply and [. . .] costly mistakes are not made by the local boys."[80] However, in the last two weeks of the year, after the wrap-up of the "Informe preliminar," the situation came to a head. As the Comité was presenting the document to the government for approval and commissioning a feasibility study, the Junta orchestrated a strategy to prevent this from happening. Before the meeting of the Board of the Empresa set for December 20, 1950, the Junta asked Currie for detailed comments on the new proposal supported by the "Informe preliminar." Currie promptly obliged.[81] The very next day, December 20, the Board of the Empresa officially rejected the possibility of undertaking a new study, claiming that this had already been discussed, with negative results, during previous contacts with other businesses (six were on the list). Unlike the Comité, the Empresa thought that a larger plant would be preferable to a smaller one for reasons of economies of scale: its excessive capacity in the beginning would, in the medium term, allow the Empresa to promptly meet an increasing market demand as needed. In addition, the Empresa underscored the serious damage to the national economy that would occur by giving up the manufacturing of assets such as railroad tracks, steel beams, armored plates, and structural steel sections "that the country urgently needs." It also emphasized the incompetence of Salem. Paz de Río announced that it would not stop construction of the plant with its already-finalized capacity of 140,000 tons per year.[82]

The resolution of the Board of Directors was made public immediately. Perhaps not entirely in good faith, the "Informe preliminar" of the Comité was treated as a published document, and Currie's letter treated as an official position of the Comité, notwithstanding the fact that he claimed to speak only on behalf of himself.[83] Thus the Junta had fabricated a public occasion to reject a proposal that should have been evaluated by the government only, whose decision should have been final. Moreover, the press mainly favored the integrated plant and interpreted the resolution of the Junta as an expression of the official position of the government, which, however, had yet to express itself.[84]

The Comité tried to present its version through the press, but it had lost the match. The Colombian government was cornered by the growing nationalistic euphoria for the country to produce some strategic goods internally. It avoided a confrontation and backed the initiative of the management of the Empresa. The government was also conditioned by international events. The Korean War, which had started on June 25, 1950, caused an increase in the price of scrap metal and greatly helped those who argued for the need to produce steel within national borders irrespective of the cost of the plant. The International Bank—in principle decidedly against the integrated plant and determined to follow its mission's report and the recommendations made to the government by the Comité based on that report—also pulled back. Obviously, the final decision about the plant was not up to the Bank, but I could not find any documents testifying to the Bank's pressure on the Colombian government or its efforts to back up the work of the Comité. In the words of the Bank's vice president, Robert Garner, "Paz de Río had become a national symbol."[85] It was therefore useless to oppose it.

STEEL AND DEVELOPMENT: REASONS FOR DISAGREEMENT

As the chronicle of events so far proves, to understand the debate about the steel plant in Colombia soon after World War II, we must discriminate between economics and technology on one hand and politics on the other. Indeed, the final decision about the plant in Paz de Río was based on politics.

The Junta Directiva was able to build a large and aggressive consensus around its own project. This gradually reduced the ability of the Comité to operate. The international situation, dominated by the Korean crisis and its repercussions on the market for raw materials, offered the Junta the excuse for a public opinion campaign based on vital national economic and military needs. The Junta skillfully hooked it to the rhetoric of the economic growth of the country: In the long run, the initially oversized plant would become economically efficient and national strategic necessities would be strengthened. The irrationality of a decision based on current (and exceptional) events was overcome by the prospect of a country on the edge of industrialization.

Beyond the political decision to push ahead with Paz de Río, it is also important to review different positions on the economic and technological suitability of the various proposals. In this regard, the Apéndice A of the "Informe de la mission para el Comité" prepared by Flesher reveals the conceptual framework within which the actors in the decision-making process, except perhaps for the Junta, developed the discussion. Apéndice A reads, "The maximum progress achievable with a 5 billion peso investment [the total available for investments, public and private, calculated by the Comité for the years 1951 to 1955] is only possible if the amount devoted to each sector, for example transportation, agriculture, or industry, is proportional to its contribution to the overall Colombian economy during this period."[86] The alternative uses of the funds required for the project at Paz de Río were also listed: a hydroelectric power station for an additional 120,000 kilowatts (half of the production of electricity in Colombia in 1950); or thermoelectric power stations for 240,000 kilowatts; or 30,000 private houses; or the purchase of 266 diesel locomotives with about 500 kilometers of new roads and railroads; or 23,000 hospital rooms; or new schools for 900,000 students, thus doubling the available primary school buildings.[87]

Two concepts emerged: (1) that the development of a sector should be proportional to the development of other sectors, and (2) that investments in different sectors were alternative to each other. These two concepts were based on the notion of balanced economic growth. The maximum possible progress for the whole economy could be reached only by preventing an exclusive use of the available resources by a single sector or business. In practical terms, this meant that investments were mutually exclusive, a zero sum game.[88]

Hirschman's and Streeten's critiques were directed specifically at such thinking, which, they maintained, led to false and misleading assumptions in investment decisions. According to Hirschman, the concern should not be about a supposed scarcity of resources, which generated the need to consider investments as mutually exclusive, but rather to understand the mechanisms to mobilize hidden yet existing resources. The proportional growth of different sectors (Paul Streeten insisted on this point), far from allowing the maximum possible progress, forced a condition of constant inadequacy in the dimensions of firms, plants, and entire industrial sectors.

Hirschman arrived in Colombia only a year after Currie, the Comité, and the Bank had surrendered to the Paz de Río project. Although Hirschman did not participate in the original debate, it is natural that, given the strategic and journalistic importance of the Paz de Río case, he was also involved.[89]

Criticizing the tendency of "international agencies" and the "economist-planner" (read: the International Bank and Lauchlin Currie) to prepare "general plans," and, specifically, their failure to support the project at Paz de Río, Hirschman stated in a 1954 speech:

> The economist-planner should bring his talent primarily to bear on the elaboration of well-planned sector projects [. . .]. In spite of all the insistence on "overall" planning, I have yet to see a project that is thus well conceived rejected by national or international agencies disposing of investment funds on the ground that the investment required is too high considering the need for monetary stability and for "balanced" development. In Colombia, the only case to my knowledge into which this kind of consideration has thus far entered at all was that of Paz de Río steel mill. Nevertheless, the report of the International Bank Mission, which objected to the project, carried only one extremely vague sentence about the fact that the money involved in Paz de Río might be put to better use elsewhere in the economy. (Hirschman [1954] 1971a, p. 49)

According to Hirschman, because of "backward" or "forward linkages," a newly founded industry could not be too big in the context of the national economy. Satellite and nonsatellite businesses would be established as a consequence, thus contributing to the growth of the country. The "rule of thumb" proposed by Hirschman was that an industry could be established in a developing country when the existing demand was equal to half of the demand needed to make it economically viable (Hirschman [1958] 1963, p. 103n4). The iron and steel industry was a good example of "backward" and "forward linkages." Hirschman concluded: "Perhaps the underdeveloped countries are not so foolish and so exclusively prestige-motivated in attributing prime importance to this industry!" (Hirschman [1958] 1963, p. 108). Hirschman was probably referring to the display of national pride as a reaction to the objections to the project at Paz de Río advanced by the Currie Mission first and then by the Comité. According to Hirschman, Paz de Río was not only a national symbol but also a potential generator of linkages and thus a powerful instrument of development for the country.

The Comité's positions were certainly different from Hirschman's views in many respects. Nevertheless, when exploring the core reasoning of the mission and the Comité, one can see how the positions converged, despite Hirschman's criticism.

Considerations of technical and geographic nature within the Currie report underscored the weak impact that the Paz de Río project would have in stimulating other industrial sectors. Its isolation would make distribution of the product very difficult and expensive. At the same time, it would impede the aggregation of other industries around the main plant. It would have been very difficult to form a "growth pole," which the mission considered the most desirable result and to which Hirschman dedicated a chapter in his 1958 book (Hirschman [1958] 1963, ch. 10), unless heavily subsidized.

When it became clear that the location of the plant could not be changed, reducing the cost of the plant became the main concern of the Comité. Despite all reasonings on possible future benefits of initially oversized projects, a single endeavor that (according to the estimates of the "Informe de la mision para el Comité") would absorb about two-thirds of all the capital available for the industrial sector in one year was deemed excessive.[90] The Comité conceived an incremental growth in size for the plant, thus linking its development to increased competence and market share. This would have limited the burden of its unfortunate location and allowed the business to gain strength despite this initial handicap. This reasoning was actually not too different from Hirschman's attempt to find the "hidden rationalities" of the process of growth. Thanks to these hidden rationalities, the economy of a sector or a country is pushed toward new paths for growth that were previously invisible or unpredictable.

Paradoxically, obstacles may play a positive role in the process of growth when they help to forge decisions and contribute to unite efforts and attempts to discard unfeasible hypotheses and to find solutions previously unthought of.

The Comité took a mediator's role between political/ideological or lobbying needs on the one hand and technological and economic issues on the other. In other words, the Comité was at the center of a process of forming and structuring decision-making processes. This is what Streeten and Hirschman highlighted as the most necessary factor for growth (but also the rarest) in developing countries.

In an environment where professional skills were often inadequate or lacking, processes of learning by doing would stimulate and set the pace for mechanisms of skills acquisition or improvement. These mechanisms could contribute to a virtuous circle of development, learning, and growth, overcoming the bottlenecks in the job and capital markets and in the output demand flowing from the manufacturing activity.

It is possible that disagreements arose over the suitability of labor-intensive (preferred by the mission) or capital-intensive production (preferred by Hirschman). Hirschman's preference was based on the principle that a labor force that was not trained for industrial manufacturing could be more productive if the production were centered on the *process* (typically capital intensive, like steelmaking) rather than on the *product* itself (typically labor intensive, like construction). However, although interesting and even important, these were not major disagreements. They referred to specific choices on how to implement a certain project or productive activity rather than to fundamental incompatibilities about the nature of the process of development.

Overall, the approaches of Currie and the Comité and the approach of Hirschman were more similar than the *ex post* reconstructions of the debates among developing economists may suggest, despite the friction and disagreements about some specifics of the question at hand. Of course, it would be wrong to maintain that there was total agreement. The point is that the positions were not diametrically opposed and that all parties supported much more similar mechanisms to guide or help the development of poor countries than they were ready to admit.[91]

Changing Alliances

The apparently irreconcilable break between Hirschman and Currie had to do with their respective frames of reference. From opposite premises, in an environment more complex and intertwined than it first appeared, they often reached similar conclusions.

AGREEMENTS AND DISAGREEMENTS

We have already mentioned how the International Bank, although increasingly favoring loans for single, well-defined projects, continued to frame them within general development plans. For example, in an official letter to Emilio Toro, Jacques Torfs underscored that a general investment program was essential for Colombia. Referring to the newly established Consejo, Torfs insisted that the new body would have to take on "the responsibility of formulating an overall investment program which would be coherent with the economic possibilities of Colombia."[92] Each individual project would be a component of the wider program: "The Government should be able to appraise the proposals within the framework of a coherent economic policy."[93]

Other issues had similar dualisms and swinging agreements and disagreements among the major participants in the debate. One example comes from the comparison between "social overhead capital" (SOC) and "directly productive activities" (DPA), as proposed by Hirschman in his book *The Strategy of Economic Development* ([1958] 1963, pp. 83–97). By social overhead capital, Hirschman meant all the services necessary to support directly productive activities: "In its wider sense, [SOC] includes all public services from law and order through education and public health to transportation, communications, power and water supply, as well as such agricultural overhead capital as irrigation and drainage systems. The hard core of the concept can probably be restricted to transportation and power" (Hirschman [1958] 1963, p. 83). According to Hirschman, this restricted SOC is the foundation of the activities promoted by the International Bank.[94] The concept of SOC in its wider sense, however— my observation, not Hirschman's—was the basis of the Currie mission's approach.

In any case, neither the restricted nor the wider concept satisfied Hirschman, who instead favored investments for DPA. This leaning was not only consistent with his doctrine of unbalanced growth, but also was a substantial element of unbalanced growth. Of course, a small investment in SOC was necessary as the initial condition for investing in DPA, but it was useless or even counterproductive to insist on social capital in a context of limited productive activity: "Excess SOC capacity is essentially permissive, [but] it invites rather than compels" (Hirschman [1958] 1963, p. 93). On the contrary, allowing DPA to flourish before investing in SOC might generate spontaneous pressures to develop the needed SOC. DPA, in other words, "yield an extra dividend of 'induced,' 'easy-to-take,' or 'compelled' decisions resulting in additional investment and output" (Hirschman [1958] 1963, p. 89). As such, progress achieved in the development of DPA generates new needs and the related pressure to satisfy them, which, at least partially, make up for the shortfall of "the power to take decisions." This, according to Hirschman and Streeten, was *the* truly scarce factor in developing countries. Through the categories of SOC and DPA, therefore, Hirschman criticized an approach attributable to both Currie and the International Bank.

In the already cited 1954 article, Hirschman proposes another set of categories for intervention in developing countries, which brings him closer to Currie. Here, Hirschman criticizes another bad habit typical of the International Bank: "Large international lending agencies [. . .] are looking for short cuts to economic development and are ready to let themselves be persuaded that they have found them in the form of a hydroelectric project, a few arterial roads or an irrigation scheme, [or] the big 'steel-and-concrete' projects" (Hirschman [1954] 1971a, p. 52). However, "the elaboration of projects in the unglamorous, but nonetheless essential, fields of education, small industry, improvement of agricultural methods, etc." was just so important that, according to Hirschman, it would be worthwhile to invest half of the available resources on them (Hirschman [1954] 1971a, p. 53).[95] Here it is useful to remember the attention devoted by the Currie mission's report to "unglamorous but nonetheless essential" fields, such as education and health or, as Currie stressed, the necessity to link "noneconomic as well as strictly economic fields" (Currie 1981, p. 55).

In sum, the positions and the disagreements between the actors involved in the strategies for Colombia's economic development between the 1940s and 1950s were not unequivocal. Table 1 helps visualize the changing alliances among the actors.

TABLE I

The changing alliances among Lauchlin Currie,
Albert Hirschman, and the World Bank

Social Overhead Capital	*vs.*	Directly Productive Activities
International Bank		Albert Hirschman
Lauchlin Currie		
Project Loans	*vs.*	Program Loans
Albert Hirschman		Lauchlin Currie
International Bank		
Shortcuts	*vs.*	Unglamorous Complications
International Bank		Albert Hirschman
		Lauchlin Currie

These dichotomies, which inspired the establishment of different and not always explicit alliances, did not appear in sequence. Rather, they overlapped over time, which makes it difficult to extrapolate a rigid opposition among the parties. The reality was much more nuanced.

A SOCIOLOGICAL INTERPRETATION OF THE DEVELOPMENT
ECONOMICS DEBATE: ROBERT K. MERTON
AND THE "KINDLE COLE" PRINCIPLE

In reviewing two concrete cases where Currie's and Hirschman's positions clashed, we have already seen that their different visions had to do mostly with tactical issues, while their essential reasoning was very similar. They differentiated themselves primarily when trying to create models.

A key to interpreting their clash comes from the sociology of science. Robert K. Merton suggests that, by its very nature, scientific research as a profession attracts self-centered individuals who are eager to gain fame and therefore particularly inclined to clash with those who disagree with them or try to disprove them. This hypothesis makes reference to the selection processes within a given group, and in principle it is subject to empirical verification (Merton [1957] 1973a). However, the real focus of Merton's analysis is the system of norms that regulates scientific research, understood as an institution.

> It is these norms that exert pressure upon scientists to assert their claims [. . .]. The way in which the norms of science help produce this result seems clear enough. On every side the scientist is reminded that it is his role to advance knowledge and his happiest fulfillment of that role, to advance knowledge greatly. [Reward] becomes socially validated testimony that one has successfully lived up to the most exacting requirements of one's role as scientist [. . .]. Recognition and fame then become symbol and reward for having done one's job well. (Merton [1957] 1973a, pp. 293–94)

Here, Merton addresses the issue of "priorities in scientific discovery," which has been the cause of many disagreements—and noble gestures— among scientists during all periods. In another contribution given several years later, referring to the discipline of sociology, Merton broadened the analysis of the conflict among scientists beyond the issue of priorities. In 1959 at the Fourth World Congress of Sociology in Stresa, Italy, Merton provided such a penetrating description of the conflict within a social science that it is worth citing a long passage:

> Much of the controversy among sociologists involves social conflict and not only intellectual criticism. Often, it is less a matter of contradictions between sociological ideas than of competing definitions of the role considered appropriate for the sociologist. Intellectual conflict of course occurs; an unremitting Marxist sociology and an unremitting Weberian or Parsonian sociology do make contradictory assumptions. But in considering the cleavages among [sociologists], we should note whether the occasion for dispute is this kind of substantive or methodological contradiction or rather the claim that this or that sociological problem, this or that set of ideas, is not receiving the attention it allegedly deserves. I suggest that very often

these polemics have more to do with the allocation of intellectual resources among different kinds of sociological work than with a closely formulated opposition of sociological ideas.

These controversies follow the classically identified course of social conflict [. . .]. Since the conflict is public, it becomes a status battle more nearly than a search for truth [. . .]. The consequent polarization leads each group of sociologists to respond largely to stereotyped versions of what is being done by the other [. . .]. Not that these stereotypes have no basis in reality at all, but only that, in the course of social conflict, they become self-confirming stereotypes as sociologists shut themselves off from the experience that might modify them. The sociologists of each camp develop selective perceptions of what is actually going on in the other. They see in the other's work primarily what the hostile stereotype has alerted them to see, and then promptly mistake the part for the whole. In this process, each group of sociologists become less and less motivated to study the work of the other, since there is manifestly little point in doing so. They scan the out-group's writings just enough to find ammunition for new fusillades. (Merton [1961] 1973b, pp. 55–56)

It is evident how this passage can refer to any other group of social scientists, including economists or development economists, as in our case. For that matter, in his book *On the Shoulders of Giants* (1965), Merton offered a witty observation that applies beyond his references to sociologists in 1959. In a takeoff on a dispute between Sir Isaac Newton and Robert Hooke about priority in the definition of the theory of color, Merton described the interaction between people in the field of science according to the principle he called the "kindle cole principle" (Merton 1965, p. 29). The principle—which should be named after Hooke, Newton, and Merton, rather than, as Merton himself pointed out, after him only—established that "though [. . .] the collision of two hard-to-yield contenders may produce light yet if they be put together by the ears of other's hands and incentives, *it will produce rather ill concomitant heat which serves for no other use but . . . kindle cole.*"[96]

Back to the specific subject of our study, the debate about the best way for poor countries to develop may also be interpreted using models of social interaction that are typical of a closed and specialized group of peers dedicated to the advancement of knowledge such as the development economists. The widely accepted theory of balanced growth was opposed, after just a few years, by a strong, explicit, and polemical position that maintained the need for unbalanced growth.[97] These positions quickly radicalized, and there is no doubt that, as Merton underscored, the supporters of each position soon projected stereotypes and self-serving interpretations onto the opinions of their adversaries, more useful for a polemical arms race than the advancement of knowledge.

Of course, this does not mean that there were not legitimate clashes strongly based on substantive issues, that is, intellectual opposition. It is also possible that the personalities of the individuals influenced the style or the direction of the debate. Merton's approach does not deny these aspects. In addition, however, it allows us to understand other issues that would otherwise be inexplicable: for example, how the debate routinely transcended the substantive differences between the different factions and why the scholars involved in these themes remained stuck in a fight that was increasingly detached from the original content of the debate. (We should remember that the debate was about *possible* policies, often situational and limited, to be implemented in developing countries.)

The problem of conflict management is common to all institutions. Conflict is not an anomaly; rather, it often reveals patterns that allow a better understanding of the internal dynamics of an institution. Also, a sociological perspective allows us to understand not only those conditions that at all times may favor the emergence of conflict (for example, seeking peer approval as proof of one's good work and the public recognition of it), but also the specific situations underlying them, which provide an explanation for the timing of a conflict.

In the 1950s, the "pioneers" of development economics, driven by the need to define their discipline as an autonomous branch of economics, constructed ponderous theories of analysis and intervention; not necessarily because, as Merton once said about "pioneering sociologists," they "happened to be system-minded men but because it was their role, at that time, to seek intellectual legitimacy" (Merton [1961] 1973b, p. 50). One likely outcome was that these intellectual constructions would oppose each other to gain internal hegemony, and indeed, so it turned out. "This was not in terms of specialization but in the form of rival claims to intellectual legitimacy, claims typically held to be mutually exclusive and at odds" (Merton

[1961] 1973b, p. 51). Hirschman's challenge to the theory of balanced development obviously comes to mind: "[This] theory fails as a theory of *development*" (Hirschman [1958] 1963, p. 51, emphasis in the original).

In a 1960 review of Hirschman's *The Strategy of Economic Growth*, Amartya
K. Sen advanced similar considerations: "Controversies on 'balanced' *versus* 'unbalanced' growth tend to leave the readers—at least, one reader—a
little puzzled. Put in their native forms, both the doctrines look right; examined from the other's point of view, each looks totally inadequate [. . .].
The 'balanced' and the 'unbalanced' growth doctrines have a considerable
amount of common ground" (Sen 1960, p. 591). It is important to also cite
Sen's conclusions: "One cannot, however, help feeling that Professor
Hirschman is overstating his case [. . .]. I have no doubt that this is how
economic thought progresses: we discover a hitherto concealed aspect of
the problem, and make it the *essence*, if not the *whole*, of the problem" (Sen
1960, p. 592, emphasis in the original).

That said, we should point out that conflict also plays a positive role, at
least when it is regulated by the group of peers comprising a scientific community. Research by minority groups or research with less visibility with
respect to the prevailing orthodoxy indeed may find it an especially advan-
tageous instrument for attracting the attention of the community. Through
these debates, the discipline overall grows and thrives.[98]

The possibility to ignite conflict, when it is not pathological, can serve
as an instrument for moderating risk of excessive conflict within a community. This is not a paradoxical note: the ability to challenge orthodoxy or at
least to make one's voice heard in a community can become the first signal
that a certain idea or issue may be strong enough to catalyze attention. On
one hand, the ability to trigger conflict discourages extreme or impractical
positions; on the other hand, it puts a limit on orthodoxy and normalizing
behaviors. The later evidence from some of the major participants in the
debate between "balanced growth" and "unbalanced growth" supports this
interpretation.

Albert Hirschman wished to placate the debate in a 1961 contribution in
which he underscored the common points between the two opposing sides.
He affirmed that the two theories could be compared to two ways to consider
the nucleus of an atom. It is possible to concentrate attention on the nucleus
itself, indivisible, or on the energy that holds it together. He maintained:

In other words I do not deny by any means the interrelatedness of various economic activities of which the balanced growth theory has made so much. On the contrary, I propose that we take advantage of it, that we probe into the structure that is holding together these interrelated activities [. . .]. To look at unbalanced growth means, in other words, to look at the dynamics of the development process *in the small.*[99]

Similarly, though less explicitly, years later Lauchlin Currie (who, despite his reputation as a "difficult" person, kept a low profile in the debate though he reiterated his conviction about the need to implement an integrated development plan) stressed the impossibility of reducing serious analysis of the problems of development to simple or one-sided solutions. In this way, he indirectly confirmed that, compared to the debate in the specialized journals, the practice of economic policy of these scholars was in fact less at odds than they themselves might have believed, taken in by their polemical enthusiasm. At a 1975 conference, Currie stated:

Although I have a great respect for the power of economic incentives and the efficacy of decentralized decision making, I am still an inveterate planner [. . .]. The "invisible hand" became two hands, the traditional one working more or less silently through economic incentives, and the more visible one of national economic policy making. The resulting strategy is a mixed one, difficult to classify.[100]

In conclusion, observing development economists in their advising capacity allows a better understanding of their theoretical positions and a reassessment of the extent of contrasts between theories. These contrasts have not disappeared, but their seemingly rigid opposition—conveyed through the testimony, in part misleading, of the scientific literature—appears nowadays out-of-date. On this shift in perspectives, Hirschman wrote:

In an interesting interview, Paul Krugman, a young MIT economist, said that certain writers, such as Arthur Lewis, Paul Rosenstein-Rodan, Gunnar Myrdal, and Albert Hirschman, should be "rehabilitated" as a group who made important contributions to economic development in the fifties. Now it is true that all of us had something in common, because we all recognized that the "underdeveloped" countries, as they were called then, needed to adopt certain public policies. Yet there was a considerable difference between my theories and those of the other members of the group. When I wrote *The Strategy of Economic Development*, my "enemies" were exactly those people with whom my name is now being associated. (Hirschman [1994] 1998, p. 109)

Today we are in a better position to appreciate the nuances of the relation between two doctrines that, at the time of the pioneers of the discipline, were described as "enemies," and today can be considered "associated." Paul Streeten, another great figure of these debates, made the following enlightening comment: "In retrospect, much of the balanced versus unbalanced growth controversy seems to me a sham dispute [. . .]. Often in practice there was much more agreement than in theory. You know the definition of an economist: when he sees something working in practice, he asks, but will it work in theory?"[101]

CHAPTER FOUR

At the Root of the Bank's Policy Advice

One goes on. And the time, too, goes on—till one perceives ahead a shadow-line warning one that the region of early youth, too, must be left behind.

—JOSEPH CONRAD, *The Shadow Line*

From the documents about the Currie mission and the later relations between Colombia and the International Bank examined in the second chapter, there is evidence of a progressive break between the multilateral institution and the leader of its first General Survey Mission, Lauchlin Currie. The Bank attributed this break to the disagreements between Currie and the Bank's officers in Colombia, primarily Albert Hirschman, although he was one of the last to arrive.

The third chapter investigated the possible reasons for this break. Given that the break was serious and could have potentially had negative consequences on the relations between the Bank and the Colombian government (Burke J. Knapp threatened to interrupt any collaboration), it was important to verify on which basis, other than the incompatible personalities of the economic advisors, the Bank decided to distance itself from Lauchlin Currie. A hypothesis is that the conflict was caused by different scientific views that also involved the Bank and that made continued collaboration impossible: Currie on one side, with Hirschman and the International Bank on the other. One could also identify a correlation between the debate that was taking place in the field of economic development and the shaping of the economic policy by a multilateral institution. However, the analysis in the third chapter disproves these hypotheses.

No doubt, the conflict took place and was passionate, but with two qualifying characteristics. First, although incompatible with each other in their rhetoric and in their methodological statements, the positions taken by the various advisors were more homogeneous than they seemed at first. Second, the division between the opposing sides was not well defined; on the contrary, it was fluid, with different parties taking different positions on different issues. The hypothesis of a conflict based on scientific disagreements and the related hypothesis of a direct link between this agreement and the economic policy of the Bank lacks solid grounding. The dispute was among scientists rather than being scientific.

Reconstructing the debate helps clarify how these discussions were in part distorted by the vehemence of the protagonists and how the debate has traditionally been reconstructed through the lens of this distortion. Of course, this *ex post* distortion of the debate was also caused by the persistence of its most controversial aspects, due to the fact that it was reported and thus "frozen" by specialized journals. Furthermore, reconstructing a debate seems easier and more accurate when its developments are reconsidered through the available publications of the time. No doubt, that is easier, but it is questionable whether it is more accurate. Although difficult to reconstruct for objective reasons (for example, scattered archives and the complexity of many situations), greater attention to the practice of economic policy would certainly help accuracy. Reconstructing these debates also helps us better understand the environment in which the economic policy of the Bank took shape: the problem of growth and development soon after World War II and the debate surrounding it.

The shaping of the economic policy of the Bank is the focus of this last chapter. With the help of archival material, I shall reconstruct the case of loans for the construction sector, which the Bank refused to support for many years. The first section deals with a case in Colombia, a program for urban development in the city of Barranquilla coordinated by Lauchlin Currie, who required the Bank's intervention. The loan was denied. The second section goes beyond this specific case and explores the Bank's initial reflections on this kind of investment. By analyzing what the Bank refused to support, one can delineate by contrast a profile of the investments that were supported. In particular, by analyzing the reasons for turning down certain loans, it is possible to better understand the convictions behind the shaping of the Bank's economic policy during those years. The third and fourth sections describe the options discarded by the Bank and the criteria that influenced the institution's choices. The fifth section records the end of this period of debate, thus the end of the transition, and the new phase that characterized the institution from the 1950s through the first half of the 1960s.

The Urban Development Plan for Barranquilla

REQUEST FOR IBRD FINANCING

In the first half of 1952, Samuel Hollopeter of the Empresas Municipales of Barranquilla approached the Bank about obtaining a loan to finance the foreign exchange cost of expanding the municipal waterworks, sewage system, and slaughterhouse facilities. In a letter to the newly appointed president of the Consejo Nacional de Planificación, Rafael Delgado Barreneche, the Bank's vice president, Robert Garner, declared that the Bank would not "be willing, as a matter of principle, to consider financing municipal projects of this nature." Garner wrote that the Bank would consider financing projects for municipal services only if "tangible evidence was provided that the projects were closely connected with the development of productive facilities." The only possible exception—he added—would be if demonstration were given of "the importance of the projects in increasing development" and if it "were considered by the Colombian Government as part of an overall municipal development program."[1]

Mindful that support from the national government was necessary, at the beginning of September 1952 a delegation from the city of Barranquilla met with the Consejo Nacional de Planificación and formally asked the Consejo to back its application for a loan of $5,089,700 from the International Bank to cover the foreign exchange burden of a wide-ranging investment plan. The minutes itemize the objectives of the plan: "Aqueduct expansion, sewer improvements and additions, local market improvements, construction of a new slaughterhouse with a meat processing plant, improvement of municipal cleaning, construction of a modern hospital, road paving, and piping standardization."[2]

The total investment was estimated at 95 million pesos, of which 25 million was for housing, 15 million for sewer systems, 9 million for water mains, 3 million for pipes and hydrants, 26 million for road resurfacing and roadwork, 5 million for a new 500-room hospital, 2 million for schools, 3.5 million for markets and a slaughterhouse, almost 7 million for rehabilitation of the Zona Negra, and 120,000 pesos for the stadium.[3] In fact, the Zona Negra—"probably the worst slum in Colombia,"[4] inhabited by black people—would have been the main beneficiary of the plan as a whole, because the housing and sewage program was targeted mainly to that area, where living conditions were a "shame for the nation."[5]

As is evident from the list, the range of interventions was very wide, and they were aimed at improving the quality of life of the poor. The people of Barranquilla and adjacent zones understood the importance of the program and its value for their well-being, and they strongly supported it. Consequently, the Consejo was confident that the increase in tariffs necessary to cover the domestic burden of the program would be well received if it led to concrete benefits. In mid-November, the Consejo submitted a financing program to the president of the Republic of Colombia, Urdaneta Arbeláez. The financing sources were to be from the citizenry (almost 40 percent of the total through service fee and property tax increases), and from the government (municipal, departmental, and national, accounting for 45 percent of the total), plus some other minor sources (for example, businesses, which would contribute 9 percent of the total).[6] The president of the Junta Asesora de Obras Publicas of Soledad, a small town a few miles from Barranquilla whose only source of water (unfiltered and nonpotable) was the Río Magdalena, wrote to the governor of the Department of Atlántico offering its (only) water tank, two turbines, and three engines used to pump water from the Magdalena River to the town in exchange for being linked to a new and bigger waterworks, which would finally bring potable water to the townspeople. The president wrote, "The majority of inhabitants of Soledad are poor people; but they are willing to pay a just price for access to potable water. [. . .] Being able to consume the same water of Barranquilla has been an old desire of the people of this municipality."[7]

With the new year, although some projects were delayed (the hospital for example) and the plan had not yet been published in its entirety, implementation began on most of the plan, mainly the new houses and sewer system for the Zona Negra.[8] The residents reacted very favorably, as the Consejo had hoped, and this made it possible to raise the municipal fees without protest.[9] Above all, it was still hoped that the International Bank would become convinced of the social and economic value of the plan. Burke J. Knapp, the first director of the Bank's operations in Latin America, was in Colombia at the time, and Currie suggested that he stop in Barranquilla to meet the local administrators and examine the situation in person. As Currie confided to Hollopeter, "It will be a good opportunity to get him interested in the whole plan."[10]

As soon as the plan was published, in early March 1953, the Consejo sent a copy to the International Bank, accompanied by a long letter soliciting the loan.[11] In this letter, Emilio Toro (who, having been an executive director of the Bank, knew the institution and its managers very well) sought to convince the skeptical Vice President Garner of the effectiveness and economic feasibility of the plan. He debated Garner's arguments for refusing the loan,[12] pointing out that the Consejo had scrupulously complied with his observations by transforming a simple aqueduct improvement project into a "general program of municipal development."[13] He stressed that it was important for a portion of the financial sources to take the form of a foreign loan, even if modest, because only thus could the Consejo guarantee uninterrupted implementation of the plan if the local administration changed.[14] Toro, well aware that the International Bank had no intention of creating a precedent for small loans to municipal facilities, emphasized the national importance of the plan.[15] At the same time, he sought to understate the "social" significance of the plan, citing the waterworks, the slaughterhouse, the public markets, and a new road between Barranquilla and Ciénaga, but neglecting to emphasize what was in fact the bulk of the plan, that is, the housing program for the Zona Negra. Also, he did not mention the hospital and the doubling of classrooms in the Atlantic Department.[16] In sum, Toro insisted on the two points that Garner wanted to hear: (1) a specific (and very modest $3.7 million) project loan set within the context of (2) an overall plan for development: "Although the aqueduct is the immediate goal of the loan, the main objective is making a 100 million peso development plan possible."[17] The Consejo thus hoped that the Bank would be willing to send a brief mission to Barranquilla before a Colombian delegation was invited to Washington, D.C., to plead directly for the Barranquilla loan.[18]

In reaction to the prolonged silence of the Bank, the Colombian government instructed its Washington Ambassador to lobby for a positive answer,[19] whereupon Garner wrote an official letter to Toro stating that the Bank would not participate in the financing of the Barranquilla plan. It is worth quoting from the letter at length:

> The Bank should concentrate its efforts on projects which will yield the greatest and quickest increase in output and productivity. As a rule, projects for municipal improvement do not meet this test. However, by lending for projects which do, we believe we can most effectively assist our member countries to develop new sources of wealth and income which would enable them to provide out of their own resources better municipal services, better housing, better health and education—in fact, all of the fruits of greater economic productivity.[20]

Garner's argument in his letter to Toro was a very clear expression of the belief widely held at the time in the close causal link between economic growth and social development. A specific instance of this belief was the "trickle-down" theory. It supported the thesis that *even* in the event of a worsening in the distribution of income owing to economic growth, in a reasonable period of time the results would be positive for society as a whole, and most of all for the less wealthy strata of population. Economic growth was both a necessary and sufficient condition for the general development of a country. It was perhaps this conviction that led Garner to write, a few lines later:

> In the case of the Barranquilla project, I am convinced that, *although the social benefits might be considerable*, the economic results would not be nearly as great as those which could be obtained from [. . .] directly productive projects.[21]

This is a surprising statement to the observer of today aware that economic growth can no longer be considered a sufficient prerequisite for social development (although still strongly related to it), but it expressed the conventional wisdom of the early years of development economics.

The Barranquilla plan was eventually published in a slightly modified version, which took account of the lack of external financing (Consejo Nacional de Planificación 1954, p. 8) but still preserved its basic characteristics. The main consequence of the lack of external financing was prolongation of the plan itself until 1958, so that it was no longer a five-year plan, but a six-year one. All in all, a minor change.

WHY DID THE BANK REFUSE FINANCING?

Once again, as was the case for the conflict between Currie and Hirschman, returning to theoretical debates does not help. Within the Bank, the debate was part of the existing, larger discussion in the new discipline of economic development, a discussion that highlighted the dichotomy between "program" or "planning" on one hand and "project" on the other. Nevertheless, the Barranquilla plan does not provide evidence that the decision to fund it or not revolved around these differences. This dichotomy, of course, set off the discussion within the institution; however, the discussion took place on grounds that were always more practical than theoretical. First, it is important to remember that the Bank began its activity with loans for reconstruction programs in Europe and not for individual projects. Second, although there was an increasing tendency to finance single projects, the Bank never lost sight of the general programs that provided the context for the single projects (IBRD 1954). The case of the Paz de Río plant is an example. Against a background of intense public argument between some politicians, industrialists, and public opinion on one side and the Comité de Desarrollo Económico on the other, Bank economist Jacques Torfs recommended to his supervisor Leonard Rist, director of the Economic Department, that the Bank should open a "conditional" line of credit with the Colombian government in order to reach a compromise solution satisfactory to the Comité.[22] This position was based on the conviction that as long as the Bank contributed to a large *program* of consistent investments, it could impose some conditions on the economic decisions of the government of the country. In this case, the Bank ultimately decided not to intervene, but during the negotiations on the Colombian loans, the Bank maintained its policy of waiting for the publication of a comprehensive plan before supporting specific projects.

Thus, the best way to understand the reasons behind loan decisions is not to see them as the result of the opposition between "projects" and a "program," but as a consequence of a more fundamental and pragmatic assessment of the very nature of the loans. Using Robert Garner's words, everything that was not "directly productive" was ineligible for Bank involvement.[23] To the extent that an investment was not directly productive, it was immediately perceived as too risky and not credit worthy.

On the other hand, people like Currie thought that the necessity to link together "non-economic as well as strictly economic fields" was obvious, as Currie wrote many years later, reflecting on his early experiences in Colombia (Currie 1981, p. 55). In his view, the need to link different fields did not conflict with the need to direct resources toward "productive" goals. Nobody, and certainly not Currie, doubted the necessity to increase productivity as an essential element in a country's development. This could only happen by developing mechanized agriculture and, especially, an increasingly large industrial sector endowed with resources and inputs (including energy, transportation, raw materials, machinery), often with a significant amount of labor, or an "unlimited supply" of labor, as Lewis observed (1954). Thus, the distinction does not seem as precise or clear as stating the need to support "directly productive" activities would suggest at first. Perhaps the emphasis should be placed on the adverb *directly*. Everything that did not belong to certain clearly identified areas of production (energy, transportation, and heavy industry first of all) was not considered productive enough. It remains unclear why the productive aspect of other areas was not recognized.

How the Bank dealt with the issue of housing construction loans from the very beginning can help clarify the issue. Thus, we must broaden the discussion from the particular case of residential and urban development in Barranquilla to the more general but more relevant issue of how the Bank financed housing. (For further considerations, see Alacevich forthcoming).

The IBRD and Housing Loans

The idea that the International Bank would offer loans for urban development and housing had arisen within the Bank itself. However, the International Labor Organization (ILO) was the first to elaborate on this idea.

THE ILO PROPOSAL AND THE FIRST IBRD COMMENTS

The ILO Building, Civil Engineering and Public Works Committee had met for its second session in Rome from March 16 to March 25, 1949. On that occasion, the Italian manufacturers' delegate,[24] Mr. Gadola, suggested that the ILO investigate the possibility of establishing a completely new institution, the International Institute for Building Loans, under the control of the two Bretton Woods institutions, the International Bank for Reconstruction and Development (IBRD) and the International Monetary Fund. According to the minutes of a subcommittee, "The function of the proposed institute would be to collect private savings by the issue of bonds in countries where such savings exist, with a view to making mortgage loans for housing construction, especially for the lower-income groups."[25] The main purpose of this proposal was to sustain and stabilize employment internationally, first by stimulating a labor-intensive activity and second by promoting a better distribution of labor among countries. On this latter point, it was stressed that the project would favor migration from countries with a surplus work force to those with deficits.[26] The construction sector could have proven to be an effective engine for growth and at the same time helped to improve living conditions of the local population. It could have combined the need to stimulate economic growth with action on social issues.

The resolution was adopted on March 25, and the ILO Governing Body was invited to contact IBRD. It did this one month after Eugene R. Black, formerly the Bank's U.S. executive director, became the third IBRD president.[27] The matter was immediately passed to the Economic Department for preliminary examination.

Under Leonard Rist, the Economic Department broke the analysis into two separate matters: (1) whether housing could be considered a sufficiently "productive" project, as required by the Bank's Articles of Agreement,[28] and (2) whether the Bank could contribute with loans, which would principally be in U.S. currency, to projects whose outlays would principally be in local currency, hence financing only a possible "indirect" need for foreign currency.[29]

As for the first issue, the answer was quite clear: "no doubt, there are areas where the housing shortage seriously hampers the development of new resources and industries, so that financing of new houses would in those areas be directly productive even within a narrow understanding of that term."[30] As for the second point, the analysis was more complicated, not least because at that very preliminary stage of communication it was impossible to understand what options were considered by the ILO. The Bank focused on three options:

1. A new institute selling bonds, which would be formally guaranteed by the IBRD
2. A new institute selling bonds, with the Bank guaranteeing the monetary policy of the government hosting the building investment, not the bonds themselves
3. A new institute, with the Bank simply acting as a sponsor without any formal commitment

The most likely option was that the Institute for Building Loans would sell bonds in the private markets of capital exporting countries under guarantees by the IBRD. However, the proceeds would be mostly in U.S. currency, which was inconsistent with the practice of financing only housing projects that required mostly local currency. It was thus assumed that this extra U.S. currency would be added to the overall foreign currency resources of the borrowing country as a supplement "necessary to absorb the inflationary pressure created by increased construction activity."[31]

As an alternative, the Bank pondered whether its intervention had been asked to persuade potential *local* investors to buy the proposed institute's bonds in the local market, offering a guarantee by the IBRD against losses due to devaluation of the local currency. Of course, the authority of the Bank would "keep the local government in line."[32] A less likely option was that the Bank would participate merely by lending its prestige and experience, without any formal guarantees of the institute's bonds.

Although these three scenarios, especially the first, were at odds with the Bank's previous loan policy of providing the foreign currency needed for specific reconstruction programs, the *Articles of Agreement* explicitly envisaged loans for "indirectly" needed foreign currency.[33] Thus, the Economic Department recommended investigating the matter further, asking the ILO to specify the nature of the involvement requested of the Bank.[34]

THE DISENGAGEMENT OF THE IBRD

Contacts between the ILO and the Bank continued for a while, but the Institute for Building Loans never saw the light. This was partly because of conflicts within the ILO, mainly between the country representatives and the technical staff.[35] Indeed, the ILO staff was highly skeptical about the feasibility of such a huge new institution, that the institution could find resources to finance housing projects, or that the Bank would really sponsor it as the ILO committee predicted in its resolution of March 1949.

On the other side, the country representatives expressed the need of many governments to cope with reconstruction or social problems, or both, and saw a new institution headed by the IBRD as a way to channel resources into the housing sector. The housing shortage was a widely discussed problem, and many proposals for programs or institutions to finance housing were put forward at least until the mid-1950s.[36]

For its part, the International Bank managed to avoid any commitment to housing projects.[37] As the Bank's president, Eugene Black, explained to his ILO counterpart, David Morse, it was a strict rule of the Bank that loans in foreign currency should be used only to finance the cost of imported goods and services, and they could not be diverted to the financing of expenditures in local currency.[38] A more general rule was that Bank loans should be for directly productive purposes. As Richard Demuth, head of the Technical Assistance and Liaison Staff Office, put it, "The first test of any project to be financed by the Bank is its productivity," and the productivity of housing investments seemed too low.[39]

Thus, the Bank granted no loans to finance activities in the fields of housing, town planning, and building materials. Only two loans concerned building construction, among other things. In a "reconstruction" loan to the Netherlands in 1947, some resources were used to finance the importing of materials used for housing. In fact, in the Netherlands, replacement of workers' houses destroyed during the war "was a step necessary for the rehabilitation of Dutch industries essential to the national economy."[40] In a loan made in 1952 to improve Iceland's agricultural production, some resources were used for the construction of farms (IBRD 1952a). However, since Iceland had to import almost all its building materials, this loan was considered consistent with the rule that only the foreign exchange requirements of a project could be financed.[41] With the exception of these two loans, in practice the Bank never considered building construction, except incidentally (for example, erecting a construction camp at the site of a dam project).

Discussions at the Bank: Impact Loans and Social Loans

In spite of this clear choice to not commit to loans that top management did not consider part of the Bank's responsibilities, the internal discussions did not stop. Discussions were centered around two different proposals: loans brought about by the consequences of the "impact" of other investments on the national economy and loans with a "social" aim.

IMPACT LOANS

The first discussion focused on a topic that the Economic Department had already studied in the context of the ILO proposal, namely the usefulness of a loan in dollars when the investments essentially needed local currency. Such a loan would have guaranteed the stability of the balance of payments, supposedly under pressure from the increase in domestic expenditures caused by those very investments. This would later be called an "impact loan," in other words a loan that did not directly support a specific project but would absorb the consequent inflationary impact of that specific project on the balance of payments of the country.

This effect was discussed in detail in the *Fifth Annual Report to the Board of Governors* of the Bank (IBRD 1950c). This document analyzed the possibility that local expenditure on labor or domestically produced equipment could increase the demand for imported consumer goods or raw materials,

or, as stated in the *Report*, "foreign exchange requirements indirectly resulting from expenditures in local currency" (IBRD 1950c, p. 10). The
conclusion of the *Report* was that, in such case, a loan from the Bank
would be appropriate because it was aimed at supporting a country during a period of expansion and removing or containing its inflationary
tendencies.

This analysis was based on a study that Paul Rosenstein-Rodan, then a
member of the Economic Department, had prepared on a loan application
for the development of southern Italy that had come to the Bank from the
Italian government toward the end of 1948. The Italian government had the
funds to undertake an investment program using domestic capital, but it
lacked foreign currency reserves. Rosenstein-Rodan estimated that additional income generated by the investment program would lead to an increase in internal demand. This, in turn, would have created additional
demand for imports. As a result, the country would be subject to inflationary
pressure and would need additional foreign currency reserves. The Bank
would have been responsible for making these additional reserves of foreign
currency available. Therefore, the loan would have financed "the impact of
an investment program which the Italian government undertakes."[42]

Interestingly, this mechanism was in many aspects similar to what was
emerging from the studies by the Economic Commission for Latin America (ECLA) and its leader, Raúl Prebisch. Albert Hirschman later reformu-
lated and highlighted this mechanism in his book *The Strategy of Economic
Development* ([1958] 1963). In both instances, the approach could be defined
as "structuralist" as opposed to "monetarist"; the problems of balance of
payments and inflation in developing countries were seen not as the consequence of irresponsible fiscal and monetary policies but instead as structural disequilibria from a lack of supply that inevitably came about during
the development process.

Prebisch's and ECLA's analysis came from the need to identify the anticyclical measures that might allow Latin American countries to industrialize without experiencing a decrease in employment and national revenue
typical of periods of depression, which originated from countries that were
at the "center" of the world economy. The ECLA solution was "import-
substitution."

During periods of growth in the "center" countries (the United States
and, after the reconstruction, western European countries), an increase in

exports (and consequently in income) occurred in the Latin American "periphery." This growth, in turn, led to an increase in internal demand and consequently of imports. The opposite happened during periods of depression: a decrease in exports led to a fall in employment and income and therefore in imports. An anticyclical policy for South American countries would reduce imports by sacrificing those that were less important (consumer goods) and focusing on the imports of capital goods. This would lead to the growth of internal supply in the medium term. This supply would have responded better to demand without causing a burden to the balance of payments, and it would have had positive effects on employment by creating new jobs. Internal production would have gradually replaced imports, thus freeing peripheral countries from cyclical dynamics generated by "center" countries.

This phase of industrialization through the substitution of imports would not have been free from inflationary pressures. ECLA's most important publication during those years maintained that "the substitution of internal production for imports requires the importation of capital goods. [. . .] To import the capital goods it would be necessary to reduce still further the coefficient of imports for current consumption, thus bringing about a further rise in the cost of living" (ECLA 1950, p. 53). However, such an obstacle "could doubtless be partly removed with the co-operation of international financial institutions" (ECLA 1950, pp. 53–54).

Several years later, Albert Hirschman further analyzed how "inflationary impulses are communicated to the economy by *certain types of development sequences*" (Hirschman [1958] 1963, p. 158; emphasis in the original) and not by incoherent monetary policies or a generalized euphoria for national spending (public or private). In countries where the entrepreneurialism is generally limited and where the elasticity of supply is low in the short term, increases in prices of specific products serve as indicators for investment opportunities. In addition, in industrializing countries, unlike in industrialized countries, new industrial production emerges in a context where competition is very limited and therefore does not contribute to containing domestic prices.

In contrast to the ECLA positions, Hirschman maintained that inflation caused by demand did not play a pivotal role in putting pressure on the balance of payments. Although he did not deny it, he saw other causes: in some cases, inflation was due to a drain of foreign currency rather than to an increase in domestic prices; as a consequence, the pressures on the balance of payments "take place *in lieu of, rather than on top of,* price rises" (Hirschman [1958] 1963, p. 166; emphasis in the original).

However, in Hirschman's analysis (in this case in agreement with ECLA positions), the real limitations in supply came from a limited internal production. Making use of resources such as foreign currency or international aid, which were not influenced by the movement of prices, would have been valuable if it allowed an increase in imports and a simultaneous rise of internal production, thus increasing the elasticity of supply under conditions of no or low inflation (Hirschman [1958] 1963, pp. 167–68). In a later publication, Hirschman maintained that "the needs of developing countries for international financial assistance do not arise so much from the fact that they are too poor to save the amounts needed to achieve some growth target [. . .] as from some disproportionalities that arise in the growth process. At some stage the need of the expanding economy for imported inputs outpaces its ability to increase exports" (Hirschman 1984, p. 103).

Despite this general consensus about an analysis that provided a rationale for international loans to improve reserves of foreign currencies in developing economies, and despite the fact that this consensus was expressed both inside and outside the Bank (the *Fifth Annual Report to the Board of Governors*, Rosenstein-Rodan, ECLA, and Hirschman), the International Bank did not want to risk a change of direction. For example, the first two loans to Italy, granted as "impact loans," were successful but were not replicated. As Rosenstein-Rodan pointed out: "It was contrary to many people's thinking, notably to [. . .] the most conservative business thinking in the Bank."[43] Bank staff generally focused on the technical aspects of projects and did not see the use or scope of a complex economic analysis. The widespread internal opposition to loans beyond the "project approach" was summarized by an anonymous Bank official quoted in Mason and Asher: "Why mess around with program loans and hard-to-appraise types of projects if you are really best at financing electric power and transportation projects, and there are still plenty of power and transport projects to finance?"[44]

SOCIAL LOANS

The second discussion complemented the first and emerged from the experience of the General Survey Missions of the Bank to developing countries. Thanks to the firsthand observations of economic and social conditions of these countries, these missions understood that in addition to the stimulus and support of activities that were directly productive, it was urgent to address issues that were social in nature. According to many of the Bank's missions, addressing social issues was fundamental to promoting a sustained and continuous process of development. Development brought about changes to the growth rates of different sectors, the structures of supply and demand, and the growth rates of urban and rural populations, thus putting pressure on the social structure of countries that were already marked by high level of stress.

For example, the mission to Cuba in 1950 recommended urgent action to increase dramatically the amount of potable water in Santiago, which was on the brink of a humanitarian disaster: "The city narrowly escaped disaster in the summer of 1950, and luck cannot be counted on to save it again" (IBRD 1951, p. 31). The mission to Jamaica gave priority to the reconstruction of at least 30 percent of the dwellings on the island (IBRD 1952b, p. 125), while the final report of the mission to Nicaragua opened with a chapter on "Sanitation, Education and Public Health," which stated:

> Expenditures to improve sanitation, education and public health should, without question, be given first priority in any program designed to increase the long-range growth and development of the Nicaraguan economy. [This] program [. . .] tackles jointly the problems of increasing the physical productivity of the country and that of improving the living standards of the people. This program is an integral part of the agricultural, industrial and transport investment program. (IBRD 1953, p. 22)

One of the most interesting cases was the Colombian mission, because Currie's extended stay in the country gave continuity to the recommendations of the mission and their implementation. The program of urban renewal of the city of Barranquilla and its Zona Negra neighborhood stemmed from the 1949 mission report, which addressed health and housing problems, the construction sector, and the problem of low school enrollment. However, as we already noted, the Bank did not want to move in this direction.

Nevertheless, the objection that the municipal facilities and, in particular, the housing sector, were not directly productive was not convincing even then. Lauchlin Currie would have proposed his "leading sector" model only during the 1970s, tellingly using the construction sector as an example; however, it is obvious that the mechanism, if not the label, was already applied in the construction program proposed for the city of Barranquilla. Therefore, it is not anachronistic to quote Currie in 1974 on the construction sector:

> The import component is low. The unskilled labour component is relatively high. The need it serves is so compelling that in the United States and Canada, despite the high level of incomes, "home operations" still capture about 30% of disposable income. The stock of houses is so large that a relatively small addition should have little effects on prices. [. . .] It is true that the stock is not so great in a developing country but this is more than offset by the high growth rate of urban population and the desirability of replacing extensive slum areas. (Currie 1974, p. 7)

Currie recommended removing all obstacles to development in the sectors where a high, if latent, demand could be expected and that predictably would have reached high rates of growth "independently of the overall rate of growth of the economy" (Currie 1974, p. 6). These conditions (a high, but latent demand) identified a sector with potential for fast growth even without an initial corresponding growth in other sectors. Such a sector would be a pilot and an engine for the economy by providing a haul for continuous and sustained growth.

Currie was not satisfied with the explanations about the vicious circle of poverty, which understood poverty in terms of general scarcity of resources and capital, nor was he persuaded by solutions based on the need for simultaneous aggregate growth in many sectors so that the economy would flourish. On the contrary, he proposed selecting one or several sectors that, if opportunely stimulated and vitalized, could serve as engines for the other sectors. One can see here a substantial convergence with Hirschman's theory of "unbalanced growth."

The case of Barranquilla was particularly interesting precisely because it merged the need to stimulate the economy by selecting a pilot sector and the need to respond to social issues. In his work as an economic consultant in Colombia, Currie was therefore able to apply his prior attempt to reconcile "the humanitarian and social aims of the New Deal [with] sound economics."[45] Not unlike Gunnar Myrdal in his reflections about the uselessness of the notions of "economic" and "non-economic" factors (Myrdal 1957, p. 21), Currie complained that the Bank "had the strange belief that water was social, not economic" (Currie 1979, p. 11). It is precisely the distinction between economic issues and social (and therefore noneconomic) issues that was pointless for development economists. As Myrdal stated, "This distinction is a useless and meaningless criterion from a logical point of view and should be substituted by the distinction between 'relevant' and 'non-relevant' factors or 'more or less relevant'" (Myrdal 1957, pp. 21–22).

However, the Bank did not feel a need to adopt these criteria and systematically rejected projects that were explicitly "social." As Vice President Robert Garner reportedly said to Currie in 1951 when Currie proposed a large and varied investment plan that was both social and economic (a natural consequence of the research and study of the 1949 mission): "Damn it, Lauch! We can't go messing around with education and health. We're a *bank!*"[46] Despite the recommendations, the Bank did not give any loans to Cuba or Jamaica during the 1950s. Of the nine loans granted to Nicaragua from the 1953 mission until the end of the decade, none of them had a social component. The Bank's position is well synthesized by Burke Knapp's words:

> Water is the first thing people want, but we have to distinguish between [. . .] amenities which raise the standard of living, and [. . .] projects which will benefit the economy. [. . .] Our emphasis should be on the latter.[47]

The Bank's Relentless Preference for Directly Productive Loans

The position of the Bank, therefore, did not change, despite the reflections and the opportunities generated by considerations of possible "impact" and "social" loans. There are four main reasons that inspired this policy: a financial reason having to do with funds available at the time for the Bank's operations, a political-cultural reason involving the Bank's top management, a political reason involving the influence of different U.S. political economic elites on the foreign economic policy of the United States, and the experience from the first loans granted by the institution. Although interrelated, these four reasons will be discussed separately.

Originally, the Bank's role was conceived mainly as a guarantor for foreign direct investments in countries undergoing reconstruction and only later in developing countries. In other words, the Bank was supposed to use its limited resources as a guarantee fund. This was a common assumption, but it was disproved by circumstances as soon as the Bank became operational. It turned out that foreign direct investment flows were insufficient to sustain European reconstruction. Thus, the Bank had to serve not only as a guarantor but also as a lending institution. At that point, it became necessary for the Bank to raise additional funds in capital markets, which would serve as the foundation for loans made by the Bank first to European, then to developing, countries.

The actual resources available to the Bank amounted only to the 2 percent in gold paid in by all member countries plus the 18 percent share in dollars from the United States. Thus, the Bank began to issue bonds whose sales enabled it to borrow from capital markets. In order to do so, it had to prove to be financially trustworthy. This was the primary task for President McCloy and his deputy, Garner, when they joined the Bank in March 1947. They worked closely with the U.S. executive director, Black, who later became head of the institution.

Even before the Bank could sell its bonds to insurance companies, investment banks, pension funds, or fiduciary funds on the U.S. market, it needed the individual U.S. states to legalize these bonds. In the interwar period there had been many cases of loans to foreign governments that were never paid back—34 percent of all loans to foreign governments in default according to Kraske et al. (1996, p. 59)—and therefore many states in the United States forbade banks, funds, and insurance companies from giving credit abroad. Since the Bank was a multilateral institution, it was necessary to convince each state, one by one, to allow its local financial institutions to buy Bank bonds.

As Garner recalled, in the beginning "there wasn't a Wall Street man who would touch the [Bank's] bonds with a ten-foot pole."[48] The opening of credit was made possible by the "information conferences" through which the institution became known in financial circles, in the press, and, in particular, by familiarity of John McCloy, Robert Garner, and Eugene Black with the U.S. financial world. In mid-July 1947, the Bank issued its first bonds on the New York Stock Exchange. The demand was much greater than the supply, and the Bank collected more than $250 million.

If in the short run the Bank's management could and did rely on personal relations within Wall Street, in the long run the institution realized that it had to prove its strength and reliability in the field. Extreme caution in making investment decisions became a signature of President McCloy, Vice President Garner, and the executive director and later third president of the Bank, Eugene Black. This provides a clear explanation for the propensity of the Bank toward individual projects that were "directly productive." Investors wanted assurance that their money would be invested in productive activities that could be easily monitored. However, such a reason is more apt to explain the preference for loans linked to single and controllable projects instead of larger investment programs characterized by multiple variables, which are more difficult to evaluate. On the other hand, it does not explain why some investments that could have led to a fair return, could be accurately designed, and were easy to monitor (for example, housing construction programs) were rejected. Therefore, to gain a broader perspective, we must also evaluate the management culture of the institution.

WALL STREET MEN

The presidents of the Bank and their staff came from similar backgrounds. Eugene Meyer, the first president of the Bank, "was a well-known figure on Wall Street" (Kraske et al. 1996, p. 19). At the age of twenty-six, he had already become wealthy from the stock market, and at the age of seventy-one, when he was offered the presidency of the Bank, he had a strong reputation as an investment banker with Republican ties (as well as a public servant on several committees and boards over the years).

John McCloy and the team that he brought with him in early 1947 had spent most of their careers on Wall Street. After studying at Harvard, McCloy became a lawyer in New York in the most exclusive circles, which exposed him to the largest corporations of the country. He belonged to the conservative, Republican high society of New York (Bird 1992; Kraske et al. 1996). Robert Garner came from the world of big North American industrialists: "In my job at Guaranty [Trust Company] I made numerous friends in Wall Street" (Garner 1972, p. 157). In 1942, he became vice president for finance at General Foods. His name as vice president of the International Bank was suggested to McCloy by Harold Stanley, one of the two associates of Morgan Stanley (Garner 1972, p. 206).

In 1949, Eugene Black became the third president of the Bank after having been the vice president of Chase National Bank, overseeing the portfolio of investments. Like Meyer, he too "had become a seasoned investment banker and a well-known and respected figure on Wall Street. Going through the letters he received when he became executive director and later president of the World Bank is like going through an edition of *Who's Who* of the financial world of the United States at that time" (Kraske et al. 1996, p. 78). Black hoped to have either Douglas Dillon or David Rockefeller as a successor, both exponents of the elite of the U.S. social and financial establishment.

This did not happen, but George Woods, who took his place in 1963, came from a similar environment. He was chairman of First Boston Corporation, an investment bank that had a solid reputation on Wall Street and was a specialist in acquisitions and underwriting, "the buying side of the investment business" (Kraske et al. 1996, p. 116).

McCloy tried to present the Bank's top managers as nonpolitical, emphasizing their links to the U.S. financial elite. This was a way to strengthen the independence of the institution. It was part of the culture of these men and their professional milieu to conceive the Bank not as an agency for development but as a *bank*, whose investments should be productive and lead to "the greatest and quickest increase in output and productivity," according to Garner.[49] This culture became stronger with the arrival of McCloy.

The issue of the basic identity of the institution had already been observed by Roy Harrod when he described the days of Bretton Woods in his biography of Keynes: "The biggest question at issue was never fully discussed, namely, whether the Bank should be a sound conservative institution on normal lines, or depart from orthodox caution in the direction of greater venturesomeness" (Harrod 1951, p. 580). With the arrival of Mc-Cloy, a decision was made: "The Bank was to be not a political or charitable agency but a financially sound lending institution, and the criteria that were to determine the conduct of its business were to be acceptable to Wall Street" (Kraske et al. 1996, p. 53).

McCloy's efforts were successful, to the point that U.S. ambassador to Chile Claude G. Bowers was concerned about the excessively close ties between the Bank and Wall Street. In discussing Bank loans to Chile, the ambassador wrote to U.S. president Harry S. Truman: "Our enemies are [. . .] charging that the International Bank is under the domination of Wall Street and that we are back to Dollar Diplomacy with the Good Neighbour Policy scrapped."[50]

Clearly, the top management's ties to Wall Street were helpful in presenting the Bank as a reliable and financially responsible institution. The top managers behaved as Wall Street men not only tactically, for the purpose of presenting the institution as trustworthy and convincing, but because they *were* Wall Street men. The culture and the jargon they introduced at the Bank was heavily criticized years later, in the first official history of the institution:

> The early literature of the Bank is full of references to "sound" economic policies, "sound" fiscal and monetary policies, and "sound" policies of various other kinds, with the clear implication that the distinction between sound and unsound policies is as obvious as the distinction between day and night [. . .]. The distinction is not always perfectly clear, however, and, in such cases, those to whom it *is* crystal clear seem irritatingly doctrinaire. (Mason and Asher 1973, p. 186; emphasis in the original)

U.S. FOREIGN ECONOMIC POLICY AND THE WANE OF THE NEW DEAL

With the end of World War II, the era of the New Deal came to an end. This had major repercussions internationally because of the role of the United States in the reconstruction of an international economic order. The Axis powers had collapsed and western European countries, including Great Britain, were going through a very difficult period. Help from North

America was of vital importance. The Soviet Union had withdrawn from any sort of international collaboration and focused instead on its own area of influence, even though it had participated in the Bretton Woods Conference. The Bretton Woods institutions were also part of this new international order.

The United States wanted to overcome trade restrictions and move toward greater integration of markets. Obvious trade interests were at the basis of this vision: U.S. producers needed an open trade policy to sell their products in new markets. However, this also came from the lesson of the 1930s: trade restrictions caused political hostilities.

Charles S. Maier (1977, p. 609) defined the United States' vision as an "eschatology of peaceful prosperity," based on the need for the rebirth of international trade relations, centered on productivity and economic growth, and rooted in the political and economic experience of the New Deal and the war economy. According to Maier, the United States' emphasis on international economic growth after the war had its background in the way the United States had handled its own social conflict in the previous fifteen years: the impossibility to eradicate the conflict led the U.S. to appease it through compromises.

For some years, the U.S. business community had backed away from the heterodox spending and planning policies promoted by the New Dealers. Indeed, it was the war economy that brought the U.S. business community back to share with the government the task of planning and managing the resources needed to support the military effort. From this coexistence sprang a sort of compromise between two profoundly different paradigms. According to this compromise, economic growth through the diffusion of generalized well-being was supposed to mitigate the distribution problem (which, in an extreme version, became a "class struggle"). The state of equilibrium and ultimately the deadlock between supporters of redistribution policies (typical of the prewar New Deal) and the representatives of the industrial and financial community (recently returned to direct political activity) pushed the political elite to embrace what was defined as the "apolitical politics of productivity" (Maier 1977, p. 613). U.S. society could then transcend the class conflict by a growth that would benefit all social levels.

Removing conflicts over distribution by resolving the problem of scarcity became the keystone of U.S. economic policy, both in-house and abroad: "The true dialectic was not one of class against class, but waste versus abundance" (Maier 1977, p. 615). It was possible to achieve abundance through an expert stimulus of the economy and its mechanisms, and it was therefore the result of *technical* rather than *political* expertise. During the Cold War, this strategy produced remarkable political dividends that, among other things, helped the anticommunist struggle (Gardner [1956] 1969). The International Bank and the International Monetary Fund were inevitably part of this picture, and they were unquestionably in tune with this "politics of productivity."

What is noteworthy is another similarity between the Bank and the U.S. political-economic world: the parallelism between the departure of the New Deal supporters from government agencies soon after the war and the ouster of "social" issues supporters during the first years of the Bank. This parallelism is important because in both cases the same forces, the same ideologies, and the same approaches to economic and social realities were facing off.

The U.S. industrial and financial elite were profoundly discredited after the 1929 crash. For a decade, they gave in the economic initiative to a new wave of heterodox politicians and economists who supported Roosevelt's New Deal. A decade later, executives in finance and industry who had not backed Roosevelt's political and economic plan were called back into the government due to the new needs and demands of wartime. By the end of the war and after a period of confrontation with the New Dealers, they found themselves in the driving seats, while the New Deal generation was on the ebb (Hirschman [1989] 1995, pp. 145–46).

The Bretton Woods institutions were born from the work of the generation of New Dealers and early Keynesians. However, the Bank's operations were managed by individuals tightly connected to Wall Street who were very critical of Roosevelt (this is clear from Garner's harsh judgment: "[Roosevelt] did more harm to this country than anyone else in history"). Supporters of the New Deal initially tried to influence the basic decisions on the economic policy of the Bank, as several proposals regarding the expansion of activities in social areas that were not directly productive testify; however, these supporters were ousted just a few years later.

From this point of view, the case of Lauchlin Currie is particularly enlightening, and it demonstrates the progressive marginalization that many exponents of the New Deal underwent when the Wall Street people took over the leadership positions at the Bank.

THE EARLY SUCCESSES OF THE BANK:
AN OBSTACLE TO CHANGE

The first loans granted by the Bank to European and developing countries proved to be successful, and in fact they were completely repaid. According to those who urged caution and considered it inappropriate for the Bank to venture into higher-risk loans in an environment where it was difficult to raise funds, there was no reason to change policy. The success of the first loans validated this position against alternative proposals of "impact" and "social loans," and contributed to perpetuating that model.

Looking back at the history of the loans made by the Bank during its first fifteen years—from the long presidency of Black (1949–62) until the beginning of George Woods's tenure—this unquestionable success is confirmed. The first two years of actual activity—from 1947 to 1948, because 1946 was dedicated to setting up the internal administrative apparatus—were devoted to loans for reconstruction in Europe for about $500 million. After slowing down during the period 1949–50 (the years of transition from reconstruction to development), the volume of annual loans granted by the Bank stabilized at an average of about $325 million until 1958, when it rose to $700 million.[51]

What is particularly noteworthy is the amount of the net transfer (disbursement minus the repayment of debt on capital minus the repayment of interest), which slightly exceeded $40 million in 1961.[52] This number means that debtor countries were repaying their loans to the Bank, whose profits grew "at an almost indecent rate" (Mason and Asher 1973, p. 407).

Coda: The End of the Debate

THE REORGANIZATION OF 1952

The season of debate came to a practical and symbolic end with the internal reorganization of 1952, the first significant reorganization of the hierarchy and the departments of the institution.

During its first years, the Bank had been organized internally by function (see Figure 9). In addition to the oversight entities, that is, the board of

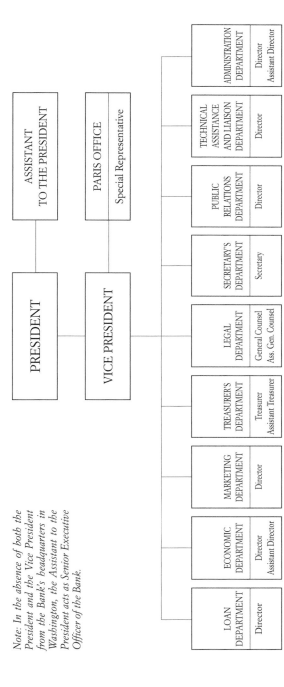

Note: In the absence of both the President and the Vice President from the Bank's headquarters in Washington, the Assistant to the President acts as Senior Executive Officer of the Bank.

PRESIDENT

ASSISTANT TO THE PRESIDENT

VICE PRESIDENT

PARIS OFFICE
Special Representative

LOAN DEPARTMENT
Director

ECONOMIC DEPARTMENT
Director
Assistant Director

MARKETING DEPARTMENT
Director

TREASURER'S DEPARTMENT
Treasurer
Assistant Treasurer

LEGAL DEPARTMENT
General Counsel
Ass. Gen. Counsel

SECRETARY'S DEPARTMENT
Secretary

PUBLIC RELATIONS DEPARTMENT
Director

TECHNICAL ASSISTANCE AND LIAISON DEPARTMENT
Director

ADMINISTRATION DEPARTMENT
Director
Assistant Director

Figure 9 IBRD organization chart through September 22, 1952.
SOURCE: IBRD, "Report of a Committee on Bank Organization," March 28, 1952, Annex, A; Organization-Report of Committee on Organization 1952; Central Files; Fonds 2; World Bank Group Archives.

governors, the executive directors, and the president, the institution was made up of a few offices organized by function. The most important ones were the Legal Department, the Loan Department, and the Research (Economic) Department. Other departments were added later: the Marketing Department, which was established alongside the existing Public Relations Department, and whose task was to make the institution known to potential investors and to maintain good relations with the financial world, and the Administration Department. In addition, there were two representative offices, one in New York and one in Paris, that facilitated, respectively, contacts with Wall Street and the European governments. Finally, there were the Secretary and the Treasurer (Mason and Asher 1973, p. 866, chart H-1).

Among these departments, the Loan Department was the operational heart of the structure: all staff members responsible for the relations with individual countries and involved in loan negotiations, together with technical and financial staff for project evaluation, were part of it. The Loan Department also employed some economists, usually specialized in the economy of a specific country. Most economists, however, worked in the Economic Department, which conducted research on creditworthiness of countries and on financial strategies.

The approval of a loan required a positive opinion by the Loan Department about the structural, technical, and financial aspects of a project and by the Economic Department about the reliability of the country under consideration. The relations between these two departments were not always harmonious. In addition, the Loan Department started taking on a very heavy workload that got heavier with the increase of loans to developing countries (Mason and Asher 1973, pp. 74–75).

The Economic Department had been created by the first president of the Bank, Eugene Meyer, as the Research Department. Its primary function was to evaluate the economic aspects of individual loan applications coming from client countries.[53] In fall 1947, tensions about the division of labor with the Loan Department, unequivocally documented in the archives of the Bank,[54] led to a first attempt to have the departments complement each other instead of compete against each other. The Loan Department would be organized geographically and conduct studies on individual countries that had approached the Bank for a loan; the Research Department would be organized functionally and conduct sectoral studies on a regional and global scale.[55] The Loan Department ultimately rejected this arrangement and issued recommendations aimed at keeping all loan-related issues under its umbrella:

> The present Loan-Research boundary, drawn between studies relating to particular applications (actual or potential) and those relating to several such applications [. . .] is artificial. There is no obvious reason why the former category should fall under the Loan Director and the latter under another Director. All studies relating to the processing of loan applications (and 90% of the research needed in the Bank falls under this heading) should be under the Loan Director.[56]

According to these recommendations, the Research Department would become a "service department [. . .] doing the work it was asked to do in the way it was asked to do it."[57] Another, more radical solution proposed by the Loan Department was the dissolution of the Research Department, which could be replaced by an economic advisor reporting directly to the president: "This Adviser should be of the first rank (someone of the calibre of the late Lord Keynes would be the ideal). He might be asked by the President to comment on reports on loan applications *after* they had passed the Staff Loan Committee stage."[58]

Obviously, the Research Department opposed these recommendations. Its role, it claimed, was not only to respond to the immediate research needs of the Bank, and the Loan Department in particular. Its most distinctive feature was its ability to conduct broader research that, albeit less immediately applicable, could stimulate effective, long-term development policies.[59] It is significant that Leonard Rist, the head of the Department, at the beginning of 1948 decided to change the unit's name from Research Department to Economic Department. Rist, a French national, said in 1961, "I discovered that research in English may mean that you collected statistics and don't interpret them yourself, which is one thing I didn't want to do."[60] Rosenstein-Rodan soberly commented that "the divisions and sections of the [Economic] Department have the responsibility of drawing the attention of other members of the Bank staff to significant developments which it is considered may be of interest to them in their work."[61]

The Economic Department went through another interesting attempt to reorganize, but in the end it "[was] never a favorite of McCloy, Garner, or Black" (Mason and Asher 1973, p. 75).[62] A new interdepartmental committee, under the direction of William Iliff, prepared a draft restructuring plan that would inform the 1952 reorganization of the institution.

As shown in Figure 10, Iliff's main innovation was the introduction of three departments organized by region: one dealing with Asia and the Middle East; another with Europe, Africa, and Australasia; and one with the Western Hemisphere (primarily Latin America). The staff that maintained relations with specific countries, independent of their specializations, joined these three regional departments, which took over most operational tasks, including some that were previously under the Economic Department. Everything to do with the preparation, management, and the evaluation of loans was now the responsibility of these regional departments. In addition, they were in charge of evaluating the reliability of a country, studying development programs "in their widest aspects," organizing the economic survey missions, and writing the final reports.[63]

Those engineers, technicians, financial analysts, and economists who had specific competences in certain sectors and worked on evaluation and supervision of projects in fields such as transportation, energy, and agriculture joined the new Technical Operations Department, which became the largest in terms of head count. The three regional departments, together with the Technical Operations Department and the Marketing Department, made up the core of the institution. Together they were called the Operational Departments.

On the other hand, the Economic Department was relieved of all of its operational responsibilities, reduced in size, and assigned only consulting duties. Strictly speaking, the department disappeared to make room for a team called Economic Advisory Staff. This "should be a very small group, [and] would be responsible for advising on the 'across-the-board' aspects of the Bank's economic approach to its operations."[64] Coordination with the economists of the regional departments would be facilitated by a permanent committee set up as a forum for "an exchange of views with regard to the economic approach adopted in each of the three Area Operational Departments."[65] Thus, the former Economic Department could play the role of consultant, but at the same time it was ousted from the decision-

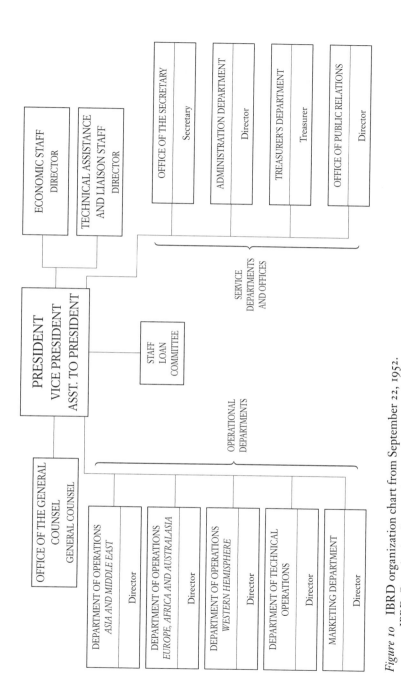

Figure 10 IBRD organization chart from September 22, 1952.
SOURCE: IBRD, Organization–Report of Committee on Organization 1952; Central Files; Fonds 2; World Bank Group Archives.

making chain: "It is our conception that the Economic Adviser would have no operational responsibility and, while he would be available to advise the Operations Officers [. . .] the line of operational responsibility would run from the Operations Officers through the Chief Operations Officer to the Directorate of the Department."[66]

Leonard Rist sarcastically pointed out that the underlying concept reflected the American military tradition and its clear separation between the line of command and auxiliary services. In the case of the Bank, operational departments would naturally be within the line of command, while the services of economic and research analysis would simply play a supporting role.[67]

The new organization became effective on September 22, 1952.[68] Many individuals had to change departments, offices, and colleagues. The morale of the staff was affected for some time, as A. S. G. Hoar, the director of the former Loan Department, had feared:

> Even if one conceded a net advantage to the proposed new arrangement (which I do not), that advantage could be bought too dearly by the disruption and shock to morale which the shake-up would entail [. . .]. I do know that almost all of my Loan Officers feel very deeply in this matter. They are welded together into a team which is confident in itself. They have appreciated the growing strength which has come from discarding weak members and recruiting stronger ones. They feel they are a winning side—as, indeed, the record proves them to be—and they do not want to be broken up.[69]

The main goal of the reorganization seemed to justify this risk. The separation between regional departments, which worked with countries, and the Technical Operations Department, which evaluated the technical and financial contents of individual projects (without a connection to the officials of individual countries) served as a system of mutual control and freed the decision-making process from any possible biases. Specifically, this guaranteed that the institution would not authorize weak projects simply because of complacency toward national officials and that technically solid projects would not go through without a thorough monitoring of the economic situation of a country. In other words, the institution "protected itself simultaneously against the technocrat and the diplomat."[70] According to Mason and Asher, "The relationship between area departments and the Technical Operations Department—'area-T.O.D.' relations—after 1952 became the Bank's most difficult and pervasive organizational problem" (Mason and Asher 1973, p. 76).

Another intentional goal, which was obvious but rarely underscored officially, was the complete reshaping of the functions and responsibilities of the economists within the institution. With reference to this period, the most recent official history of the Bank states that the administrative reorganization of 1952 precisely had this goal: "To cut the size and authority of the Economic Department" (Kapur, Lewis, and Webb 1997, p. 130). Leonard Rist, who was then director of the Economic Department, stated in 1961: "That was a deliberate intention to humiliate people in that thing, and to this day I've been humiliated by this term [. . .]. I can only interpret [it] as a voluntary slap."[71]

The Economic Department, in fact, had become increasingly stronger. It had acquired a fundamental position in deciding the loans of the institution and in shaping the Bank's economic policy, and it tried to do so with a broad vision. As Rist remembered,

> I had a great fight to force my economists to think in social and political terms and to force the others to accept that this was part of the economist's job. I didn't say it was exclusively the economist's job. That was the big fight. In effect I said: "I want to have my views about Mexican economic policies tomorrow but that doesn't mean to say that you can't have yours. Then at least we can discuss them." There was a time when the theory would have been: "You don't have any right to have any views about the future of Mexican policy." It was never put quite in that form, but that was the implication. And this was very largely the difficulty in the famous fight between the loan department and the economic department.[72]

The research activity and heterodox proposals coming from this department were accepted with an annoyance that at times was only barely concealed. Robert Garner, commenting in 1961 about Rosenstein-Rodan's contribution to the Bank, stated:

> I frankly never felt that the Bank was his dish of tea, and he's finally gone to Harvard—to the academic world, where I think his talents lie. I came

to the conclusion that the Bank was not the place for the development of broad economic policies or studies, that our job was applied economics, that the world is full of theoretical economists [. . .] and that for us to try to get into that field was unwise.[73]

Albert Waterston added about Rosenstein-Rodan that "someone like Bob Garner wouldn't even talk to him."[74] Moreover, Garner gave instructions that Burke Knapp should replace Rosenstein-Rodan as deputy director of the Economic Department.[75] Rosenstein-Rodan finally left the Bank in 1954.[76]

Only during the 1960s did the role of economists within the institution become appreciated: "Woods gave Bank economists, for the first time, equal weight in the lending process with the loan officers and project analysts" (Kamarck 1995, p. xii).

BLACK'S BANK

During the 1950s and through 1962, the International Bank was led by Eugene Black, who was appointed in 1947 as the U.S. executive director and president in 1949 to replace McCloy, who was sent to Germany as high commissioner. During these years, the institution grew constantly and consistently and acquired an undisputed and successful profile.

The primary activity of the Bank became the financing of infrastructure projects, which were often large in size and capital intensive, destined to last a long time: dams, roads, railroads, and power plants. During the 1950s, more than 80 percent of the investments to developing countries went to the energy and transport sectors (Kapur, Lewis, and Webb 1997, p. 109). In addition, despite acknowledging the need of a program framework for interventions in the member countries, the Bank reiterated its preference for financing single and well-defined development *projects*. The view was that a loan for a single project, because it is easily defined and monitored, would be more easily repaid than a large program, which is more difficult to oversee. By financing large public works projects, the Bank acquired the leverage to influence the macroeconomic variables of a country, whose good conditions were considered vital for a positive return on investment. De facto conditionality always existed to the extent that the institution found it necessary to protect its investments.

The ability to plan projects and the technical and engineering skills to complete them became the essential functions for achieving these goals. The role of economists was drastically reduced, and Black's Bank essentially became a bank of engineers. As Mason and Asher put it, the Bank was "overly concerned with the engineering aspects of projects" (Mason and Asher 1973, p. 78). Other sectors, including health, education, and access to water sources, were not considered. Agriculture only received a small amount of total investments.[77] As per Black's approach, development necessarily occurred through the growth of aggregate indices of the economy, and shortcuts in alleviating poverty through welfare programs would be counterproductive. An internal report about India, dated July 1958, stated: "Not least amongst the dangers to be guarded against in the present stage of India's development is the pursuit of welfare at the expense of efficiency. The government policy of progressively reducing inequalities, if carried beyond a certain point, may be difficult to reconcile with the aim of rapid economic development."[78]

What certainly did not change was the extreme prudence of the Bank in granting loans. Black was very careful not to let the lending discipline relax, even though Wall Street was by then confident in the soundness of the institution and the high quality of its staff.[79]

Even the U.S. administration was sometimes unhappy with this extreme caution. The government expected the Bank to participate more directly in social initiatives with an anticommunist function. Although the Bank did not want to tarnish its reputation as a rigorous institution, it did its part. Indeed, several loans betray the political basis of their assessments in a way that can only be explained in the context of the Cold War.[80]

Black always tried to resist political pressure that would push the institution outside its rigid financial discipline. Only in 1960, toward the end of his long presidency, did Black decide to found an organization to support developing countries whose macroeconomic conditions made them ineligible for IBRD loans. The International Development Association (IDA) was created as the "soft window" of the Bank—the window for countries that had special difficulties with finances and balance of payments. Another affiliate organization that Black and primarily Garner supported with conviction and energy was the International Finance Corporation (IFC), established in 1956. Its task was to participate (always as a minority shareholder) in foreign direct investment in developing countries, which was barred to the Bank. The participation of an IBRD affiliate would facilitate the movement of private capital to investment opportunities in the most disadvantaged countries. The IFC answered the need to stimulate the transfer of private entrepreneurial capacity to countries that had the potential for sustained growth, and this was consistent with Black's political vision (Haralz 1997).

By 1963, when Black left the presidency and George Woods took the reins, the Bank had grown for more than a decade with a solid conviction that development had to be promoted through financing individual projects for infrastructure and directly productive activities. "This, in the opinion of the IBRD management, was about what could be expected of a soundly managed international development institution" (Mason and Asher 1973, p. 462).

Conclusions

This research has attempted to describe the economic policy choices of the International Bank between the 1940s and the 1950s. It has tried to outline the shape taken by the action of the Bank in its early years. These were years in which the internal structure of the institution was still growing, in which the functional relations among the various actors had to be adjusted more than once, in which the Bank learned by trial and error. This process was complicated by the sudden need for the institution to redirect its mission from European reconstruction to development of disadvantaged countries, inventing a new trade for itself and acquiring new expertise. I tried to evaluate how this particular historical and institutional context influenced the lending policies of the Bank.

This methodology can fruitfully be applied in the study of all institutions: institutions can only be fully understood through the lens of a historical analysis that digs below the official positions and that documents the processes of change, the dynamics between the various actors, and the relative weight that these actors have over time. The lucid reflections of Leonard Rist, albeit in a different context, are once again very useful:

> To some people, you see, you can judge policy merely by looking at the nose of the fellow who makes it. If you like his face, then his policies will be good, especially if you like his public utterances. Now, public utterances are made for the public and [are] not necessarily a guide to what his decisions will be. And getting that element of personalities out and putting the elements of history first, social pressures and traditions of the country, where they belong [. . .] which is only a background, as a guide, and then going into the analysis of which are the forces which are actually at work. This I think the boys [at the Economic Department] have learned. And I think they have enjoyed it.[1]

Such an analysis is useful to reveal and examine the disputes between different ways of understanding and managing the work of the International Bank, and it shows the rise and fall of an approach that was not alternative to, but instead complementary to, the mainstream policies of the institution.

The transition from reconstruction to development opened a window through which one can see the appearance of new perspectives and ideas on development that challenged the somewhat one-dimensional perspective of senior Bank management. Kapur, Lewis, and Webb spoke about this as "cracks in the marble" (1997, p. 130). The Bank generated from within opinions that were different from the model of "directly productive loans," and that contaminated the supposed integrity and unity of thought and action. The moment of crisis, when the tension between different perspectives reached its peak, was described through the specific but exemplary case of the Bank's work in Colombia.

Eventually, the window closed following the expulsion or the normalization of incompatible positions, or those considered as such. Although the debate between various options continued after 1952, and Paul Rosenstein-Rodan remained at the Bank for another two years, the reorganization of 1952 played a significant role. The elimination of the Economic Department, that is, its reduction to a merely consultative role, unequivocally signaled a desire by management to curb forces perceived as centrifugal. Obviously, in a complex organization that is constantly growing, the processes under way have their inertia, and changes do not occur overnight. However, the reorganization of 1952 indicated the end of a season. The season that began after 1952 featured great continuity and stability under the direction of Eugene Black, whose presidency still stands as the longest in the history of the institution.

Analyzing the years before 1952 allows us to better understand the roots of the power later shown by Black's long and stable tenure. It was a power forged, at least partially, through the conflict with positions that in Roy Harrod's words, tried to "depart from orthodox caution in the direction of greater venturesomeness" (Harrod 1951, p. 580). Still, my analysis helps not only to understand the strengths of this long season but also to reveal a deep reason for the Bank's subsequent crisis. That strength and the growing success in managing loans prevented the Bank fifteen years later from recognizing the failure of the hopes for developing countries that the first season of development economics had raised.

The failure of the hopes for greater well-being as a result of the efforts to promote growth during the 1950s, a failure that became unquestionable during the 1960s, was twofold. For one, it was exposed by a series of empty promises: improvement in the well-being of the poorest people, who were the object of these policies, did not occur; the unemployment rate in many countries increased; and the benefits from growth were more unevenly distributed than originally expected. For another, this failure was exposed by the dramatic, unintended consequences of policies that were thought to be virtuous. Albert Hirschman remembered that "it look[ed] increasingly as though the effort to achieve growth, whether or not successful, brings with it calamitous side effects in the political realm, from the loss of democratic liberties at the hand of authoritarian, repressive regimes to the wholesale violation of elementary human rights" (Hirschman [1979] 1981c, pp. 98–99).

These signs of the "futility" and "perversity" of the policies to pursue growth fortunately did not take on the form of reactionary rhetoric, that is, rhetoric that would discourage an intervention considered useless or dangerous (Hirschman 1991). Instead, they generated a widespread need for revision and discussion. Hans Singer wrote that, in the 1950s,

economic development became the big growth sector in the economic
science. In the flush of enthusiasm, economists tended to think in terms of
economic growth models. Those were the great days of the Harrod-Domar
formula, of average and incremental capital-output ratios, of rates of
savings and investment, of closing and widening gaps in gross national
product (GNP). But then came the days of disillusionment. Doubts began
to creep in whether the matter was as simple as that. What was the
meaning of GNP gaps when the GNP concept was applied to countries
with subsistence economies? [. . .] The problem of the underdeveloped
countries is not just growth, but development. Development is growth *plus*
change; change, in turn, is social and cultural as well as economic, and
qualitative as well as quantitative. The key concept must be the improved
quality of people's life. (Singer 1965, pp. 3 and 5)

While the scientific and academic world discussed these problems (David
Morse, director general of the ILO for twenty-two years spoke of the "de-
thronement of the GNP" [1971, p. 7]), the International Bank persevered
with the line imposed by Black and Garner in the early 1950s. Woods made
a tentative opening toward loans that previously would not have been
granted, but only because the Bank was forced, for political reasons, to re-
invest its earnings, which everybody considered excessive. But overall, the
Bank lagged behind the turmoil and studies taking place in the field of
economic development.

Only with Robert McNamara, the fifth president of the Bank (1968–81)
and the first manager-turned-politician to lead it, did the Bank try to catch
up with the new frontiers in development, especially during his second
term.[2] The Bank undertook the study and implementation of policies directly related to the fight against poverty, and thus loans that were "poverty
biased" and not only "directly productive." The most obvious fruits of this
change of perspective were the strategy of *Redistribution with Growth*
(Chenery et al., 1974) and later the strategy of basic needs (launched by the
ILO [1976, 1977] and embraced by the Bank).[3]

Although born from an initiative by Lord Keynes and the New Deal
thinkers, from the very beginning the Bank had a strong cultural imprint-
ing that can be traced to conservative and Republican circles of U.S. high
finance. This explains its long-held conservative attitudes on development
problems and policies toward disadvantaged countries. However, as my

research has shown, during its early years the Bank was also exposed to different points of view that addressed more closely the complex economic and social realities of the less developed countries. However, the Bank rejected these points of view and actively distanced itself from them.

The echoes of these discussions within the institution had almost faded when, in the mid-1960s, the debate within economic development emphasized the need for complementary approaches to economic growth. The Bank had forgotten its early studies on development issues, and so it was unable to adapt readily to new demands. The profile of success that the Bank had given itself during the long presidency of Black kept the institution from understanding and addressing the changes that were occurring around it. Its success was the basis of its inability to change. When the Bank later discovered that it was out of step with the times, it reacted to regain an edge.

This oscillating movement, from the cutting edge of the discipline to its backwaters and vice versa, was not exclusive of this one period of the institution's history. On the contrary, it is a mechanism that may be found in other decades and that may help explain the highs and lows of the sixty-year-long history of the Bank.

REFERENCE MATTER

Notes

ABBREVIATIONS

For practical reasons, in the notes references to some archival sources have been shortened.

Colombia 1: Colombia, General Negotiations 1; Country Operational Files; Fonds 1; World Bank Group Archives.

Colombia 2: Colombia, General Negotiations 2; Country Operational Files; Fonds 1; World Bank Group Archives.

Colombia 3: Colombia, General Negotiations 3; Country Operational Files; Fonds 1; World Bank Group Archives.

Currie Mission: Currie Mission–Colombia, General Survey Mission (CURRIE) 1949–1952, Country Operational Files; Fonds 1; World Bank Group Archives.

Colombia Mission I: Colombia, General Survey Mission–Report I, Country Operational Files; Fonds 1; World Bank Group Archives.

Colombia Tech. Ass. III: Colombia Technical Assistance III, Country Operational Files; Fonds 1; World Bank Group Archives.

Housing 1: Housing and Urban Development vol. 1; Central Files; Fonds 2; World Bank Group Archives.

LBCP: Lauchlin B. Currie Papers, Rare Book, Manuscript, and Special Collections Library, Duke University, Durham, NC.

Oral Hist. 44: Fonds 01, Columbia University Project; WB IBRD/IDA 44 Oral Histories; World Bank Group Archives.

Org. Econ. Dept.: Organization-Economic Department General, 1947–1964; Central Files; Fonds 2; World Bank Group Archives.

Org. Report: Organization-Report of Committee on Organization 1952; Central Files; Fonds 2; World Bank Group Archives.

CHAPTER ONE

1. Regarding the initial difficulty of the Bank and especially the closing of U.S. financial markets to international bonds, see the interesting reflections of Davison Sommers, general counsel of the World Bank in those years. Davidson Sommers, oral history interview, June 22, 1989, Truman Presidential Museum and Library, http://www.trumanlibrary.org/oralhist/sommersd.htm.

2. For example, the case in Oliver (1990).

3. For example, the cases in Mason and Asher (1973) and Kraske et al. (1996).

4. For a discussion about the static and ahistoric character of the marginalistic approach, see Dasgupta (1985). For historical and institutional approaches, see for example Rutherford (1994) and Hodgson (2001).

5. I must admit a simplification in quoting this text. Instead of the suspension of the quote, I should have reported the words "than the sociologist." The contrast that Hirschman proposed was therefore between "the historian" and "the sociologist." Eliminating the comparison is not meant to make Hirschman's words explain something different from the original. More simply, it is useful to avoid making a particular polemic from twenty-five years ago more visible than the more substantial message of his work. His goal was not to directly oppose a sociological to a historic sensitivity, but to restore some degree of freedom in social analysis.

6. As a demonstration of this sensitivity, Hirschman's memory about his first reading of Karl Marx's works is important: *"The Eighteenth Brumaire of Louis Bonaparte* was a particularly fine work. His historical books were much less orthodox than his economic ones [. . .] I like to understand how things happen, how change actually takes place" (Hirschman [1994] 1998, p. 67).

7. As quoted in Canfora (2004, p. vii).

8. Stan Liebowitz and Stephen Margolis questioned the historical value of the examples given to prove the thesis of path-dependence. Liebowitz and Margolis (1995) discuss the example of the formats of Beta and VHS video recorders. In Liebowitz and Margolis (1998), it is possible to find a discussion about both Beta and VHS formats, as well as the QWERTY keyboard for typewriters.

9. Oral history interview, Leonard Rist, July 19, 1961, p. 47, *Oral Hist. 44.*

CHAPTER TWO

1. November 5, 1947. Cited in Kapur, Lewis, and Webb (1997, p. 83).

2. During the mission to Colombia, the Bank also sent missions to Central American countries: Guatemala, Nicaragua, Costa Rica, El Salvador, Honduras, Panama, and the Dominican Republic. See "Economic Technology Meeting," December 16, 1948, *Colombia 1.*

3. "IBRD Relations with Colombia—Confidential," Mr. Gordon, January 19, 1950, *Colombia 2.*

4. "Outgoing Wire," John J. McCloy to Professor Lionel Robbins, March 1, 1949, *Currie Mission*.

5. Officially the head of the mission was the only one responsible for the content of the final report of the mission. It was also explicitly reported that the opinions and the interpretations included in the report did not necessarily correspond to those of the Bank. The reason that the Bank kept its distance was to give the mission diplomatic freedom and allow the Bank to freely express itself. Nevertheless it was clear that the institution would have strongly supported the mission and its work.

6. For some reflections on this topic, see the introduction by Pier Francesco Asso and Marcello De Cecco to Hirschman's writings from the 1930s (Asso and De Cecco [1945] 1987).

7. See for example the issue dedicated to Currie of *HOPE—History of Political Economy*, vol. 10, no. 4 (1978), or the session on the economists of the New Deal at the annual meeting of the American Economic Society, in *American Economic Review: Papers and Proceedings*, vol. 62, no. 1–2 (1972).

8. "Translation of the text of a cable from the President of Colombia, addressed to Mr. McCloy, received April 28," Marcus H. Elliott to Mr. A. S. G. Hoar, April 30, 1947, *Colombia 1*.

9. "Office Memorandum—Colombia," Mr. A. S. G. Hoar to Mr. D. Crena de Iongh, May 2, 1947, *Colombia 1*.

10. "Office Memorandum—Colombia, Review of Current Problems," Latin-American Division to Mr. A. S. G. Hoar, August 5, 1947, p. 3, *Colombia 1*.

11. Gonzalo Restrepo-Jaramillo, Ambassador of Colombia, to Mr. John McCloy, President IBRD, February 25, 1948, *Colombia 1*. The conference ended on May 2, 1948, see "Ratification by the United States of the *Pact of Bogotá*," November 22, 1948, attached to Paul C. Daniels for the Secretary of State to the Diplomatic Missions in the American Republics, January 12, 1949, in *Foreign Relations of the United States, 1949*, vol. 2 (Washington, D.C.: Government Printing Office, 1975), pp. 419–24.

12. Oral history interview, Sir William Iliff, August 12, 1961, p. 1, *Oral Hist. 44*.

13. "Office Memorandum—President's Latin American Tour—Colombia," W. A. B. Iliff to Mr. J. J. McCloy, 22 March 1948, *Colombia 1*.

14. The reason for the homicide is unknown. In fact, a crowd tore him out of police custody and lynched him. The U.S. secretary of state, George Marshall, was in Bogotá to observe the work of the conference that had just begun. In agreement with the Colombian authorities, Marshall declared that the crime was due to the international Communist conspiracy; see "Memorandum of Conversation, by the Secretary of State," Dean Acheson, Washington, D.C., April 19, 1949, in *Foreign Relations of the United States, 1949*, vol. 2 (Washington, D.C.: Government Printing Office, 1975), pp. 605–7; and Yépez (1994, p. 42). But the hypothesis of an assassination

orchestrated by the "right" seems much more plausible because a "larger number of victims are Liberals"—as reported by the American Ambassador to Bogotá, Willard L. Beaulac, to the Secretary of State, Bogotá, November 2, 1949, in *Foreign Relations of the United States, 1949*, vol. 2 (Washington, D.C.: Government Printing Office, 1975), pp. 616–18—and because the Liberal Party was the one "whose policy greatly appeals to the working classes and the under-privileged," "File Copy—Recent Events in Colombia," Victor L. Urquidi to Mr. A. S. G. Hoar, April 13, 1948; *Colombia 1*. The U.S. ambassador also added that "Liberals allege Conservative government has combined with Conservative Party to oppose Liberals and there is evidence to support allegation," Willard L. Beaulac to the Secretary of State, Bogotá, November 2, 1949, in *Foreign Relations of the United States, 1949*, vol. 2 (Washington, D.C.: Government Printing Office, 1975), pp. 616–18.

15. Among many aspects of this revolt, the oil workers of Barrancabermeja established a soviet. The *Bogotazo* was one of the most significant events in contemporary Colombian history. This often appears in many fictional stories, and in a discussion about the fundamental characteristics of urban fiction in postwar Colombia. Torres G. considers it a transition from tradition to modernity for the Colombian capital (Torres G. 1998).

16. "File Copy—Recent Events in Colombia," Victor L. Urquidi to Mr. A. S. G. Hoar, April 13, 1948, *Colombia 1*.

17. "Office Memorandum—Colombia," Jacques Torfs to Mr. G. H. Clee, Loan Officer, April 28, 1948, *Colombia 1*.

18. "Memorandum of Conversation by the Secretary of State," Washington, D.C., July 12, 1948, in *Foreign Relations of the United States, 1948*, vol. 9 (Washington, D.C., Government Printing Office, 1972), pp. 440–44, cited on page 441.

19. The original amount was allocated as follows: $5 million for agricultural equipment; $10 million for irrigation and electrification, rivers and ports, railroads, and salt mines, respectively; and $15 million for roads. "Office Memorandum—Colombia," Marcus H. Elliott to Files, June 1, 1948, *Colombia 1*. The additional amount of $28 million was for a new iron and steel plant, which McCloy was told about during his visit to the Latin American country; see "Colombia—Report and Recommendations," prepared by Loan Department in consultation with Economic Department, November 18, 1948, *Colombia 1*.

20. Gilbert Clee had responsibility for the entire process, and he shared it with his principal advisor, Jacques Torfs, who was already familiar with the country. "File Copy—Colombia, Discussions with officials of," Gilbert H. Clee to Mr. M. Elliott, June 15, 1948, *Colombia 1*; "Office Memorandum—Colombia, Discussions with officials," Jacques Torfs to Mr. Gilbert H. Clee, June 16, 1948, *Colombia 1*; "Office Memorandum—Colombia, Discussions with officials," Jacques Torfs to Mr. Gilbert Clee, June 22, 1948, *Colombia 1*; "Office Memorandum—Colombia,

Discussions with officials," Jacques Torfs to Mr. Gilbert Clee, June 29, 1948, *Colombia 1*; "Office Memorandum—Colombia, Interview with the representatives of the Colombian Government, July 8, 1948," Jacques Torfs to Mr. M. Elliott, July 14, 1948, *Colombia 1*; "Office Memorandum—Colombia, Meeting with Colombian Representatives, Tuesday, July 20," Jacques Torfs to Mr. Marcus H. Elliott, July 21, 1948, *Colombia 1*; "Office Memorandum—Colombia, Interview with the representatives of the Colombian Government, July 8, 1948," Jacques Torfs to Mr. M. Elliott, July 14, 1948, *Colombia 1*; "Office Memorandum—Colombia, Discussions with officials," Jacques Torfs to Mr. Gilbert Clee, June 22, 1948, *Colombia 1*; "Office Memorandum—Colombia," Gilbert H. Clee to Mr. W. A. B. Iliff, July 2, 1948, *Colombia 1*; "Office Memorandum—Colombia, Meeting with Colombian Representatives, Tuesday, July 20," Jacques Torfs to Mr. Marcus H. Elliott, July 21, 1948, *Colombia 1*.

21. In a report prepared by Jacques Torfs for Gilbert Clee, the following institutions and companies are mentioned: American and Foreign Power and its South American Subsidiary (Sapco), Standard Oil of New Jersey and its Colombian subsidiary Tropical Oil Co., Foreign Bondholders Council, National City Bank, and finally Raymond Concrete Pile Co., "Office Memorandum—Colombia," Jacques Torfs to Mr. G. H. Clee, Loan Officer, April 28, 1948, *Colombia 1*.

22. See several letters from individual businessmen in response to the questions posed by ANDI regarding these loans: Eduardo Uribe Uribe, manager of Cía. Antioquena de Telares S. A. to ANDI, June 1, 1948, *Colombia 1*; "Re: Financiaciones externas," Hijos de Eleazar Ospina & Cía. to ANDI, July 1, 1948, *Colombia 1*; "Ref: Financiaciones externas," Gaseosas Posada Tobon to ANDI, July 1, 1948, *Colombia 1*; "Ref: Financiaciones externas," Gaseosas Colombianas S. A. to ANDI, July 2, 1948, *Colombia 1*.

23. The official exchange rate was 1.75 pesos per dollar, but it was unsustainable. On the black market the exchange rate was between 2.50 and 2.85 pesos per dollar between August and September 1948. It was clearly a symptom of the scarcity of the strong currency. See "Colombia—Report and Recommendations," prepared by Loan Department in consultation with Economic Department, November 18, 1948, *Colombia 1*. The peso was devalued by approximately 10 percent on December 17, 1948, from 1.75955 to 1.94991 pesos per dollar. See "Colombia: Foreign Exchange Rates, Recent Modifications to System," J. Torfs to Mr. Leonard B. Rist, December 22, 1948, *Colombia 1*.

24. "Colombia—Conference with Financial Mission of Colombia," Gilbert H. Clee to Files, September 7, 1948, *Colombia 1*.

25. Other objectives of the Colombian mission included the discussion with the American investors about a program to eliminate debt incurred by departmental and municipal authorities in Colombia on the international market during the previous years and the possible entrance of the country into GATT. See David M. Clark,

Commercial Attaché for the U.S. Ambassador in Colombia (Beaulac), to the Secretary of State, Bogotá, December 17, 1948, in *Foreign Relations of the United States, 1948*, vol. 9 (Washington, D.C.: Government Printing Office, 1972), pp. 476–78.

26. "Office Memorandum—Reply furnished by Colombian Mission on July 20, 1948 to IBRD Questionnaire," Laura B. Hughes to Dr. Harold Larsen, August 4, 1948, *Colombia 1*.

27. "Office Memorandum—Preliminary Report on Colombia," Dr. Larsen to Dr. Rosenstein-Rodan, March 31, 1949, *Colombia 1*.

28. "Colombia," Gilbert H. Clee to Mr. W. A. B. Iliff, September 23, 1948, *Colombia 1*.

29. "Office Memorandum—Colombia, Meeting between the Colombian Financial Mission and the IBRD," W. A. B. Iliff to Files, September 23, 1948, *Colombia 1*.

30. "File Copy—Colombia," G. Lincoln Sandelin to Mr. A. Broches, October 20, 1948, *Colombia 1*; "File Copy—Colombian negotiations," Gilbert H. Clee to Mr. A. S. G. Hoar, November 1, 1948, *Colombia 1*; "Office Memorandum—Colombia, Enabling legislation to provide a Government guarantee for IBRD loans," A. S. G. Hoar to Mr. Robert Garner, November 17, 1948, *Colombia 1*; Gilbert H. Clee to Sr. Don Jose Camacho-Lorenzana, November 18, 1948, *Colombia 1*.

31. "Colombia—Report and Recommendations," prepared by Loan Department in consultation with Economic Department, November 18, 1948, *Colombia 1*.

32. "Staff Loan Committee—Minutes of Staff Loan Committee Meeting," November 24, 1948, *Colombia 1*; "Colombia—Report and Recommendations," prepared by Loan Department in consultation with Economic Department, November 18, 1948, *Colombia 1*.

33. "Colombia," Robert L. Garner to Mr. Emilio Toro, December 1, 1948, *Colombia 1*.

34. "Colombia," Robert L. Garner to Mr. Emilio Toro, December 1, 1948, *Colombia 1*; "File Copy—Terms of reference of proposed technical mission to Colombia," date unavailable, *Colombia 1*.

35. "Incoming Wire," Emilio Toro to IBRD Mr. Garner, December 6, 1948, *Colombia 1*.

36. "Economic Technology Meeting," December 16, 1948, *Colombia 1*; "Colombian Loan Application—Memorandum on Meeting of Working Party, Tuesday, March 8," M. F. Verheyen and P. A. Kanters to Mr. Crena de Iongh, March 10, 1949, *Colombia 1*; "Office Memorandum," H. B. Ripman to Mr. D. Crena de Iongh, July 19, 1949, *Colombia 1*; John J. McCloy to Don Gonzalo Restrepo-Jaramillo, March 17, 1949, *Colombia 1*; Gonzalo Restrepo-Jaramillo to Mr. McCloy, March 21, 1949, *Colombia 1*; Gonzalo Restrepo-Jaramillo to Mr. McCloy, March 25, 1949, *Colombia 1*; "File Copy," R. L. Garner to Dr. Lauchlin Currie, August 22, 1949, *Currie Mission*.

37. Paul Rosenstein-Rodan taught economics at the University of London from 1930 to 1947. During World War II, he organized an intergovernmental commission sponsored by the British government to analyze the economic growth of less developed allied countries. After the end of the war, he was asked by the British government to join the International Monetary Fund, but he chose the Bank instead. See oral history interview, Paul Rosenstein-Rodan, August 14, 1961, pp. 1–2, *Oral Hist. 44*.

38. "Office Memorandum—Mission to Colombia," Paul F. Craig-Martin to Dr. Rosenstein-Rodan, December 21, 1948, *Colombia 1*; "A Short Description of the Agricultural Economy of Colombia," prepared by Maurice F. Perkins, December 21, 1948, *Colombia 1*.

39. In the 1930s, Bogotá had reached a population of 330,000, and it grew to 650,000 during the following decade. In the 1930s, Barranquilla had a population of 150,000. Cali grew from 100,000 in 1940 to 280,000 by 1950 (Casetta 1991).

40. "Memorandum of Conversation, by Mr. Albert H. Gerberich of the Division of North and West Coast Affairs," Washington, September 24, 1948, in *Foreign Relations of the United States, 1948*, vol. 9 (Washington, D.C.: Government Printing Office, 1972), pp. 456–60, cited from pp. 457–58.

41. The U.S. multinational arrived in Colombia during the first decade of the 1900s when U.S. capital was used for easy investments in the Latin American continent. The local governments were particularly accommodating in order to attract these investments. Apropos, the strike in 1928 against the United Fruit in Santa Marta—which is also narrated by Gabriel García Márquez in *One Hundred Years of Solitude*—ended with the killing of more than 100 workers by the local police (Casetta 1991).

42. "Office Memorandum—Colombia, Minerals," Charlotte Katz to Mr. Samuel Lipkovitz, February 11, 1949, *Colombia 1*; "Office Memorandum—The Role of Minerals in the Colombian Economy and Some Suggestions in Connection with the Bank Mission," Samuel Lipkowitz to Dr. Rosenstein-Rodan, December 21, 1948, *Colombia 1*.

43. "Office Memorandum—Proposed Colombian Development Program," A. D. Spottswood to Dr. P. N. Rosenstein-Rodan, February 11, 1949, *Colombia 1*. For example, in 1943 the Peruvian government established the Peruana Santa Corporation for the development of the city of Chimbote based on the example of the U.S. Tennessee Valley Authority (see Alacevich and Costa 2009).

44. "Memorandum," transmitted by Gonzalo Restrepo-Jaramillo to Mr. John McCloy, January 11, 1949, *Colombia 1*.

45. "Memorandum," transmitted by Gonzalo Restrepo-Jaramillo to Mr. John McCloy, January 11, 1949, *Colombia 1*.

46. "Mission to Colombia—Letter no. 9," Lauchlin Currie to Mr. Robert Garner, September 5, 1949, *Currie Mission*.

47. This was also due to high cost of internal transport that made importing expensive (IBRD 1950a, p. 90).

48. The uncertainty is because the document does not speak about the role that Williams would have had in the mission, although Williams's importance leads one to believe that he would have been the mission's head. The same document mentions the appropriateness of involving Williams considering that two Bank staff members, Dick Demuth and Harold Larsen, had the necessary competence to fill the position for which Williams had been proposed. Demuth and Larsen belonged to the Bank's senior management (Demuth later became head of the Technical Assistance Department). Their skills were not similar to Williams's, so they could not have been considered alternatives for any specific task except perhaps for overall responsibility for the mission. The document, from Rist to Garner, states: "I have as yet not contacted Professor Williams, of the New York Federal Reserve Bank. Before doing it I think we should be absolutely sure that nobody from this Bank can assume that load. As you know, there are two persons in our staff who appear competent to do so: Messrs. Demuth and Larsen." From "File Copy—Confidential—Colombia," Leonard B. Rist to Mr. Robert L. Garner, January 10, 1949, *Colombia 1*.

49. His position, which was shared by the minority, hinged on the concept of "key currency." Williams maintained that a period of global stabilization of "key currencies" was needed to introduce the U.S. plan, which was prepared by White. Such stabilization would have established a more solid, albeit gradual, international monetary order. See Asso and Fiorito (2009).

50. Douglas H. Allen to Mr. John J. McCloy, February 25, 1949, *Currie Mission*; Earl B. Schwulst to Mr. John J. McCloy, February 25, 1949, *Currie Mission*.

51. "Outgoing Wire," John J. McCloy to Professor Lionel Robbins, March 1, 1949, *Currie Mission*; "Incoming Wire," Robbins to McCloy IBRD, March 8, 1949, *Currie Mission*. In his biography of Keynes, Roy Harrod writes: "Professor Robins proved a highly skilled negotiator and won great esteem in the United States. Keynes came to rely on him and to value his judgement. Robbins often played the role of conciliator." From Harrod (1951, pp. 554–55).

52. Leonard B. Rist to Mr. Laughlin [sic] Currie, April 22, 1949, *Currie Mission*; Dr. Harold Larsen to Mr. J. Torfs, May 9, 1949, *Currie Mission*. John H. Williams had been Currie's Ph.D. supervisor at Harvard, 1927–31, so the case may be made that Williams recommended Currie as an alternative. I am grateful to Roger Sandilands who brought this to my attention.

53. The interpretation of this book is still debated: Sandilands (1990) highlights the arguments that accuse the Federal Reserve of having caused the Great Depression in the 1930s through an unjustifiably passive monetary policy; Kindleberger (1991) is doubtful of this interpretation and highlights Currie's analysis of the multiplier.

54. "I was, I am happy to say, responsible for bringing Ken Galbraith to Washington." From Currie (1972, p. 141).

55. Mason (1982) writes that Viner considered Currie and White too good for Harvard. Galbraith (1971) maintains that Currie did not obtain tenure at Harvard also because he was judged not to be erudite enough. In the 1970s, Currie was still remembered and celebrated for his great statistical contributions during the 1930s, as he tried to develop more solid instruments for analysis, evaluation, and intervention (Jones 1978, Currie and Krost 1978; Currie 1978a, 1978b).

56. "Memorandum on Full Employment," Currie to Roosevelt, March 18, 1940, Franklin D. Roosevelt Presidential Library, Hyde Park, New York, cited in Barber (1996, p. 130).

57. "Memorandum on Full Employment," Currie to Roosevelt, March 18, 1940, Franklin D. Roosevelt Presidential Library, Hyde Park, New York, cited in Barber (1996, p. 130).

58. The speech was delivered on January 6, 1945. Available at http://www.presidency.ucsb.edu/ws/index.php?pid=16595.

59. Currie's only known publication during this period is a transcript of a conference held on March 5, 1946, in his role as president of the Council for Italian American Affairs at the *Istituto di Studi Internazionali* based in Milan. It was entitled "Post-War Italy in the Economic World."

60. In 1936, the *New York Daily News* published, thanks to the intervention of a powerful exponent of the Republican Party, "A Declaration of Independence by Democrats," written by Garner against Roosevelt (Garner 1972, p. 166).

61. Currie was the first head of the mission who did not come from within the institution. See "IBRD Press Release No. 139," June 30, 1949, *Currie Mission*.

62. Lauchlin Currie to Professor Alvin Hansen, June 3, 1949, *Currie Mission*; Alvin H. Hansen to Lauchlin Currie, IBRD, June 4, 1949, *Currie Mission*.

63. "File Copy—Confidential—Colombia," Leonard B. Rist to Mr. Robert L. Garner, January 10, 1949, *Colombia 1*.

64. "Colombia: Currie Mission Report," G. Gondicas to Mr. A. S. G. Hoar, July 6, 1950, *Currie Mission*.

65. Oral history interview, Leonard Rist, July 19, 1961, pp. 26–27, *Oral Hist. 44*.

66. Actually, the collaboration between the Fund and the Bank ended up being reduced to a joint library, some shared translation services, and a joint Annual Meeting.

67. "Outgoing Wire," John J. McCloy to Professor Lionel Robbins, March 1, 1949, *Currie Mission*.

68. Currie was a talented writer. This is evident from the pages of his autobiography when he describes his first twenty years of life. Sandilands opportunely brought these complete pages into the first chapter of his biography on Currie (Sandilands 1990).

69. Lauchlin Currie to Mr. Robert L. Garner, July 24, 1949, *Currie Mission.*

70. Lauchlin Currie to Mr. Robert L. Garner, August 8, 1949, *Currie Mission.*

71. Lauchlin Currie to Mr. Robert L. Garner, August 10, 1949, *Currie Mission.*

72. Lauchlin Currie to Mr. Robert L. Garner, September 12, 1949, *Currie Mission.*

73. "Address by Dr. Lauchlin Currie, chief of mission of the International Bank for Reconstruction and Development, on the occasion of a farewell luncheon tendered the mission by the Banco de la Republica, October 28, 1949," October 28, 1949, *Currie Mission.* This is the original text written by Currie in English. In the World Bank archives the Spanish translation is also available, which was read by Currie at the farewell luncheon: "Discurso del Dr. Lauchlin Currie, Jefe de la Misión del Banco Internacional de Reconstruccion y Fomento pronunciado el 28 de octubre de 1949, con motivo del almuerzo de despedida ofrecido por el Banco de la Repubblica," October 28, 1949, *Currie Mission.*

74. For example, the Pan American Sanitary Bureau of Washington, D.C., the FAO, and the American and foreign enterprises. See John R. Murdock to Mr. Laughlin [*sic*] Currie, November 17, 1949, *Currie Mission*; Herbert Broadley to Mr. Lauchlin Currie, 27 April 1950, *Currie Mission*; Mary McDonnell to Miss Agnes Maher, September 5, 1950, *Currie Mission.*

75. "Presentation of Colombian Report," William L. Ayres to Mr. Robert L. Garner, July 14, 1950, *Colombia 1* (emphasis in the original).

76. A 1948 report from the Bank was more pessimistic about this point: "In view of the rate of population increase the problem may, in fact, not to be how to raise real income per head, but how to maintain it." From "Economic Technology Meeting—Colombia," December 27, 1948, *Colombia 1.*

77. "Interview with C. Edwin Halaby. Manufacturer's Representative in Colombia," Lauchlin Currie, June 14, 1949, *Colombia 1.*

78. This was the equivalent of U.S. $2.5 billion, with a little more than $500 million for imports. In 1951, however, Colombia had a very drastic devaluation, which caused the exchange rate to change from 1.95 pesos to 2.51 pesos per dollar.

79. Herbert Broadley to Mr. Lauchlin Currie, 27 April 1950, *Currie Mission.* I was unable to find other documents about criticism of Currie's proposal in the agricultural sector and especially the regressive tax. Albert O. Hirschman wrote a very interesting study about the various agricultural reforms that took place successively in Colombia in his book *Journeys Toward Progress* (1968).

80. John R. Murdock, WHO Assistant Director, to Mr. Richard H. Demuth, June 26, 1950, *Currie Mission.*

81. "The Need for Foreign Capital in the Development Program for Colombia," Jacques J. Polak, attached to "Memorandum," J. J. Polak to Dr. Rodan, June 22, 1951, *Colombia Tech. Ass. III.*

82. Polak reports to Rosenstein-Rodan that Torfs, to whom he showed his written critique, answered that there were precise and strong reasons why some conclusions from the report were taken out. See "Memorandum," J. J. Polak to Dr. Rodan, June 22, 1951, *Colombia Tech. Ass. III.*

83. In a conversation that took place on December 3, 2004, Jacques J. Polak confirmed his conviction that at the time "the Bank was not the place for economists."

84. "IBRD Relations with Colombia—Confidential," Mr. Gordon, January 19, 1950, p. 5, *Colombia 2.*

85. A loan of $3,500,000, signed on November 2, 1950, was used for the electric power station at Anchicaya. "Colombia," date unavailable (probably end of May 1951), *Colombia 2.* Underlying the decision to lend money for the electric power stations was a concern that rejection would compromise the Colombian government's acceptance and implementation of the general development plan presented in the Currie report. See "IBRD Relations with Colombia—Confidential Draft," W. A. B. Iliff, January 23, 1950, *Colombia 2.*

86. S. W. Anderson to Files, January 30, 1950, *Currie Mission.* Several Bank documents underscore the intention of the Bank to postpone approving specific project loans pending the Mission's report on a global strategy—even though, in practice, things went differently. See, for example, "Colombia: Conversation with Ambassador re Projects under Consideration by the Bank," D. W. Smyser to Files, September 22, 1949, *Colombia 2.*

87. Willard L. Beaulac to the Secretary of State, Bogotá, July 25, 1949, in *Foreign Relations of the United States, 1949,* vol. 2 (Washington, D.C.: Government Printing Office, 1975), pp. 609–11. The Export-Import Bank (Eximbank) was founded in 1934 from the merger of two government banks established by Franklin D. Roosevelt to stimulate trade with the Soviet Union and Cuba. Eximbank's mandate was to help U.S. capital cross national borders while avoiding competition with private banks. Over the years, Eximbank linked the financial and commercial interests of private investors with the political-diplomatic interests of the U.S. government. For a history of this institution, see Becker and McClenahan (2003).

88. Martín del Corral to Mr. Eugene Black, October 3, 1950, *Colombia 2.* "Office Memorandum—Study of Report in Colombia," Lauchlin Currie to Eugene Black, March 17, 1950, *Currie Mission.*

89. "File Copy," R. L. Garner to Mr. Richard H. Demuth, November 21, 1950, *Colombia Mission I.*

90. "Press Release," IBRD, August 2, 1950, *LBCP.*

91. "However"—notes Sandilands—"neither railroad nor water transport has been very well used or managed in Colombia. The more flexible road transport system has always been more fully utilized, and increasingly so as the network developed" (Sandilands 1990, p. 170).

92. This topic will be further discussed in Chapter 3.

93. "Colombia: Agriculture Needs an Increase of Bank Credit," S. W. Anderson to Mr. A. S. G. Hoar, February 3, 1951, *Colombia Mission I*; "Colombia: Agriculture Needs an Increase of Bank Credit," E. deVries to Mr. A. S. G. Hoar, February 9, 1951, *Colombia Mission I.*

94. Urdaneta Arbeláez had replaced Laureano Gómez, who had been very ill. See Sandilands (1990, p. 168).

95. Jacques Torfs to Mr. Rist, January 29, 1951, *Colombia 2.*

96. "Confidential—Copy of undated airmail letter from Mr. Torfs, received in Bank on February 8, 1951," Jacques Torfs to Mr. Rist, February 8, 1951, *Colombia 2.*

97. "IBRD—Inter Office Memorandum," G. Grayson to Files, February 16, 1951, *Colombia 2.*

98. "Notes on Meeting of Staff Loan Committee Held 2:30 P.M., Thursday, March 22, 1951—Confidential," *Colombia 2.*

99. E. G. Burland to Mr. A. S. G. Hoar, February 19, 1951, *Colombia 2.*

100. R. L. Garner to Mr. E. G. Burland, February 28, 1951, *Colombia 2.*

101. E. C. Burland to Mr. A. S. G. Hoar, March 1, 1951, *Colombia 2.*

102. "Draft," Martín Del Corral, June 3, 1951, *LBCP.*

103. A statement requested by Torfs from the economic advisor to the president of Colombia leads us to believe that the situation had already reached uncomfortable levels, as can be read in the following: "Given that, according to what you informed me, there can be a possibility that someone may wrongly think you have had some involvement related to the services provided by Dr. Lauchlin Currie, I take this opportunity to hereby state that such involvement has never taken place." Alfonso Patiño to Jacques Torfs, June 27, 1951, *Colombia 2.*

104. "File Copy," R. L. Garner to H. E. Señor Dr. Don Cipriano Restrepo-Jaramillo, Ambassador of Colombia, January 16, 1952, *Colombia 2.* Information on the Consejo is from R. L. Garner to Dr. Emilio Toro, May 13, 1952, *Colombia 2*; E. G. Burland to Mr. A. S. G. Hoar, Loan Director, March 21, 1952, *Colombia 2*; "Colombia," Jacques Torfs to Dr. Harold Larsen, March 25, 1952, *Colombia 2*; E. G. Burland to Mr. A. S. G. Hoar, Loan Director, March 1, 1952, *Colombia 2.*

105. "Excerpts from a proposed letter from Mr. Hirschman to Messrs. Toro and Delgado in response to a request for some ideas concerning the staffing of the Planning Office," without date (probably beginning of April 1952), *Colombia 2.*

106. R. L. Garner to Dr. Emilio Toro, May 13, 1952, *Colombia 2.*

107. R. L. Garner to Dr. Emilio Toro, May 13, 1952, *Colombia 2.*

108. A. S. G. Hoar to Mr. E. G. Burland (Tommy), March 14, 1952, *Colombia 2.*

109. E. Toro to Mr. Garner, May 20, 1952, *Colombia 2.*

110. "File Copy—Personal and Confidential," R. L. Garner to Dr. Emilio Toro, May 26, 1952, *Colombia 2.*

111. Lauchlin Currie to Bill Howell, August 21, 1952, *Colombia 2.*

112. Albert O. Hirschman to Mr. Richard H. Demuth, August 23, 1952, *Colombia 2*.

113. "Hirschman's position is very difficult since Currie has entered the picture. He seems very much concerned, and I have a strong feeling that we have left him alone too much [. . .] [Currie]'s only support in high circles comes from Toro." From Willem Koster to Orvis, September 14, 1952, *Colombia 2*.

114. Albert O. Hirschman to Mr. J. Burke Knapp, September 20, 1952, *Colombia 2*.

115. Albert O. Hirschman to Mr. J. Burke Knapp, September 20, 1952, *Colombia 2*. It is worth noting that Currie, in later reflections about those events, manifested a much more positive opinion of the confrontations inside the Consejo: "the discussions on short policy memoranda were vigorous and probing, preparing the members of the committee for their meetings with the president" (Currie 1981, p. 180).

116. Albert O. Hirschman to Mr. J. Burke Knapp, September 20, 1952, *Colombia 2*.

117. Albert O. Hirschman to Mr. J. Burke Knapp, September 20, 1952, *Colombia 2*.

118. "Functions and Organization of the Colombian Planning Office," J. Burke Knapp to Mr. Robert L. Garner, October 7, 1952, *Colombia 3*.

119. As Knapp wrote to Hirschman: "Albert, I wish that we had been able to work out something which would be more clearly satisfactory to you. I do want to assure you that the points made in your letter to me, dated September 20, received full consideration. I do believe that under the arrangements which Jacques will outline to you in more detail you will find an excellent opportunity to apply your great talents," J. Burke Knapp to Mr. Albert Hirschman, October 10, 1952, *Colombia 3*.

120. "Outgoing Wire," Garner to Chairman Consejo Economico de Planificación, October 10, 1952, *Colombia 3*.

121. Emilio Toro to Mr. Robert L. Garner, October 10, 1952, *Colombia 3*.

122. J. Burke Knapp to Mr. Jacques Torfs, November 7, 1952, *Colombia 3* (emphasis in the original), and J. Burke Knapp to Mr. Albert O. Hirschman, November 7, 1952, *Colombia 3*.

123. J. Burke Knapp to Mr. Jacques Torfs, November 7, 1952, *Colombia 3*.

124. Knapp wrote to Hirschman: "However, Albert, the main purpose of this letter is to let you know that we in the Bank feel that, so far at least, you have had a rotten deal and that we understand and sympathize with the extraordinary difficulties which you have had to confront. I find myself wondering to what extent your experiences have soured you on the general situation in Colombia and your prospects for satisfactory future work there. If you feel you want to stay on under the improved circumstances which I hope will soon attain, we shall be delighted to have your continued support in Colombia. On the other hand, I want you to know,

if you decide to leave, that I would be eager to have you join the regular staff of the newly created Western Hemisphere Department in the Bank." From J. Burke Knapp to Mr. Albert O. Hirschman, November 7, 1952, *Colombia 3*. Torfs assured Knapp that Hirschman was reacting well: "Albert Hirschman seems to be regaining heart. While he realizes fully that he is bound to become the No. 2-man in the advisory staff, he seems, to my great surprise, to accept the situation willingly." From "Colombia Mission Report #2 with Planning Office," Jacques Torfs, November 10, 1952, *Colombia 3*.

125. J. Burke Knapp to Mr. Jacques Torfs, November 7, 1952, *Colombia 3*.

126. R. L. Garner to Dr. Emilio Toro, November 17, 1952, *Colombia 3*; J. Burke Knapp to Dr. Emilio Toro, December 3, 1952, *Colombia 3*.

127. "Colombia Mission Report #3 with Planning Office. Week of November 10th to 17th," Jacques Torfs, November 18, 1952, *Colombia 3* (emphasis in the original).

128. "Colombia Mission Report #2 with Planning Office," Jacques Torfs, November 10, 1952, *Colombia 3*.

129. "Colombia Mission Report #3 with Planning Office. Week of November 10th to 17th," Jacques Torfs, November 18, 1952, *Colombia 3*.

130. In Torf's opinion, the president was not up to date about the problems of the Consejo because Toro filtered information. The Bank should have bypassed him: "Concerning Dr. Currie, I can only report that everything is happening here as if Dr. Toro had not received any communication from Washington [. . .]. I am convinced that communications between the Bank and Dr. Toro, regarding the activities of Dr. Currie, will remain dead letter, because Dr. Toro will simply keep them for himself, or 'interpret' the opinions of the Bank, when presenting them to the Government. As long as there will be no direct communication between the Bank and the Government, i.e. the President of the Republic, on this problem, it will remain forever unresolved. It would be extremely desirable for the Bank to take such steps as rapidly as possible. Dr. Currie will return here by the end of the next week. Both Albert and I will be deeply involved in our long-term projects [. . .]. It will be relatively easy for Dr. Currie to start undoing all that we have started in the last few weeks." From "Colombia Mission Report #5 with Planning Office. Week from November 23rd to November 29th," Jacques Torfs, December 5, 1952, *Colombia 3*.

131. Emilio Toro to Mr. Robert L. Garner, November 28, 1952, *Colombia 3*.

132. J. Burke Knapp to Dr. Emilio Toro, December 3, 1952, *Colombia 3*; J. Burke Knapp to Mr. Jacques Torfs, December 3, 1952, *Colombia 3*.

133. Jacques Torfs to Mr. Burke Knapp, December 12, 1952, *Colombia 3*.

134. "Seventh Report on Mission with Planning Office—Weeks from December 8 to 13 and from December 15 to 20," Jacques Torfs, December 20, 1952, *Colombia 3*.

135. Emilio Toro to Lauchlin Currie, July 28, 1953, *LBCP* (emphasis in the original).

CHAPTER THREE

1. Quoted in Sandilands (1990, p. 166).

2. R. L. Garner to Dr. Emilio Toro, November 17, 1952, *Colombia 3*.

3. "He venido a estudiar los problemas del pais: Currie," August 28, 1950, *LBCP*.

4. In order to reconstruct this debate, I will use some publications that fall outside the time period of the events in this book. It may seem anachronistic, but it is not. Research that was published at the end of the 1950s or at the beginning of the 1960s had broadly circulated within institutions and academia and at conferences. For example, Ragnar Nurkse published *The Formation of Capital in Underdeveloped Countries* in 1958, but he based this volume on several presentations that he made in Rio de Janeiro in 1951. A similar case involving Albert Hirschman will be extensively discussed in this chapter.

5. See for example the excellent synthesis of Charles Oman and Ganeshan Wignaraja (1991).

6. As Walt Rostow wrote: "As a matter of historical fact a reactive nationalism—reacting against intrusion from more advanced nations—has been a most important and powerful motive force in the transition from traditional to modern societies, at least as important as the profit motive. Men holding effective authority or influence have been willing to uproot traditional societies not, primarily, to make more money but because the traditional society failed—or threatened to fail—to protect them from humiliation by foreigners [. . .]. And so also, of course, with the colonial areas of the southern half of the world" (Rostow [1960] 1990, pp. 26–27).

7. Later, Paul Rosenstein-Rodan toned down this position by taking sides in favor of a sequence that would expect to develop social overhead capital first. In 1984 he maintained that "before building consumer goods factories, a major indivisible block of social overhead capital or infrastructure must be built and sponsored because private market initiatives will not create it in time" (Rosenstein-Rodan 1984, p. 208).

8. Massachusetts Institute of Technology, Center for International Studies, *The Objectives of United States Economic Assistance Programs* (Cambridge, Mass.: Massachusetts Institute of Technology, Center for International Studies, 1957), p. 70.

9. Among the contributors to the concept of "external economies," which, as we have seen, is central to the idea of balanced growth, it is worth remembering Tibor Scitovsky. Scitovsky, in turn, took an argument from the work of James Meade (1952), which focused on developed countries, and extended the argument to developing countries. Specifically, Scitovsky highlighted the difference between pecuniary

external economies and technological external economies of direct interdependence and their implications (Scitovsky 1954, 1959).

10. Hirschman notes how he and Streeten, despite working independently, gave their works very similar titles. The working title of Hirschman's volume was *The Economics of Unbalanced Growth* before it finally became *The Strategy of Economic Development*. Streeten's article was entitled "Unbalanced Growth" (Hirschman 1984, p. 87n1).

11. See the reflections of Andrea Ginzburg (1983), who affirmed: "If, using an ancient metaphor, we wanted to encapsulate Hirschman's thinking into one of the three forms of social thought classified by W. Stark, he would be among those who see society not as an organism or a mechanism, but as a process" (Ginzburg 1983, p. 16).

12. Albert O. Hirschman to André Gunder Frank, August 18, 1959, in Hirschman (1984, p. 105; emphasis in the original).

13. Hirschman presented the concept of "linkages" more concretely than is presented here. See for example his discussion of satellite industries (Hirschman [1958] 1963, chapter 6). On the same topic, see Streeten's observations: "Choose projects which, (i) while advancing some sectors, concentrate the pressure of unbalance on groups and sectors whose response to a challenge is likely to be strongest; (ii) while creating bottlenecks, also break them; (iii) while providing products and services for industry, agriculture, and consumers, also induce new development to take place in other directions [. . .]; (iv) while providing a new product or service require consequential investments in other lines" (Streeten 1959, p. 183).

14. Quoted from J. Schumpeter, *Business Cycles* (New York and London: McGraw Hill Book Company, 1939), p. 102.

15. Galbraith, a trained agricultural economist, served as the U.S. Ambassador to India during the Kennedy administration.

16. Nehru, educated from a young age by primarily British private tutors, left for England at the age of fifteen. He studied at Harrow for two years before being admitted to Trinity College in Cambridge in 1907, where he completed his degree in 1910. That same year, he began his doctoral program in law at the Inner Temple in London. Certified as a lawyer in 1912, he returned to India after seven years of education in the most exclusive schools of the United Kingdom. See Brecher (1959).

17. *Articles of Agreement*, Article III, Section 4 (vii).

18. The frequent disputes between Rosenstein-Rodan and senior management at the Bank forced the economist to leave the institution soon after the general reorganization of 1952 (Oliver 1975, pp. 272–73).

19. Oral history interview, Paul Rosenstein-Rodan, August 14, 1961, pp. 1–2, *Oral Hist. 44*. Burke Knapp's thought was in line with Rosenstein-Rodan's with

respect to U.S. loans to postwar Europe within the frame of the Marshall Plan. In a later recollection, Knapp said: "The creditworthiness of countries has to be determined on the basis of their total capacity to service debt, rather than according to what particular commodities they are going to receive under an aid program. [. . .] The question of whether you lend hard money or soft money should depend upon the country that you're dealing with and its overall capacity to mobilize resources and make repayment, not upon the particular nature of the project." From oral history interview, J. Burke Knapp, July 24 and 30, 1975, available at www.trumanlibrary.org/oralhist/knappjb.htm, paragraphs 92 and 94.

20. "Ensanches del acueducto de Bogotá," March 26, 1953, *LBCP*. See also "Resumen del Plan para Bogotá," Lauchlin B. Currie, May 28, 1953, *LBCP*.

21. "As [the electric] company is in a better position to contract foreign loans than is the Waterworks, it is recommended that the application for a foreign loan be limited to the electric company." From "Waterworks," January 1, 1953, p. 4, *LBCP*. See also "Expansion of Electric Power for Bogotá," January 1, 1953, *LBCP*.

22. Equivalent to $2.4 billion in 1994 (Kraske et al. 1996, p. 55).

23. Oral history interview, Robert L. Garner, July 19, 1961, p. 6, *Oral Hist. 44*.

24. "Memorandum sobre el concepto de los medios de pago y la política monetaria," Lauchlin Currie, May 21, 1952, *LBCP*.

25. "Memorandum sobre el concepto de los medios de pago y la política monetaria," Lauchlin Currie, May 21, 1952, *LBCP*.

26. "Situacion monetaria—Analisis y recomendaciones," Albert Hirschman, June 21, 1952, *LBCP*.

27. "Situacion monetaria—Analisis y recomendaciones," Albert Hirschman, June 21, 1952, *LBCP*.

28. "Analisis del presupuesto para la vigencia de 1.952 y de su probable efecto sobre la situacion economica y monetaria en los meses restantes de 1.952," Albert Hirschman, August 22, 1952, *LBCP*.

29. "Analisis del presupuesto para la vigencia de 1.952 y de su probable efecto sobre la situacion economica y monetaria en los meses restantes de 1.952," Albert Hirschman, August 22, 1952, *LBCP*.

30. "El presupuesto para la vigencia 1.953," Albert Hirschman, August 27, 1952, *LBCP*.

31. "Conclusiones de los tres memoranda. Sobre la situación monetaria, Sobre la ejecución del presupuesto de 1952 durante los meses restante de este año, y Sobre el presupuesto para 1953," Albert Hirschman, August 27, 1952, *LBCP*.

32. "El presupuesto para la vigencia 1.953," Albert Hirschman, August 27, 1952, *LBCP*.

33. "El presupuesto para la vigencia 1.953," Albert Hirschman, August 27, 1952, *LBCP*; "Memorandum preliminar sobre el presupuesto," Lauchlin Currie y Enrique Peñalosa, September 20, 1952, *LBCP*. After the *Bogotazo*, the Colombian

army had grown from 12,000 to 30,000 men. See "Memorandum of Conversation by the Secretary of State," Washington, July 12, 1948, in *Foreign Relations of the United States, 1948*, vol. 9 (Washington, D.C.: Government Printing Office, 1972), pp. 440–44. The Colombian government insisted on the necessity to fight the "Communist enemy from within in the Americas" and asked the United States for substantial help to increase its military equipment. From "Memorandum of Conversation, by the Secretary of State," Dean Acheson, Washington, April 19, 1949, in *Foreign Relations of the United States, 1949*, vol. 2 (Washington, D.C.: Government Printing Office, 1975), pp. 605–7. The reluctance of the United States did not discourage the Colombian authorities, at least according to the U.S. Ambassador in Bogotá: "I told [. . .] that I did not foresee any danger that the Colombian army would become a menace to Colombia's democracy. What I was afraid of was that the Government's economic policy, which was resulting in still higher living costs, was helping to create another situation of social tension which might explode at any moment [. . .]. All Latin Americans agreed that the arms transfers did not have a disturbing effect on domestic peace. Revolutions and coups d'état took place before the United States ever sent arms to Latin America and would continue to take place." From "Memorandum of Conversation, by the Ambassador in Colombia (Beaulac)," Bogotá, February 15, 1949, attached to Willard L. Beaulac to the Secretary of State, February 16, 1949, in *Foreign Relations of the United States, 1949*, vol. 2 (Washington, D.C.: Government Printing Office, 1975), pp. 603–5; the quote is on page 604.

34. "Memorandum preliminar sobre el presupuesto," Lauchlin Currie y Enrique Peñalosa, September 20, 1952, *LBCP*; "El presupuesto para la vigencia 1.953," Albert Hirschman, August 27, 1952, *LBCP*.

35. "Memorandum preliminar sobre el presupuesto," Lauchlin Currie y Enrique Peñalosa, September 20, 1952, *LBCP*.

36. "Memorandum preliminar sobre el presupuesto," Lauchlin Currie y Enrique Peñalosa, September 20, 1952, *LBCP*.

37. "Memorandum preliminar sobre el presupuesto," Lauchlin Currie y Enrique Peñalosa, September 20, 1952, *LBCP*.

38. "Interes del Consejo en el presupuesto," Albert Hirschman, October 20, 1952, *LBCP*.

39. "Memorandum," Albert Hirschman, October 31, 1952, *LBCP*.

40. "Memorandum," Albert Hirschman, October 31, 1952, *LBCP*.

41. "Memorandum," Albert Hirschman, October 31, 1952, *LBCP*; "Notas sobre estimativos y politica del presupuesto," Lauchlin Currie, November 6, 1952, *LBCP*; "Politica presupuestal," Albert O. Hirschman and Jacques Torfs, November 10, 1952, *LBCP*; "Comentarios especificos sobre el memorandum del Dr. Hirschman de Noviembre 10 de 1952," November 10, 1952, *LBCP*; "Comentarios sobre el memorandum acerca de la Politica Presupuestal por lo Señores Torfs y Hirschman," Lauchlin Currie, November 15, 1952, *LBCP*.

42. Comité de Desarrollo Economico, "Informe preliminar sobre el establecimiento de una planta siderurgica," Bogotá, December 14, 1950, pp. 2–3, *LBCP*.

43. "We had our final luncheon with the President today, but apart from a lot more pressure on the Paz de Río project, nothing noteworthy happened," Lauchlin Currie to Robert Garner, October 14, 1949, *LBCP*.

44. With Garner's approval, Currie sent Flesher to Chile with the task of evaluating in person the situation of the Compañia de Acero del Pacifico, a private company with some state participation whose plants were under construction thanks to an initial $28 million loan from the Export-Import Bank out of an estimated total of $53 million. At the time of Flesher's visit, the estimate had increased to $90 million. Flesher estimated the final cost to be over $140 million. See Lauchlin Currie to Robert Garner, October 18, 1949, *LBCP*; Carl Flesher to Lauchlin Currie, October 25, 1949, *LBCP*.

45. Moreover, the transportation costs of the imported machinery would be lower due to the coastal location of Barranquilla.

46. *El Tiempo*, August 15, 1950, *LBCP*; *El Espectador*, August 18, 1950, *LBCP*; *El Liberal*, August 25, 1950, *LBCP*; *El Tiempo*, September 1, 1950, *LBCP*.

47. "Office Memorandum—Colombia," W. L. Jago to Mr. S. Aldewereld, July 25, 1950, *Colombia 2*.

48. "Guarantee Agreement," August 19, 1949, quoted in Wiebe Glastra to Mr. Jacques Torfs, May 25, 1951, *Colombia 2*.

49. "Office Memorandum—Colombian Working Party—Contracts entered by Colombian private companies controlled by the Government, with foreign concerns," M. Verheyen to Mr. Crena de Iongh, August 7, 1950, *Colombia 2*.

50. Robert L. Garner to Mr. Hernan Jaramillo Ocampo, August 22, 1950, *Colombia 2*.

51. Robert L. Garner to Mr. Hernan Jaramillo Ocampo, August 22, 1950, *Colombia 2*.

52. Robert L. Garner to Mr. Hernan Jaramillo Ocampo, August 22, 1950, *Colombia 2*.

53. "Colombia," without date (probably the end of May 1951), *Colombia 2*.

54. Martín del Corral to Mr. Eugene Black, October 2, 1950, *Colombia 2*; Martín del Corral to Mr. Eugene Black, October 3, 1950, *Colombia 2*.

55. Lauchlin B. Currie to Robert L. Garner, November 9, 1950, *LBCP*; "Memorandum," D. G. Singer to Lauchlin Currie, November 10, 1950, *LBCP*.

56. Proof of this concern was the effort to understand which information about the feasibility of the project of the Paz de Río was in Currie's hands (and therefore presumably of the Comité). Among others, Currie had a copy of a letter in which the Gerente General (the managing director) of the Colombian Armco, Edward J. William, assured the management of the Empresa Siderúrgica Paz de Río that Armco had not passed any meaningful information when the Currie mission had

requested clarification on an earlier consultancy to the Empresa Paz de Río. See Edward J. Williams to Roberto Jaramillo, November 15, 1950, *LBCP*.

57. "Situation in Colombia," Jacques Torfs to Mr. Leonard B. Rist, December 18, 1950, *Colombia 2*.

58. Lauchlin B. Currie to Robert L. Garner, November 9, 1950, *LBCP*.

59. "Notas que pueden servir de base a un acuerdo unanime sobre Paz del Río" (probably a draft, with a date written in pencil), Rafael Obregón, November 27, 1950, *LBCP*.

60. "Notas que pueden servir de base a un acuerdo unanime sobre Paz del Río" (probably a draft, with a date written in pencil), Rafael Obregón, November 27, 1950, *LBCP*.

61. "Informe de la mision para el Comité. Fomento de una industria colombiana de acero" (probably a draft, with a date written in pencil), Comité de Desarrollo Economico, December 15, 1950, p. 3, *LBCP*.

62. "Informe de la mision para el Comité. Fomento de una industria colombiana de acero" (probably a draft, with a date written in pencil), Comité de Desarrollo Economico, December 15, 1950, p. 4, *LBCP*.

63. "The President of the Republic himself has ordered the suspension of all foreign purchases for the projected steel plant at Paz de Río." From "Situation in Colombia," Jacques Torfs to Mr. Leonard B. Rist, December 18, 1950, *Colombia 2*.

64. "Informe de la mision para el Comité. Fomento de una industria colombiana de acero," Comité de Desarrollo Economico (probably a draft, with a date written in pencil), December 15, 1950, pp. 5–6, *LBCP*.

65. "Informe de la mision para el Comité. Fomento de una industria colombiana de acero," Comité de Desarrollo Economico (probably a draft, with a date written in pencil), December 15, 1950, p. 7, *LBCP*.

66. "Informe de la mision para el Comité. Fomento de una industria colombiana de acero" Comité de Desarrollo Economico (probably a draft, with a date written in pencil), December 15, 1950, p. 10, *LBCP*.

67. "Informe de la mision para el Comité. Fomento de una industria colombiana de acero," Comité de Desarrollo Economico (probably a draft, with a date written in pencil), December 15, 1950, p. 11, *LBCP*.

68. "The Committee's objection to this project is that it does not contemplate the development of an integrated steel plant, which has been considered a desideratum." From Comité de Desarrollo Economico, "Informe preliminar sobre el establecimiento de una planta siderurgica," Bogotá, December 14, 1950, p. 3, *LBCP*.

69. "Informe de la mision para el Comité. Fomento de una industria colombiana de acero," Comité de Desarrollo Economico (probably a draft, with a date written in pencil), December 15, 1950, p. 13, *LBCP*.

70. "Informe de la mision para el Comité. Fomento de una industria colombiana de acero," Comité de Desarrollo Economico (probably a draft, with a date written in pencil), December 15, 1950, p. 14, *LBCP*.

71. "Informe preliminar sobre el establecimiento de una planta siderurgica," Comité de Desarrollo Economico, Bogotá, December 14, 1950, p. 4, *LBCP*. Only one member of the Comité, Juan Pablo Ortega, had a different position and asked that his disagreement be included in the minutes of the meeting. Ortega actually opposed the case for the plant for imported scrap metal in Barranquilla, which the committee had already dismissed in the very document that Ortega did not want to sign. It seems that Ortega's gesture was merely obstructionist.

72. A. Brassert to G. A. Pizza, December 5, 1950, in *LBCP*, Box 32, Carpeta 4; Frank Engineering, radiogram to Lauchlin Currie, December 7, 1950, *LBCP*; Samuel Keener, radiogram to Lauchlin Currie, December 8, 1950, *LBCP*.

73. "Informe preliminar sobre el establecimiento de una planta siderurgica," Comité de Desarrollo Economico, Bogotá, December 14, 1950, p. 3, *LBCP*; Currie to Flesher, December 15, 1950, *LBCP*; Samuel Keener, radiogram to Lauchlin Currie, December 6, 1950, *LBCP*; Samuel Keener, radiogram to Lauchlin Currie, December 9, 1950, *LBCP*.

74. "Flying Ohio Businessman to Fly Own DC-4 Plane on Round-World Business Trip," Salem Engineering Company, July 10, 1949, p. 1, *LBCP*.

75. "Development of Steel Industry in Colombia, South America," Samuel Keener for Salem Engineering Company to Committee for Economic Development, December 12, 1950, p. 2, *LBCP*.

76. "For its wartime contribution to the development of the Atom Bomb through the Manhattan Project, Salem Engineering Company was presented an award for engineering achievement." From "Press Release," Salem Engineering Company (date in pencil), December 12, 1950, p. 3, *LBCP*.

77. "Development of Steel Industry in Colombia, South America," Samuel Keener for Salem Engineering Company to Committee for Economic Development, December 12, 1950, pp. 4–5, *LBCP*.

78. "Development of Steel Industry in Colombia, South America," Samuel Keener for Salem Engineering Company to Committee for Economic Development, December 12, 1950, pp. 5 and 7, *LBCP*.

79. "Informe preliminar sobre el establecimiento de una planta siderurgica," Comité de Desarrollo Economico, Bogotá, December 14, 1950, pp. 3–4, *LBCP*.

80. Currie to Flesher, December 15, 1950, *LBCP*.

81. The request followed a letter from Currie to the Empresa dated December 18, 1950, in which Currie informed the Empresa that the government would have asked the Empresa to work with Salem. Salem made itself available for the new Flesher project; see Roberto Jaramillo Ferro to Lauchlin B. Currie, December 19, 1950, *LBCP*; Lauchlin B. Currie to Roberto Jaramillo Ferro, December 19, 1950, *LBCP*.

82. Empresa Siderúrgica Nacional de Paz de Río, "The Board of Directors of the Empresa . . . ," December 20, 1950, pp. 1–3, *LBCP*. Salem's alleged incompetence seems almost preposterous and confirms the opportunistic nature of the position of the Junta. The IBRD had good and trustworthy references about Salem

from the vice president of Bethlehem Steel Company, which used Salem's plants: "They are specialists in steel heating problems of all kinds." From Slater to Currie, December 15, 1950, *LBCP*.

83. Lauchlin B. Currie to Roberto Jaramillo Ferro, December 19, 1950, *LBCP*.

84. Lauchlin Currie to Mauricio Obregon, December 22, 1950, *LBCP*.

85. R. L. Garner to Mr. Elmer G. Burland (Tommie), February 13, 1951, *Colombia 2*. In retrospect, Currie highlighted how on this occasion a treasure in knowledge was squandered. This know-how could have been exploited much more effectively: the mission and its experts had developed reasoned and well-grounded opinions, and they had identified a feasible solution. The Bank probably could have shown more determination in defending the positions of the mission, even though it is true that "if a government is determined on a course of action on noneconomic grounds, there are obviously limits on what an economic adviser, especially a foreigner, can or should attempt to do to stop it" (Currie 1981, pp. 153–58; the quotation is on p. 158). However, until 1955 more than $150 million was invested in the project, and almost $200 million by 1959. "The 'infant industry' ha[d] remained an infant" (Currie 1981, p. 157).

86. "Informe de la mision para el Comité. Fomento de una industria colombiana de acero," Comité de Desarrollo Economico (probably a draft, with the date in pencil), December 15, 1950, p. 15, *LBCP*.

87. "Informe de la mision para el Comité. Fomento de una industria colombiana de acero," Comité de Desarrollo Economico (probably a draft, with the date in pencil), December 15, 1950, pp. 16–17, *LBCP*.

88. A proper interpretation of "balanced" growth, therefore, does not imply that all sectors should grow at the same rate. Rather, balance is understood as attempting to reshuffle existing resources to adequately meet the different potential increases in demand in each sector.

89. Because the International Bank granted a loan to the steel plant in Paz de Río in 1956 (Sandilands 1990, p. 397n9), the possibility exists that Hirschman directly influenced the change of opinion by the institution. This should be verified through additional research in the archives of the Bank.

90. "Informe de la mision para el Comité. Fomento de una industria colombiana de acero," Comité de Desarrollo Economico (probably a draft, with the date in pencil) December 15, 1950.

91. There was probably another disagreement between Currie and Hirschman. According to Krugman, Hirschman based his concept of "backward linkages" on "the idea of economies of scale at the level of the individual plant [which] translated into increasing returns at the aggregate level through pecuniary external economies" (1993, p. 22). Ramesh Chandra and Roger Sandilands (2005), on the contrary, maintain that the importance of economies of scale is marginal if compared to increasing returns. Sandilands interprets Hirschman's formulation more as a refer-

ence to technological external economies and only marginally to pecuniary external economies, which were at the center of Currie's analysis. Specifically, Sandilands holds that Hirschman's "backward" and "forward linkages" tend to be mainly technological (framed in an input-output relation), whereas Currie focused on the size of potential demand. I would like to thank Roger Sandilands for having brought this point to my attention. Regardless, it seems to me that the different views on what was at the basis of Hirschman's "backward linkages" demonstrate how the theoretical debate can magnify differences that at a practical level are actually much less defined and not so far apart.

92. Jacques Torfs to Dr. Toro, April 10, 1952, *Colombia 2*.

93. Torfs added: "When expected to formulate a decision on expenditures to be undertaken by the Nation [. . .], the Government should be satisfied on the following points: (a) Is the project good, per se? [. . .] (b) How does the project fit within the general pattern of the Colombian power supply? [. . .] (c) How does the power supply scheme for Colombia fit into the national pattern of investment? [. . .] (d) How does the overall investment program fit within the forecast of national accounts?" Jacques Torfs to Dr. Toro, April 10, 1952, *Colombia 2*.

94. For example, Torfs wrote: "Top priority should be given to TRANSPORT, POWER, and AGRICULTURAL RESOURCES." From Jacques Torfs to Harold (without last name, probably Harold Larsen), September 10, 1951, *Colombia 2* (capitalization in the original).

95. In a letter from Bogotá, Hirschman stated the need for improvements in housing and social security, Albert O. Hirschman to Mr. Richard H. Demuth, August 23, 1952, *Colombia 2*.

96. Robert Hooke to Isaac Newton, year 1670, quoted in Merton (1965, p. 28; emphasis added by Merton). Merton honored Newton with coauthorship of his principle based on a letter from Newton to Hooke where the sender declared: "What's done before many witnesses is seldom without some further concern than that for truth: but what passes between friends in private usually deserves ye name of consultation rather than contest" (February 5, 1675–76, quoted in Merton [1965, p. 23]).

97. Hirschman's bibliography is rich with articles or autobiographical notes, and this may also be read as an additional comment: "One often writes against someone, even if unconsciously [. . .]. Speaking of enemies, I have had quite a few, especially in the years I worked on the problem of development [. . .] I had written largely against the theory of balanced growth proposed by Rosenstein-Rodan and by Ragnar Nurkse [. . .]. This just goes to show that one often has *intimate* enemies and to tell who they were" (Hirschman [1994] 1998, pp. 108–9; emphasis in the original).

98. We can add "one last remark, on the impact of new ideas" in the early years of development economics, from Hirschman (1984, p. 110): "Since my

thoughts on development were largely dissents, critical of both old and new orthodoxies, they have led to lively debates, thus helping, together with the contributions of others, to make the new field of development economics attractive and exciting."

99. Quoted in Hirschman ([1958] 1963, p. ix; emphasis in the original).

100. Lauchlin Currie, conference held in Panama, 1975, quoted in Sandilands (1990, p. 372). Currie's approach seems more complex than an oversimplified stereotype of the planning approach, still today perceived as an "excessive and knee-jerk dirigisme" (Bhagwati 2004, p. 21). Jagdish Bhagwati would probably consider Currie's eclectic approach as an exception: "The problem with many [developing] countries was that Adam Smith's invisible hand was nowhere to be seen" (Bhagwati 2004, p. 21).

101. Paul P. Streeten to Michele Alacevich, e-mail, October 15, 2004.

CHAPTER FOUR

1. Robert L. Garner to Rafael Delgado B., July 31, 1952, *LBCP*.

2. "Acta No. 40," Consejo Nacional de Planificación, September 11, 1952, *LBCP*.

3. At that time the official rate of exchange was 2.51 pesos per $1 U.S. Thus, the total investment corresponded to almost $38 million.

4. Emilio Toro to Robert L. Garner, April 7, 1953, *LBCP*.

5. "Plan preliminar de cinco años, con el objeto de remediar la más urgentes necesidades del Departamento del Atlántico y en particular de la ciudad de Barranquilla," Consejo Nacional de Planificacion, November 13, 1952, p. 2, *LBCP*.

6. Emilio Toro to Próspero Carbonell, December 13, 1952, *LBCP*; Emilio Toro to Rafael Vásquez, December 11, 1952, *LBCP*; "Plan preliminar de cinco años, con el objeto de remediar la más urgentes necesidades del Departamento del Atlántico y en particular de la ciudad de Barranquilla," Consejo Nacional de Planificacion, November 13, 1952, *LBCP*.

7. Diógenes Baca Gomez to Próspero Carbonell, November 27, 1952, *LBCP*.

8. Lauchlin B. Currie to Samuel L. Hollopeter, January 20, 1953, *LBCP*; Emilio Toro to Samuel L. Hollopeter, February 20, 1953, *LBCP*; Emilio Toro to Samuel Hollopeter, February 7, 1953, *LBCP*; Samuel L. Hollopeter to Emilio Toro, February 14 de 1953, *LBCP*; Emilio Toro to Próspero Carbonell, February 25, 1953, *LBCP*.

9. The only protest was raised by street traders, who wanted the market's rents to be reduced rather than increased. See Samuel L. Hollopeter to Lauchlin B. Currie, January 19, 1953, *LBCP*.

10. Lauchlin B. Currie to Samuel L. Hollopeter, January 20, 1953, *LBCP*.

11. Emilio Toro to Samuel L. Hollopeter, March 9, 1953, *LBCP*.

12. See the already cited letter of Robert L. Garner to Rafael Delgado B., July 31, 1952, *LBCP*.

13. Emilio Toro to Robert L. Garner, March 10, 1953, *LBCP*.

14. It is worth noting that Toro omitted to say that, on Currie's suggestion, a "watchdog committee" had already been established to deal with the problem of constant changes in local administration personnel. The committee proved to be very efficient (Sandilands 1990, p. 176).

15. "We understand that normally the Bank is not interested in financing a municipal aqueduct. Nonetheless, we expect that the Bank will be interested in making a contribution to a coordinated regional development plan." From Emilio Toro to Robert L. Garner, March 10, 1953, *LBCP*.

16. Also, Emilio Toro was not completely honest when describing the efficiency of the municipal offices that would implement the program. Toro informed Garner thus: "The Municipal Utilities of Barranquilla have an outstanding record in terms of their efficiency and the fulfillment of their obligations." From Emilio Toro to Robert L. Garner, March 10, 1953, *LBCP*. Indeed, during a meeting of the Consejo, when the Barranquilla plan was still taking shape, Toro stated that the facilities managed by the municipal services verged on a "deplorable state." From "Acta No. 43," Consejo Nacional de Planificación, September 23, 1952, *LBCP*.

17. Emilio Toro to Robert L. Garner, March 10, 1953, *LBCP*.

18. Emilio Toro to Samuel L. Hollopeter, March 9, 1953, *LBCP*.

19. Emilio Toro to Cipriano Restrepo Jaramillo, Embajador de Colombia, April 20, 1953, *LBCP*. Toro wrote passionately to the ambassador: "A positive response is key for the Council's future work and its influence [. . .]. A negative [response] to the loan would have a very negative impact for our future endeavors."

20. Robert L. Garner to Emilio Toro, April 21, 1953, *LBCP*.

21. Robert L. Garner to Emilio Toro, April 21, 1953, *LBCP* (emphasis added).

22. Jacques Torfs to Leonard Rist, December 18, 1950, *LBCP*.

23. The same can be said for a more complex, yet similar, case of a plan to develop the Colombian capital of Bogotá. A comprehensive history of the *Plan para Bogotá*, which considers all aspects of the plan, from housing to energy, does not yet exist. For an initial analysis, see Michele Alacevich and Andrea Costa (2009).

24. With the support of the French and the Italian government delegates, Messrs. Guerard and Visentini, respectively.

25. "Report of the Subcommittee on Instability of Employment," International Labour Organization, Rome, March 16–25, 1949, p. 9, *Housing 1*.

26. "Report of the Subcommittee on Instability of Employment," International Labour Organization, Rome, March 16–25, 1949, p. 10, *Housing 1*. Government delegates from eastern European countries opposed the proposal, provoking a split

among trade union delegates: those representing Communist trade unions opposed the proposal or abstained, while those representing Catholic or otherwise "Atlantic seaboard" trade unions (the expression used by the Belgian Workers' delegate, Mr. Smets) were in favor; see "Report of the Subcommittee on Instability of Employment," International Labour Organization, Rome, March 16–25, 1949, p. 6, *Housing 1*, and "Proposed Resolution Concerning the Establishment of an International Institute for Building Loans," International Labour Organization, Rome, March 25, 1949, *Housing 1*. In the Italian case, for example, the delegate for the General Italian Confederation of Labor (the majority of whose officials and members voted for the Communist Party), Mr. Agostini, opposed not only the proposal but the whole report, while the delegate for the Free Federation of Italian Workers (with a majority of Catholic members), Mr. De Caterini, approved the report and the proposal.

27. "Resolution Concerning the Establishment of an International Institute for Building Loans," International Labour Organization, Rome, March 25, 1949; David A. Morse to Eugene R. Black, August 12, 1949, *Housing 1*.

28. *Articles of Agreement*, Article I (i).

29. "An International Institute for Building Loans," Svend Andersen, Economic Department, General Studies, August 26, 1949, *Housing 1*.

30. "An International Institute for Building Loans," Svend Andersen, Economic Department, General Studies, August 26, 1949, *Housing 1*.

31. "An International Institute for Building Loans," Svend Andersen, Economic Department, General Studies, August 26, 1949, *Housing 1*.

32. "An International Institute for Building Loans," Svend Andersen, Economic Department, General Studies, August 26, 1949, *Housing 1*.

33. *Articles of Agreement*, Article IV, Section 3 (c).

34. "ILO—Proposal for an International Institute for Building Loans," Svend Andersen to Leonard B. Rist, August 25, 1949, *Housing 1*.

35. "Conversation with ILO Staff in Geneva Relating to the Suggested Creation, under the Control of IBRD, of an International Institute for Building Loans," Walter Hill to Robert L. Garner, Report H 105, Paris, October 17, 1949, *Housing 1*.

36. For example, an International Loan Bank for Building, by the International Federation of Building Trade Employers and Civil Engineering Contractors in October 1951; a European Credit Institute for Housing, by the Council of Europe's Consultative Assembly in December 1951; a report by the United Nations Economic Commission for Europe on methods and techniques of financing housing in various European countries, which aroused interest in the other two UN regional Economic Commissions, namely ECLA and ECAFE; see Ernest Weissmann to Davidson Sommers, January 9, 1952, *Housing 1*.

37. See, for example, Walter Hill to Leonard B. Rist, January 17, 1951, *Housing 1*.

38. Eugene R. Black to David A. Morse, December 13, 1949, *Housing 1*.

39. "Financing of Housing," Richard H. Demuth, May 22, 1952, *Housing 1*.

40. A. S. G. Hoar to Jacob L. Crane, April 21, 1952, *Housing 1*.

41. A. S. G. Hoar to Jacob L. Crane, April 21, 1952, *Housing 1*.

42. Paul Rosenstein-Rodan, oral history interview, August 14, 1961, p. 14, *Oral Hist. 44*.

43. Paul Rosenstein-Rodan, oral history interview, August 14, 1961, p. 13, *Oral Hist. 44*.

44. Anonymous, quoted in Mason and Asher (1973, p. 78).

45. "Memorandum on Full Employment," Lauchlin B. Currie to Franklin D. Roosevelt, March 18, 1940, Franklin D. Roosevelt Presidential Library, Hyde Park, New York, quoted in Barber (1996, p. 130). This is the reason why Currie was considered a pioneer by many economists who, in the 1960s and 1970s, shifted from an idea of development as maximization of economic growth to a concept that included social dimensions such as "basic needs" or policies of redistribution of wealth. Paul Streeten, editor of *World Development*, asked Currie for a testimony about his pioneering years. Interestingly, Currie's paper for *World Development* proposed a much less enthusiastic view on the basic needs approach than those that were then advocated in much of the literature that Streeten helped to stimulate (Currie 1978c).

46. Quoted in Currie (1981, p. 61).

47. From a contribution by Burke J. Knapp, 1960, quoted in Kapur, Lewis, and Webb (1997, p. 167). Anne Salda's statement (1997) according to which the Bank's activities in water resources began in the 1950s is not sufficiently proven. The Colombian case, in addition to others, appears to disprove it.

48. Quoted in Oliver (1995, p. 41).

49. Robert L. Garner to Emilio Toro, April 21, 1953, *LBCP*.

50. Quoted in Kraske et al. (1996, p. 60).

51. Table 7-1, *World Bank Loans and IDA Credits by Fiscal Years through June 30, 1971*, in Mason and Asher (1973, p. 192).

52. Table 7-8, *Flow of World Bank Funds, by Type of Flow and Country Group, Fiscal Years 1947–70*, in Mason and Asher (1973, p. 219).

53. "Memorandum—Organization of Research Department," Leonard B. Rist to Harold D. Smith, October 3, 1946, *Org. Econ. Dept.*; "Elaboration of a Project of Statistic Documentation," J. Torfs to Mr. Rist, October 22, 1946, *Org. Econ. Dept.*

54. "Research Department—Loan Department Meeting," Martin M. Rosen to Files, July 17, 1947, *Org. Econ. Dept.*; "Research Department—Loan Department Meeting," Martin M. Rosen to Files, July 22, 1947, *Org. Econ. Dept.*

55. "Suggested Relationship Between the Loan Department and the Research Department of the IBRD," October 1, 1947, *Org. Econ. Dept.*; "Proposed division of work between the Loan and the Research Departments," Walter Hill to Mr. R. L. Garner, October 14, 1947, *Org. Econ. Dept.*

56. "Demarcation Between Loan and Research," Loan Dept., December 4, 1947, *Org. Econ. Dept.*

57. "Collaboration Between Loan and Research Departments," Loan Department, December 22, 1947, *Org. Econ. Dept.*

58. "Demarcation Between Loan and Research," Loan Dept., December 4, 1947, *Org. Econ. Dept.* (emphasis in the original).

59. "Economic (Research) and Loan Departments," Leonard B. Rist, March 11, 1948, *Org. Econ. Dept.*

60. Oral history interview, Leonard Rist, July 19, 1961, p. 16, *Oral Hist. 44.*

61. "Role of the Economic Department in Supplying Information to the Bank," P. N. Rosenstein-Rodan to All Division and Section Heads, Economic Dept., August 20, 1948, *Org. Econ. Dept.*

62. This was attempted between 1950 and 1952 by Burke Knapp, who was appointed in December 1949 to work with Rosenstein-Rodan as assistant director of the Economic Department. See "For the Press," December 5, 1949, *Org. Econ. Dept.* Knapp tried to maintain the responsibilities of his department while marginalizing the role of Rosenstein-Rodan and the group that he oversaw, which dealt with "special studies." See "Office Memorandum—Economic Department Organization," Donald D. Fowler to Files, February 21, 1950, *Org. Econ. Dept.*; "Organization and Staffing Requirements of the Economic Department," Mr. J. Burke Knapp to Messrs. Black and Garner, March 6, 1950, *Org. Econ. Dept.*; "Wider Distribution by the Bank of economic Information," J. Burke Knapp to Mr. R. L. Garner, October 18, 1950, *Org. Econ. Dept.*

63. "Report of a Committee on Bank Organization," International Bank for Reconstruction and Development, March 28, 1952, p. 4, *Org. Econ. Dept.*

64. "Report of a Committee on Bank Organization," International Bank for Reconstruction and Development, March 28, 1952, p. 10, *Org. Econ. Dept.*

65. "Report of a Committee on Bank Organization," International Bank for Reconstruction and Development, March 28, 1952, p. 11, *Org. Econ. Dept.*

66. "Report of a Committee on Bank Organization," International Bank for Reconstruction and Development, March 28, 1952, p. 7, *Org. Econ. Dept.*

67. Oral history interview, Leonard Rist, July 19, 1961, pp. 59–60, *Oral Hist. 44.*

68. "Administrative Circular," International Bank for Reconstruction and Development, September 5, 1952, *Org. Econ. Dept.*

69. "Office Memorandum—Proposed Reorganization of the Bank," A. S. G. Hoar to Mr. R. L. Garner, March 28, 1952, *Org. Econ. Dept.*

70. John H. Williams, "International Bank for Reconstruction and Development," an unpublished paper presented at the Fourth Maxwell Institute on the United Nations, Bretton Woods (August 27 to September 1, 1967), quoted in Mason and Asher (1973, p. 76).

71. Oral history interview, Leonard Rist, July 19, 1961, p. 60, *Oral Hist. 44.*

72. Oral history interview, Leonard Rist, July 19, 1961, p. 19, *Oral Hist. 44*.

73. Oral history interview, Robert L. Garner, July 19, 1961, p. 98, *Oral Hist. 44*.

74. Quoted in Kapur, Lewis, and Webb (1997, p. 130).

75. A role that Knapp held from October 29, 1947. See "Acting Assistant Director," Director, Research Department to All Members of the Research Department, October 29, 1947, *Org. Econ. Dept.*; "Office Memorandum—Economic Department—Organization," Donald D. Fowler to Mr. C. G. Parker, March 6, 1950, *Org. Econ. Dept.*

76. Oliver (1975, p. 272).

77. $100 million out of almost $4 billion from 1948 to 1961 (Kapur, Lewis, and Webb 1997, p. 86, table 3-1). This amount tends to underestimate the *number* of projects in the agricultural sector out of the total. It is necessary to consider that agricultural loans were generally small compared to other sectors. Therefore one-fifth of the total number of loans in the Bank's first decade of operation went to agriculture (Kapur, Lewis, and Webb 1997, p. 111).

78. Quoted in Kapur, Lewis, and Webb (1997, p. 118).

79. Black established a Marketing Department, based in New York and active until 1963, as a privileged communication channel with financial investors (Kapur, Lewis, and Webb 1997, p. 89).

80. For example, a loan given to Iran in 1956 did not offer adequate guarantees and did not convince the management of the institution, especially Black, but was nevertheless granted after pressure by the U.S. administration. The case is well presented in Kapur, Lewis, and Webb (1997, pp. 104–5).

CONCLUSIONS

1. Leonard Rist, oral history interview, July 19, 1961, p. 17, *Oral Hist. 44*.

2. A discussion of the results of McNamara's presidency, albeit very interesting, is beyond the current research.

3. See in particular Streeten et al. (1981).

Bibliography

Abel, Christopher, and Marco Palacios. 1991. "Colombia, 1930–58." In *The Cambridge History of Latin America*, vol. 8. Cambridge: Cambridge University Press.

Alacevich, Michele. Forthcoming. "The World Bank's Early Reflections on Development: A Development Institution or a Bank?" *Review of Political Economy* 21.

Alacevich, Michele, and Andrea Costa. 2009. "Developing Cities: Between Economic and Urban Policies in Latin America After World War II." In Richard Arena, Sheila Dow, and Matthias Klaes (eds.), *Open Economics*. London: Routledge.

Asso, Pier Francesco, and Marcello De Cecco. 1987. "Introduzione." In Albert O. Hirschman, *Potenza nazionale e commercio estero: Gli Anni trenta, l'Italia e la ricostruzione*. Bologna, Italy: Il Mulino. [Original edition: Albert O. Hirschman. 1945 (extended edition 1980). *National Power and the Structure of Foreign Trade*. Berkeley, Calif.: University of California Press.]

Asso, Pier Francesco, and Luca Fiorito. 2009. "A Scholar in Action in Interwar America: John H. Williams' Contributions to Trade Theory and International Monetary Reform." In Robert Leeson (ed.), *American Power and Policy*. Basingstoke: Palgrave Macmillan.

Barber, William J. 1996. *Designs Within Disorder: Franklin D. Roosevelt, the Economists, and the Shaping of American Economic Policy, 1933–1945*. Cambridge: Cambridge University Press.

Bardhan, Pranab. 1993. "Economics of Development and the Development of Economics." *Journal of Economic Perspectives* 7 (spring):129–42.

Becker, William H., and William M. McClenahan, Jr. 2003. *The Market, the State, and the Export-Import Bank of the United States, 1934–2000*. New York: Cambridge University Press.

Bhagwati, Jagdish. 2004. *In Defense of Globalization*. Oxford: Oxford University Press.

Bird, Kai, 1992. *The Chairman: John McCloy. The Making of the American Establishment.* New York: Simon and Schuster.

Boughton, James. 2001. "The Case Against Harry Dexter White: Still Not Proven." *History of Political Economy* 2 (33):219–39.

Brecher, Michael. 1959. *Nehru: A Political Biography.* London: Oxford University Press.

Canfora, Luciano. 2004. *Giulio Cesare: Il dittatore democratico.* Rome and Bari, Italy: Laterza.

Casetta, Giovanni. 1991. *Colombia e Venezuela: Il progresso negato (1870–1990).* Florence, Italy: Giunti.

Chabod, Federico. [1961] 1989. *Storia dell'idea d'Europa.* 9th ed. Rome and Bari, Italy: Laterza.

Chandler, Alfred D., Jr. 1970. "Comment." In Ralph L. Andreano (ed.), *The New Economic History: Recent Papers on Methodology.* New York: John Wiley and Sons.

Chandra, Ramesh, and Roger J. Sandilands. 2005. "Does Modern Endogenous Growth Theory Adequately Represent Allyn Young?" *Cambridge Journal of Economics* 29 (3):463–73.

Chenery, Hollis B., Montek S. Ahluwalia, C. L. G. Bell, John H. Duloy, and Richard Jolly. 1974. *Redistribution with Growth.* London: Oxford University Press for the World Bank.

Consejo Nacional de Planificación. 1954. *Plan de fomento para el Atlántico.* Barranquilla, Colombia: Emprenta Departamental.

Currie, Lauchlin B. 1934. *The Supply and Control of Money in the United States.* Cambridge, Mass.: Harvard University Press.

———. 1950. "Some Prerequisites for Success of the Point Four Program." Address before the American Academy of Political and Social Sciences, Bellevue Stratford Hotel, Philadelphia, Pa., on April 15. Mimeo, published in *Annals of the American Academy of Political and Social Sciences* 270 (July):102–9.

———. 1972. "Discussion." *American Economic Review Papers and Proceedings* 62 (1–2):139–41.

———. 1974. "The 'Leading Sector' Model of Growth in Developing Countries." *Journal of Economic Studies* 1 (1):1–16.

———. 1978a. "Comments on Pump Priming (Circa February–March 1935)." *History of Political Economy* 10 (4):525–33.

———. 1978b. "Comments and Observations." *History of Political Economy* 10 (4):541–48.

———. 1978c. "The Objectives of Development." *World Development* 6 (1):1–10.

———. 1979. "A Talk by Lauchlin Currie: Hotel Tequendama." Mimeo, August 31.

———. 1981. *The Role of Economic Advisers in Developing Countries.* Westport, Conn.: Greenwood Press.

Currie, Lauchlin B., and Martin Krost. 1978. "Federal Income-Increasing Expenditures, 1932–1935 (Circa November 1935)." *History of Political Economy* 10 (4):534–40.

Dasgupta, Amiya Kumar. 1965. *Planning and Economic Growth.* London: George Allen & Unwin.

———. 1985. *Epochs of Economic Theory.* Oxford: Basil Blackwell.

David, Paul A. 1985. "Clio and the Economics of QWERTY." *American Economic Review. Papers and Proceedings* 75 (2):332–37.

Duesenberry, James S. 1949. *Income, Saving, and the Theory of Consumer Behavior.* Cambridge, Mass.: Harvard University Press.

Easterly, William. 2002. *The Elusive Quest for Growth: Economists' Adventures and Misadventures in the Tropics.* Cambridge, Mass.: MIT Press.

Echeverri Cortés, Carlos. 1951. "La Agricultura Tiene Necesidad de Aumento del Crédito Bancario." *El Siglo* (Bogotá, Colombia), January 2, 1951, No. 5.342.

Economic Commission for Latin America (ECLA). 1950. *The Economic Development for Latin America and Its Principal Problems.* Lake Success, N.Y.: United Nations Department of Economic Affairs.

Galambos, Louis, and David Milobsky. 1995a. "Organizing and Reorganizing the World Bank, 1946–1972: A Comparative Perspective." *Business History Review* 69 (summer):156–90.

———. 1995b. "The McNamara Bank and Its Legacy: 1968–1987." *Business and Economic History* 24 (winter):167–95.

Galbraith, John K. 1958. "Rival Economic Theories in India." *Foreign Affairs* 36 (4):587–96.

———. 1971. "How Keynes Came to America." In *Economics, Peace and Laughter: A Contemporary Guide.* Boston: Houghton Mifflin.

Gardner, Richard N. [1956] 1969. *Sterling-Dollar Diplomacy.* New York: McGraw-Hill.

Garner, Robert L. 1972. *This Is the Way It Was with Robert L. Garner.* Chevy Chase, Md.: Chevy Chase Printing.

Gerschenkron, Alexander. 1962. *Economic Backwardness in Historical Perspective.* Cambridge, Mass.: The Belknap Press of Harvard University Press.

Ginzburg, Andrea. 1983. "Introduzione." In Albert O. Hirschman, *Ascesa e declino dell'economia dello sviluppo e altri saggi.* Turin, Italy: Rosenberg and Sellier.

Granovetter, Mark. 1990. "Interview." In Richard Swedberg, *Economics and Sociology.* Princeton, N.J.: Princeton University Press.

Haralz, Jonas. 1997. "The International Finance Corporation." In Devesh Kapur, John P. Lewis, and Richard C. Webb, *The World Bank: Its First Half Century,* vol. 1. Washington, D.C.: Brookings Institution Press.

Harrod, Roy F. 1951. *The Life of John Maynard Keynes.* London: Macmillan.

Hirschman, Albert O. [1958] 1963. *The Strategy of Economic Development*. 4th ed. New Haven, Conn.: Yale University Press.

———. 1968. *Journeys Toward Progress: Studies of Economic Policy-Making in Latin America*. New York: Twentieth Century Fund.

———. [1954] 1971a. "Economics and Investment Planning: Reflections Based on Experience in Colombia." In *A Bias for Hope: Essays on Development and Latin America*. New Haven, Conn.: Yale University Press.

———. [1968] 1971b. "Foreign Aid: A Critique and a Proposal." In *A Bias for Hope: Essays on Development and Latin America*. New Haven, Conn.: Yale University Press.

———. [1965] 1971c. "Obstacles to Development: A Classification and a Quasi Vanishing Act." In *A Bias for Hope: Essays on Development and Latin America*. New Haven, Conn.: Yale University Press.

———. 1981a. "The Rise and Decline of Development Economics." In *Essays in Trespassing: Economics to Politics and Beyond*. Cambridge: Cambridge University Press.

———. [1977] 1981b. "A Generalized Linkage Approach to Development, with Special Reference to Staples." In *Essays in Trespassing: Economics to Politics and Beyond*. Cambridge: Cambridge University Press.

———. [1979] 1981c. "The Turn to Authoritarianism in Latin America and the Search for Its Economic Determinants." In *Essays in Trespassing: Economics to Politics and Beyond*. Cambridge: Cambridge University Press.

———. 1984. "A Dissenter's Confession: Revisiting the Strategy of Economic Development." In Gerald M. Meier and Dudley Seers (eds.), *Pioneers in Development*. Washington, D.C.: The World Bank.

———. [1980] 1986. "In Defence of Possibilism." In *Rival Views of Market Society and Other Recent Essays*. New York: Elizabeth Sifton Books–Viking.

———. 1991. *The Rhetoric of Reaction: Perversity, Futility, Jeopardy*. Cambridge, Mass.: The Belknap Press of Harvard University Press.

———. [1989] 1995. "How the Keynesian Revolution Was Exported from the United States." In *A Propensity to Self-Subversion*. Cambridge, Mass.: Harvard University Press.

———. [1994] 1998. "Trespassing: Places and Ideas in the Course of a Life." In *Crossing Boundaries: Selected Writings*. New York: Zone Books.

Hirschman, Albert O., and Gorge Kalmanoff. 1955. *Colombia: Highlights of a Developing Economy*. Bogotá, Colombia: Banco de la Republica Press.

Hodgson, Geoffrey M. 2001. *How Economics Forgot History: The Problem of Historical Specificity in Social Science*. New York: Routledge.

Horsefield, J. Keith. 1969. *The International Monetary Fund, 1945–1965: Twenty Years of International Cooperation*. Washington, D.C.: International Monetary Fund.

International Bank for Reconstruction and Development (IBRD). 1948. *Third Annual Report to the Board of Governors, 1947–1948.* Washington, D.C.: International Bank for Reconstruction and Development.

———. 1949. *Fourth Annual Report to the Board of Governors, 1948–1949.* Washington, D.C.: International Bank for Reconstruction and Development.

———. 1950a. *The Basis of a Development Program for Colombia: Report of a Mission Headed by Lauchlin Currie, and Sponsored by the International Bank for Reconstruction and Development in Collaboration with the Government of Colombia.* Washington, D.C.: International Bank for Reconstruction and Development.

———. 1950b. *The Basis of a Development Program for Colombia: Report of a Mission. The Summary.* Washington, D.C.: International Bank for Reconstruction and Development.

———. 1950c. *Fifth Annual Report to the Board of Governors, 1949–1950.* Washington, D.C.: International Bank for Reconstruction and Development.

———. 1951. *Report on Cuba: Findings and Recommendations of an Economic and Technical Mission Organized by the International Bank for Reconstruction and Development in Collaboration with the Government of Cuba in 1950.* Washington, D.C.: International Bank for Reconstruction and Development.

———. 1952a. *Seventh Annual Report to the Board of Governors, 1951–1952.* Washington, D.C.: International Bank for Reconstruction and Development.

———. 1952b. *The Economic Development of Jamaica.* Baltimore, Md.: Johns Hopkins University Press for the International Bank for Reconstruction and Development.

———. 1953. *The Economic Development of Nicaragua.* Baltimore, Md.: Johns Hopkins University Press for the International Bank for Reconstruction and Development.

———. 1954. *The International Bank for Reconstruction and Development, 1946–1953.* Baltimore, Md.: Johns Hopkins University Press for the International Bank for Reconstruction and Development.

International Labour Organization (ILO). 1976. *Employment, Growth and Basic Needs: A One-World Problem.* Geneva, Switzerland: International Labour Organization.

———. 1977. *Meeting Basic Needs: Strategies for Eradicating Mass Poverty and Unemployment.* Geneva, Switzerland: International Labour Organization.

Jones, Byrd L. 1972. "The Role of Keynesians in Wartime Policy and Post-war Planning, 1940–1946." *American Economic Review Papers and Proceedings* 62 (1–2):125–33.

———. 1978. "Lauchlin Currie, Pump Priming, and New Deal Fiscal Policy, 1934–1936." *History of Political Economy* 10 (4):509–24.

Kamarck, Andrew M. 1995. "Foreword." In Robert W. Oliver, *George Woods and the World Bank.* Boulder, Colo.: Lynne Rienner Publishers.

Kapur, Devesh, John P. Lewis, and Richard C. Webb. 1997. *The World Bank: Its First Half Century.* Washington, D.C.: Brookings Institution Press.

Kindleberger, Charles P. 1991. "Review of the Life and Political Economy of Lauchlin Currie: New Dealer, Presidential Adviser, and Development Economist, by Roger Sandilands." *Journal of Political Economy* 99 (5):1119–22.

Kraske, Jochen, William H. Becker, William Diamond, and Louis Galambos. 1996. *Bankers with a Mission: The Presidents of the World Bank, 1946–1991.* Oxford: Oxford University Press.

Krugman, Paul. 1993. "Toward a Counter-Counterrevolution in Development Theory." In Lawrence H. Summers and Shekhar Shah (eds.), *Proceedings of the World Bank Annual Conference on Development Economics 1992.* Washington, D.C.: The World Bank.

Laidler, David, and Roger Sandilands. 2002a. "An Early Harvard Memorandum on Anti-Depression Policies: An Introductory Note." *History of Political Economy* 34 (3):515–32.

——— (eds.). 2002b. "Memorandum Prepared by L. B. Currie, P. T. Ellsworth, and H. D. White (Cambridge, Mass., January 1932)." *History of Political Economy* 34(3):533–52.

Leijonhufvud, Axel. [1973] 1981. "Life Among the Econ." In *Information and Coordination: Essays in Macroeconomic Theory.* Oxford: Oxford University Press.

Lewis, William Arthur. 1954. "Economic Development with Unlimited Supply of Labour." *Manchester School of Economic and Social Studies* 22 (May):139–91.

Liebowitz, Stan J., and Stephen E. Margolis. 1995. "Path Dependence, Lock-in and History." *Journal of Law, Economics and Organization* 11 (1):205–26.

———. 1998. "Path Dependence." Entry in *The New Palgrave's Dictionary of Economics and the Law.* Basingstoke: Palgrave Macmillan.

Maier, Charles S. 1977. "The Politics of Productivity: Foundations of American International Economic Policy After World War II." *International Organization* 31 (4):607–33.

Mason, Edward S. 1982. "The Harvard Department of Economics from the Beginning to World War II." *Quarterly Journal of Economics* 97 (3):383–433.

Mason, Edward S., and Robert E. Asher. 1973. *The World Bank Since Bretton Woods.* Washington, D.C.: The Brookings Institution.

Meade, James. 1952. "External Economies and Diseconomies in a Competitive Situation." *Economic Journal* 62 (245):54–67.

Meier, Gerald M., and Dudley Seers (eds.). 1984. *Pioneers in Development.* Washington, D.C.: The World Bank.

Merton, Robert K. 1965. *On the Shoulders of Giants.* New York: The Free Press.

———. [1957] 1973a. "Priorities in Scientific Discovery." In *The Sociology of Science: Theoretical and Empirical Investigations.* Chicago: University of Chicago Press.

———. [1961] 1973b. "Social Conflict over Styles of Sociological Work." In *The Sociology of Science: Theoretical and Empirical Investigations.* Chicago: University of Chicago Press.

Moore, Frederick T. 1960. "The World Bank and Its Economic Missions." *Review of Economics and Statistics* 42 (February):81–93.

Morse, David A. 1971. "The Employment Problem in Developing Countries." In Ronald Robinson and Peter Johnston (eds.), *Prospects for Employment Opportunities in the Nineteen Seventies: Papers and Impressions of the Seventh Cambridge Conference on Development Problems, 13th to 24th September 1970 at Jesus College, Cambridge.* London: Foreign and Commonwealth Office, Overseas Development Administration, Cambridge University Overseas Studies Committee, London, Her Majesty's Stationery Office.

Myrdal, Gunnar. 1957. *Economic Theory and Under-developed Regions.* London: Gerald Duckworth and Co.

———. 1968. *Asian Drama. An Inquiry into the Poverty of Nations*, vol. 1. New York: Twentieth Century Fund.

Nurkse, Ragnar. 1952. "Some International Aspects of the Problem of Economic Development." *American Economic Review. Papers and Proceedings* 42 (May):571–83.

———. [1953] 1962. *Problems of Capital Formation in Underdeveloped Countries.* 3rd ed. Oxford: Basil Blackwell and Mott Ltd.

Oliver, Robert W. 1975. *International Economic Co-operation and the World Bank.* London: Macmillan.

———. 1990. "Interview by Loma Karklins." California Institute of Technology, Oral History Project, Caltech Archives, Pasadena, Calif.

———. 1995. *George Woods and the World Bank.* Boulder, Colo.: Lynne Rienner Publishers.

Oman, Charles P., and Ganeshan Wignaraja. 1991. *The Postwar Evolution of Development Thinking.* Paris: Organisation for Economic Co-Operation and Development.

Rosenstein-Rodan, Paul N. 1943. "Problems of Industrialisation of Eastern and South-Eastern Europe." *Economic Journal* 53 (209):202–11.

———. 1961. "Notes on the Theory of the *Big Push*." In Howard S. Ellis (ed.), *Economic Development for Latin America: Proceedings of a Conference Held by the International Economic Association.* London: Macmillan.

———. 1984. "Natura Facit Saltum: Analysis of the Disequilibrium Growth Process." In Gerald M. Meier and Dudley Seers (eds.), *Pioneers in Development.* Washington, D.C.: The World Bank.

Rostow, Walt W. [1960] 1990. *The Stages of Economic Growth: A Non-Communist Manifesto.* 3rd ed. Cambridge: Cambridge University Press.

Rutherford, Malcolm. 1994. *Institutions in Economics: The Old and the New Institutionalism.* Cambridge: Cambridge University Press.

Salda, Anne C. M. 1997. *Historical Dictionary of the World Bank.* Lanham, Md.: Scarecrow Press.

Sandilands, Roger. 1990. *The Life and Political Economy of Lauchlin Currie: New Dealer, Presidential Adviser, and Development Economist.* Durham, N.C.: Duke University Press.

———. 2000. "Guilt by Association? Lauchlin Currie's Alleged Involvement with Washington Economists in Soviet Espionage." *History of Political Economy* 32 (3):473–515.

———. 2004. "New Light on Lauchlin Currie's Monetary Economics in the New Deal and Beyond." *Journal of Economic Studies* 31 (3/4):171–93.

———. 2009. "An Archival Case Study: Revisiting *The Life and Political Economy of Lauchlin Currie.*" In Robert Leeson (ed.), *American Power and Policy.* Basingstoke: Palgrave Macmillan.

Sandilands, Roger, and David Laidler. 2002. "An Early Harvard Memorandum on Anti-Depression Policies: An Introductory Note." *History of Political Economy* 34 (fall):515–52.

Sapelli, Giulio. 1990. "L'impresa come soggetto storico e come istituzione: competizione e nuova sovranità." In Giulio Sapelli (ed.), *L'impresa come soggetto storico.* Milan, Italy: Saggiatore.

Scitovsky, Tibor. 1954. "Two Concepts of External Economies." *Journal of Political Economy* 62 (April):143–51.

———. 1959. "Growth—Balanced or Unbalanced?" In M. Abramovitz (ed.), *The Allocation of Economic Resources.* Stanford, Calif.: Stanford University Press.

Sen, Amartya K. 1960. "Review of *The Strategy of Economic Development,* by A. O. Hirschman; *The Struggle for a Higher Standard of Living: The Problems of the Underdeveloped Countries,* by W. Brand; and *Public Enterprise and Economic Development,* by A. H. Hanson." *Economic Journal* 70 (September):590–94.

Singer, Hans W. 1965. "Social Development: Key Growth Sector." *International Development Review* 7 (1):3–8.

Spengler, Joseph J. 1954. "IBRD Mission Economic Growth Theory." *American Economic Review. Papers and Proceedings* 44 (2):583–99.

Streeten, Paul P. 1959. "Unbalanced Growth." *Oxford Economic Papers* 11 (2):167–90.

Streeten, Paul P., Shahid J. Burki, Mahbub ul Haq, Norman Hicks, and Frances Stewart. 1981. *First Things First.* London: Oxford University Press.

Sweezy, Alan. 1972. "The Keynesians and Government Policy, 1933–1939." *American Economic Review. Papers and Proceedings* 62 (1–2):116–24.

Torres G., Carlos L. 1998. "Una aproximación al carácter de la novela urbana: el caso de la ciudad de Bogotá." *Espéculo–Revista Electrónica Cuatrimestral de Estudios Literarios*, Facultad de Ciencias de la Información, Universidad Complutense de Madrid, 9 (July–November):1998. Available at http://www.ucm .es/OTROS/especulo/numero09/n_urbana.htm.

Yépez, Freddy. 1994. *Crónicas: Guerra y Paz en Colombia*. Mérida, Venezuela: Universidad de Los Andes/Ediciones del Rectorado.

Index of Names

Abbott, J., xv
Allen, D. H., 28
Anderson, R., 33f
Anderson, S. W., 36
Angelini, A., xv
Arango, L. A., 36, 59
Argemi, L., xv
Asher, R. E., 6, 7, 126, 136, 143
Asso, P. F., xv

Bardhan, P., 66
Bentley, E., 31
Bethea, C., xv
Bhagwati, J., 178n100
Bird, K., xv
Black, E. R., 40f, 120, 122, 130, 131, 132, 136, 140, 144–145, 146, 149, 150, 151, 183n80
Bossone, B., xv
Bourguignon, F., xv
Bowers, C. G., 133
Brecht, B., 9
Broadley, H., 44
Buckingham, B., xv
Burland, E., 51

Ceballos, J. de D., 33f, 36
Chandler, A. D., 6, 7, 8
Chandra, R., 176n91
Clee, G. H., 158n17, 159n20
Cordoba, J. F., 33f
Corral, M. del, 35f, 52
Cortés, C. E., 44
Craver, E., xv
Croci Angelini, E., xv
Currie, E., xv

Currie, L. B., xv, 14, 15, 22, 29, 31, 32, 33, 33f, 35f, 36, 38, 39, 41, 43, 44, 45, 47, 48–53, 54–56, 58–60, 61, 62, 64, 65, 66, 79, 82, 83, 84–87, 90–93, 94–96, 97, 98, 100, 101, 102, 103–105, 110, 112, 116, 118, 119, 127–129, 135, 163n54–56, 163n68, 164n79, 164n80, 166n103, 167n113, 168n130, 169n1, 173n43, 173n55, 173n56, 174n57, 174n58, 175n80–83, 176n84, 176n85, 179n14, 181n45

Dasgupta, A. K., 77
David, P., 9
Delgado Barreneche, R., 49, 53, 59, 114
Demuth, R. H., 122, 162n48
Dethier, J.-J., xv
Devetag, G., xv
Dillon, D., 132
di Marzo, F., xv
di Marzo, Marina, xv
di Marzo, Marino, xv
Domar, E., 71
Dow, S., xv
Duesenberry, J. S., 70
Dunn, E., xvi

Easterly, W., 72
Eccles, M., 14, 30
Ellsworth, P. T., 29

Faison, H. R., 33f, 36, 37
Flesher, C. W., 32, 33f, 37, 47, 87, 88, 95, 99, 173n44
Foa, B., 58, 60
Fodor, G., xv